UNCOVERED

UNCOVERED

HOW THE MEDIA GOT COZY
WITH POWER, ABANDONED
ITS PRINCIPLES, AND
LOST THE PEOPLE

Steve Krakauer

**CENTER
STREET**

NEW YORK   NASHVILLE

Center Street
Hachette Book Group
1290 Avenue of the Americas, New York, NY 10104
centerstreet.com
twitter.com/centerstreet

First Edition: February 2023

Center Street is a division of Hachette Book Group, Inc.
The Center Street name and logo are trademarks of Hachette Book Group, Inc.

The publisher is not responsible for websites (or their content) that are not owned by the publisher.

The Hachette Speakers Bureau provides a wide range of authors for speaking events. To find out more, go to www.hachettespeakersbureau.com or call (866) 376-6591.

Library of Congress Cataloging-in-Publication Data

Names: Krakauer, Steve, 1984- author.
Title: Uncovered : how the media got cozy with power, abandoned
    its principles, and lost the people / Steve Krakauer.
Description: First edition. | Nashville ; New York : Center Street, 2023. |
    Includes index.
Identifiers: LCCN 2022042122 | ISBN 9781546003472 (hardcover) |
    ISBN 9781546003496 (ebook)
Subjects: LCSH: Mass media—Political aspects—United States. |
    Mass media—Social aspects—United States.
Classification: LCC P95.82.U6 K73 2023 | DDC 302.230973—dc23/eng/20220927
LC record available at https://lccn.loc.gov/2022042122

ISBNs: 9781546003472 (hardcover), 9781546003496 (ebook)

Printed in the United States of America

LSC-C

Printing 1, 2022

For what really does matter...
Jack, Mia, and Meghan

CONTENTS

UNCOVERED

The Laptop

IN MANY WAYS IT WAS the culmination of one embarrassing journalistic era and the beginning of a new, even more alarming one.

The *New York Post*, the oldest newspaper in America, which was founded by the suddenly-cool-again Alexander Hamilton, splashed a giant scoop on its tabloid front page on the morning of October 14, 2020: "Biden Secret Emails." The cover promised "exclusive" details over a several-page spread.

While a *New York Post* cover may be one of the last vestiges of old print media relevance, the current medium of power for the modern media is digital. The *New York Post*'s web story was headlined "Smoking-gun email reveals how Hunter Biden introduced Ukrainian businessman to VP dad."[1]

It was the first of what would eventually be several stories by the *New York Post*, then the *Daily Mail*, then other outlets, based on what is now known as "Hunter Biden's laptop." Entire emails were published, but the sourcing was unquestionably sketchy. The owner of a Delaware computer repair shop told the *Post* that a customer brought in a "water-damaged MacBook Pro for repair," and never picked it up. Then it was turned over by the repair shop owner to the FBI in December 2019, according to the *Post*, and a copy of the hard drive was given to former New York City mayor Rudy Giuliani's lawyer, Robert Costello. The *Post* got a copy of it after first hearing about it from Steve Bannon in September 2020, and then being provided it by Giuliani shortly before publication.

You could then perhaps understand how national media might tread lightly into this particular story, rather than rush to aggregate the *Post*'s reporting without verifying it themselves. A presidential election was about to take place in mere weeks, between Hunter's dad, Joe Biden, and Donald Trump.

But treading lightly was very different from how the story was handled by the press. Instead, what took place was perhaps the most egregious and obvious example of the elite censorship collusion racket between tech companies, government forces, and the national media that we've ever seen. Almost instantly, Twitter, media members' favored social platform for talking and listening—often to one another—made the link to the *New York Post*'s exclusive inaccessible to be shared publicly, or privately through direct messages. Twitter explained this unprecedented action as a response to its "hacked material policy"—assuming, or perhaps concluding, the material the *Post* published had been obtained through some sort of hack. Meanwhile Twitter locked the *New York Post* out of its account until it deleted its tweet linking to the report. In fact, it locked other "blue-check" journalists (verified users with a checkmark next to their Twitter account name) until they deleted their tweets linking to the article. The journalists were far more willing to comply. "I tweeted a link to the NYP story right after it dropped yesterday morning. I immediately reached out to the Biden campaign to see if they had any answer. I wish i had given the story a closer read before tweeting it," tweeted reporter Jake Sherman, then of Politico. "my goal was not to spread informatoin. my goal was to raise questions about the story—as i did in subsequent tweets—and see how the biden campaign was going to respond. They later did respond." He continued, "My account is clearly no longer suspended. I deleted the tweet."[2]

You can see the utter panic from Sherman's tweet with the spelling and capitalization issues. He dared to link to the *New York Post*—the horror!—and couldn't tweet for a little while.

Facebook took similar extreme actions against the report. Andy Stone, a comms exec at the company who previously served on Democratic staffs, tweeted the company would be "pre-ducing" the reach of the story—reducing the spread of the story in advance of a fact check: "While I will intentionally not link to the *New York Post*, I want [to] be clear that this story is eligible to be fact checked by Facebook's third-party fact checking partners. In the meantime, we are reducing its distribution on our platform."[3]

That sentiment was shared by journalists too, who urged others to pretend the article simply did not exist. Kyle Griffin, a prolific tweeter who moonlights as a top producer of MSNBC TV shows, tweeted, "No one should link to or share that NY *Post* 'report.' You can discuss the obvious flaws and unanswerable questions in the report without amplifying what appears to be disinformation."[4]

Ignore the story, directed Griffin. Linking to the *New York Post* would be "amplifying" potential "disinformation." This was the instinctual response of a media community that had become conditioned over the past few years to suppress anything that could potentially help a figure and political movement it deemed to be unacceptable and an existential threat to democracy itself. An industry that suppressed and ultimately abandoned its own inclination toward curiosity, in the service of a mission it deemed greater and more important. We can't let the readers themselves decide—what if they draw the wrong conclusions?!

But it was even deeper. The media wasn't overly outraged about the egregious overreach from Twitter and other social platforms against a media outlet because it had journalistic PTSD from 2016. There were two factors at the core of the media's relative silence on the matter: guilt and fear. The press truly believed they were partly responsible for Donald Trump's shocking victory over Hillary Clinton four years earlier, thanks to their coverage of her emails, the early easier treatment they gave him during the primary, and more. They felt guilty—and were not going to make that same mistake again.

And then there was the fear. The social media ostracization. The attacks from their colleagues. Maggie Haberman of the *New York Times* previously worked at the *Post*, and she dared to link to the story early on the fourteenth, even though she was questioning the sourcing of it. By the afternoon she was trending on Twitter as "MAGA Haberman" for her supposed crime.

Twitter ultimately reversed itself and made the link accessible by that night. But the *New York Post* wasn't "unlocked" and able to use its account for more than two weeks. In the days that followed, the media would pivot to a new storyline—that the laptop story was part of a Russian disinformation campaign. This was spun from a group of former intelligence officials, some of whom were paid contributors at the media organizations. "US authorities investigating if recently published emails are tied to Russian disinformation effort targeting Biden" was the headline of a massive, six-bylined report published by CNN two days after the *Post*'s story and discussed incessantly for days to come on air.[5]

"It seemed to me an absolutely classic case of a liberal, skewed mainstream media and social media, and tech giant empire, all conspiring to suppress a story which could have damaged Joe Biden's chances of being president had they pursued it with the same vigor that they're pursuing it now," Piers Morgan, former CNN host and now a host at TalkTV and a *New York Post* columnist, told me, in one of more than two dozen exclusive interviews I conducted for this book.

"I think there's a really, really worrying tendency on the left and the mainstream media and the Democratic Party to censor anything undesirable as if that would make it go away," Shawn McCreesh, who worked at the *New York Times* at the time the *Post* published its first Hunter Biden story in October 2020, and now works for *New York* magazine, told me. "...The media writ large, and certainly the *New York Times*, was so scarred and filled with regret by the way it covered Hillary's emails. So when Hunter's laptop came along, they were just so weary of it. But instead of either burying the story inside the paper, or just touching it lightly, the way they tried to wiggle out of covering it was by insinuating that it might not have even been real, which was a huge mistake, because of course everybody knew it was real. It was knowable. It was so obviously real."

But McCreesh sees another reason for the lack of coverage: Trump himself. "As usual, Trump is so ham-fisted and moronic about the way he goes about stuff. To have Rudy [Giuliani] out there, frothing at the mouth, was so disgusting that nobody wanted to cover it because it just felt so plainly like you'd be doing their bidding if you did. Yes, damaging stories and campaigns are often the result of reporters accepting oppo, but Trump World was so vile in the way that they pushed it that nobody wanted to touch it. Except of course the *Post,* which should not have been censored by Twitter. I think that should have alarmed more liberals, and it mystifies me as to why it has not."

What would have happened if the roles were reversed?

Maybe if it was some emails obtained through dubious means by the Biden campaign about, say, Donald Trump Jr.? And what if Twitter applied that same "hacked material policy" and locked that juicy scoop down? "Flip the political polarity of the story and see what would have happened," Bob Ley, longtime ESPN anchor, told me. "It would have been a five-alarm fire."

The lack of journalistic outrage was most notable to Salena Zito, a former *New York Post* reporter. "If you ignore something that's happening in your profession, because it's happening to someone you're competing with that maybe doesn't share your ideological views...Because it's happening to one and it's not happening to you, [it] doesn't mean they're not going to come for you eventually," she told me. "That's the first thing that as a journalist, you should be concerned [about] is your profession, not as the team you work on, but your profession as a whole."

Fox News host Tucker Carlson told me he knew instantly the laptop was real, because emails between him and Hunter Biden were on it. "The second those emails started circulating among reporters, someone sent me one from me, because I had known him," he told me. "He had quit drinking. I had quit drinking. I was talking about sobriety. He was struggling with it, you know, and I still feel sorry for him actually. I always liked him, for the record, until he went off the deep end and started doing a ton of blow; his life fell apart."

Carlson was one of the few in the media who took it seriously at the time—and took heat for giving this potential "disinformation" a platform. "To see that suppressed and then dismissed by these intel community figures told you… the censorship regime is total," Carlson told me. "Like, we don't live in a free country, if you can't read that in the weeks before a presidential election. I mean, highly relevant information, then is that a free and fair election? The answer is no, it's not a free and fair election."

Will Cain of Fox News agrees it "swayed" the 2020 election. "Hunter Biden's story should send shivers up the spine of every American because it was the canary in the coal mine," he told me.

John Roberts is a longtime Fox News reporter and host, but spent even longer at CNN and CBS News before that. He wasn't shocked by the way the story unfolded. "It was no surprise to me that most of the elements of the so-called mainstream media didn't want to touch it with a ten-foot pole," he told me. "But what bothered me as a journalist is the fact that there was evidence out there, and the evidence was real. I saw it…The evidence that I saw looked like it was credible and legitimate, and so many people in the mainstream media just dismissed it out of hand and went with the talking point from the Biden campaign that this was all Russian disinformation, because it was something that was easy for the left to digest."

"I think it's a really dangerous proposition," former *New York Times* reporter Amy Chozick told me. Chozick has covered many presidential campaigns and wrote a book on her time covering Hillary Clinton. "We're dismissing things that could be damaging toward the people we perceive as the 'good guys' or the 'bad guys.' However you feel about Trump or Biden, I do think it further diminishes, further erodes, the trust in the media, when it looks like you're hammering Russia, Russia, Russia, Russia. Russia, on the Trump side, and then there's one little hint of impropriety on the Biden side, and it's like, 'we can't even talk about that. We can't even acknowledge that, God forbid, because the other side is so bad.' I think it's dangerous."

Ben Smith, formerly the lead media columnist at the *New York Times* and longtime editor of BuzzFeed, told me the Hunter Biden story stands out because it's something of an isolated incident. "It is the iconic story about the tech industry suppressing a piece of journalism that favored conservatives and you're still talking about it two years later, because I've not seen a series of other examples of it," he told me. But, he said, "People thought it was some kind of Russian intelligence operation, which was an overreaction, which there wasn't evidence for, which I never really bought."

Rich McHugh, a longtime investigative journalist previously at NBC News and other outlets, sees the tech suppression as a huge problem. "It's shameful. It shouldn't be happening with Big Tech," he told me. "...It's this curious time where these major corporations are dictating what news we get. And I think there's inherent problems in that. It shouldn't be that way."

The Hunter Biden laptop story would ultimately be verified as authentic and not "Russian disinformation" by outlets like the *New York Times* and *Washington Post*—close to eighteen months later. But the damage was done. The moment exposed the truth about the decline of the media, and the reality of its erosion of principles. It was in many ways the end of the Trump Era of journalism, and the beginning of an even more corrosive era of censorship that was to come.

INTRODUCTION

A T SOME POINT, THE AMERICAN media shifted from reality to reality show. There are without a doubt myriad reasons this could be the case, but the fact remains that it's no longer really about reporting the truth, and instead it's about—well, a lot of other factors.

This book will attempt to figure out what those are, how we got here, and how we can get ourselves back on track.

Because make no mistake—things are off track. According to the most recent Gallup poll in October 2021, trust in "mass media" is at its second lowest point ever, with just 36 percent of Americans saying they have either a "great deal" or even a "fair amount" of trust in the media.[1]

Gallup has been tracking this number for decades. Back in the 1970s, somewhere between 68 and 72 percent of Americans trusted the media. In 2003, that number was down to a much lower but still respectable 54 percent. But since then it hasn't cracked 50 percent, dipping to 32 percent at its lowest point in 2016. Unsurprisingly, there's a split along party lines. 68 percent of Democrats trusted the media in 2021, while only 11 percent of Republicans did.

But perhaps most concerning in the latest poll is the independents line. That growing group of independents in America have reached a near-record low of just 31 percent trusting the media—that's down eleven points from 2018.

That poll is not an outlier, it's the norm. The PR giant Edelman puts out an annual "trust barometer" across various industries, and they found in 2021 that trust in traditional media hit record lows (same for trust in social media).[2] In a recent *USA Today*/Suffolk poll, independents were asked which media outlets they trusted the most, and the number one response, with 38 percent of the vote, was "none."[3]

Uncovered will lay out five overarching problems with the media, from a form of bias that's more alarming than political, to a broken incentive structure leading to self-inflicted wounds, to coziness with the powerful elite the industry is supposed to cover from a distance. Following each of the five chapters on the problems, I'll show various examples of how each of these problems play out in practice. In between, I'll introduce some case studies, talk through some concepts that help illustrate the current state of the media, and dive into specifics. At the end we'll see if we can fix this thing. Okay—that's a little ambitious, but I'll try to lay out some tangible ways the media can improve.

Along the way I'll bring you perspectives from more than two dozen current and former members of the media, all bringing their own real-world experience to the discussion. Unlike other books, there will be no "on background" quotes in here—where I give someone the anonymity of a "TV insider" to dish some dirt or to hide behind the curtain. That's a bad behavior of the press, and it's part of the reason the public trusts the media less. So I'm not going to contribute to that.

Instead, these individuals will share their unvarnished opinions and bring you the truth—at least the truth as they see it. And I'll do the same. I've been in and around the media world for more than a dozen years—with stops at CNN, TheBlaze, NBC, Fox News, and as a media reporter for Mediaite and TVNewser. I'm outside the media apparatus now, living in Dallas, but working as the executive producer of *The Megyn Kelly Show*. I love the media—I want it to be better. But it's not going to get better unless it gets serious about what's wrong in the first place.

Before we get too far down the road of talking about "the media," let's define what we're talking about.

Concept: Acela Media

Sometime around 2014 I thought I invented a term called the "Acela Media." After a Twitter search, I saw I wasn't the first one to use it. But I've adopted it as the most precise explanation of a certain kind of "media" I'm largely talking about. The Acela is the high-speed Amtrak train that flies down the Acela Corridor—starting at Boston in the north and going down to Washington, DC, in the south.

Sorry, Boston, but my version of the Acela Corridor is New York City to Washington—NYC to DC. It's a trip that many in the media make with great regularity. So much of the media apparatus operates between the two cities, and the Acela is the easiest way to hop between the two metropolises. I took the Acela from NYC to DC and back many times working at CNN, especially during the 2012 election season (although I also flew down to Atlanta about twenty times, back when that was the hub of the network).

So the Acela Media is basically the media that's situated in NYC and DC—which are all your major TV networks, most of your major newspapers, most major digital outlets. But the Acela Media also represents something else. There are lots of towns and neighborhoods between NYC and DC on the Acela that are not part of the "elite" media environment. They aren't getting invited to the fancy parties. They aren't even riding the Acela. The Acela speeds right past these towns. It's not interested in the local stops. It has places to go—fast. And so the Acela Media brings with it a level of egotism and self-absorption.

There are other terms you might see that describe the media. There's the "establishment media," largely represented by older outlets both in TV and print. There's the "legacy media," which is encapsulated by the broadcast networks in particular. There's the "corporate media," which includes a broader range of media outlets that are particularly beholden to either shareholders or investors, and therefore editorial decisions must on some level be financially motivated. There's the "mainstream media," which is similar to the Acela Media, but is more boring.

I also want to tell you where I come from—my philosophy and mission. I started the Fourth Watch newsletter in December 2019, covering the media, which was the precursor to this book. "Fourth Watch" refers to the Fourth Estate, or fourth power. The "Fourth Estate" refers to the press, or news media. In America, the Fourth Estate is often referred to in contrast to the three branches of government. But I prefer the European definition. The Fourth Estate was a separate entity from the nobility, the clergy, and the commoners. There were two ends of the spectrum when it came to the elite, and then there was the people—and the press was the conduit in between, the distiller.

Fourth Watch launched with four key pillars: intellectual honesty, intellectual consistency, intellectual curiosity, and intellectual discomfort. Honesty and consistency—independence from either political party, independence from any established belief. And curiosity and discomfort—a never-ending desire to be challenged, to interrogate our own beliefs. Disagreement strongly welcomed.

In that spirit, I'll try to live up to that philosophy here. Nuance over nonsense.

One of the first pieces of business to wrestle with is whether any of this matters at all. Is the media important, or is it frivolous? I have mixed feelings. On one hand, journalists are not saving the world. Most are not doing work that makes a difference, like a firefighter or a social worker or a doctor. The media, by and large, takes itself too seriously. There are countless examples, but one that sticks out is MSNBC's Katy Tur, appearing on a late night show shortly after Trump was inaugurated in 2017, saying "like firefighters who run into a fire, journalists run towards a story."[4]

But at the same time, when working properly, the press can serve a valuable function in society. The public relies on the media to tell them the truth—to inform them. People are busy, now more than ever. They have families, and lives, and jobs. If they want to know "the news," they should be able to get it—and get it from a place that they trust, and that deserves their trust. It is a responsibility in that sense. And the public relies on the press to hold power to account.

And then, on some level, the media of today has a job to do when it comes to entertaining the public. I know we don't want to talk about that, but what happens in the news has become more a part of our culture than ever before. The media should know that sometimes people sit in front of the TV to watch twenty minutes of cable news because they think it's fun, or funny, and hey, if they find out a little information, even better.

I also think there's an inherent privilege in being able to think about these issues, and talk about them, and write about them—for a living. I feel very lucky to be able to do this, and I don't take this opportunity lightly. It's not easy, but it's also what I love, and not many people get to make a living doing what they love.

I don't have all the answers—and I'm not going to try to come to some overriding conclusions when they aren't there. I'll try to live by example and approach this with humility and introspection, and let the mess and nuance happen naturally, rather than try to pretend everything is neat and tidy. Nothing is black-and-white—the world is full of gray areas. Doesn't that make it more fun?

So here we go. I'm excited to begin this conversation with you, and I hope you're open to the journey too.

CHAPTER 1

The Way It Was, and How It Got Weird

WHATEVER YOU THINK OF WHEN you recall the story of Ferguson, it's very likely wrong. On August 9, 2014, an eighteen-year-old Black man in Ferguson, Missouri, Michael Brown, was shot and killed by a white police officer, Darren Wilson. This was after Trayvon Martin, but before much of what would come with the social justice movement. And notably, this was before Donald Trump took an escalator ride down and announced he was running for president.

But this was the moment I believe the media changed—or at least began the metamorphosis into what it would become during the Trump Era.

Perhaps what you remember of Ferguson was the phrase "hands up, don't shoot." It became a rallying cry for the early social justice protests. It was what Michael Brown was reported to have said to Officer Wilson before Wilson shot and killed him. An iconic segment on CNN in December

2014 featured three white pundits holding up their hands in the same solidarity gesture as others around the country.[1]

The next month a CNN journalist would write that " 'Hands up, don't shoot' has become shorthand for police mistreatment of minorities, one that's spreading beyond traditional protest scenes," under the headline "Why 'Hands Up, Don't Shoot' Resonates, Regardless of Evidence."[2]

In March 2015, the Obama justice department would issue their report on the incident, and the Ferguson police department generally. They cleared Wilson of wrongdoing, concluding Wilson's version of the events was accurate: Brown punched him, tried to grab his gun, started running away, then turned and charged at him. And most notably, there was no evidence that "hands up, don't shoot" was ever uttered.[3]

In fact, the *Washington Post* would describe the "hands up, don't shoot" storyline as one of the biggest Pinocchios of 2015—or biggest lies of the year.[4] In a powerful *Post* column, Jonathan Capehart concluded, "We must never allow ourselves to march under the banner of a false narrative on behalf of someone who would otherwise offend our sense of right and wrong. And when we discover that we have, we must acknowledge it, admit our error and keep on marching. That's what I've done here."[5]

How many people who saw all the media coverage in 2014 and early 2015 still believe Michael Brown said "hands up, don't shoot"?

But that's not the end of the story either. Because while the DOJ investigation into the Ferguson police department cleared Wilson in the shooting of Brown, and also found no evidence of Wilson's racial animus, it found countless examples of racism and poor policing in the department as a whole. Racist emails were sent between police and other city officials. Arrest warrants were seemingly used as threats for payments. Over a two-year period, every single person arrested for "resisting arrest" was Black.[6]

The DOJ concluded that the disparities in arrests, tickets, and use of force existed because of an "unlawful bias" in the department.[7] If anything, the one officer accused of being a racist was apparently one of the few in the city who wasn't. The media made Wilson out to be a racist—a bad apple. But in the end, it turns out the story was more complicated and nuanced—and implicated the entire department.

Separately, the Ferguson story revealed the crackdown on journalism by those in power—like the cops. *Washington Post* reporter Wesley Lowery was arrested while covering the protests, as was Huffington Post's Ryan Reilly.[8] Trey Yingst, a journalist for News2Share, who went on to work at Fox News, was arrested too.[9] In fact, outrageously, nearly a dozen journalists were arrested or detained during the post-shooting protests.[10] It's an example for why we need a reliable, trustworthy press—when the system works, the public can rely on journalists to go and get the story, despite the risks to their own safety.

The cases against Lowery and Reilly continued after 2014 too, with them being charged in 2015 and ultimately having the charges dropped in 2016.[11]

That sort of criminalization of journalism should outrage all Americans. And it's important for the press to cover these stories. But to what degree? I later interviewed Lowery while the George Floyd protests were sweeping the country, and he described how the media coverage—especially the TV coverage—could drift into "riot porn" territory.[12] One journalist who has been on the ground for many of these social justice protests, and the tangential riot offshoots, is MSNBC's Ali Velshi, who was there in Ferguson and later in the summer of 2020 protests.

"You cannot hold people to account if you do not expose yourself to the bearing of witness. Sometimes you just gotta show it, and it may take days or weeks or months or years to determine what 'it' that you showed the viewer is—what's actually happening there," Ali Velshi told me. "When we say the shooting of Michael Brown wasn't racially motivated—I think there's a distinction in my mind between someone who's a racist who does something or something that happens because of structures in our society that are unfair. So I think the second applies in that case. And I think that's what we've learned—that there's a lot of nuance about this. Something can be borne out of a system that's unfair, that may not make every participant in it a racist or culpable of racism...I do think the only contribution I can have to this is constantly bearing witness, and then allowing for that conversation on an ongoing basis."

Few stories are uncomplicated. Nothing is easy. And the media doesn't serve us well to treat complicated stories with nuance-free coverage.

A few months before Ferguson, an eye-opening article in *National Journal* and CBS News from Major Garrett exposed a side of the media-government relationship like few other stories do. With the headline "The Pen, the Phone, and Stray Voltage," Garrett went on to peel back the curtain of a political strategy spearheaded by one of President Obama's top aides, David Plouffe, known as the "stray voltage" theory. "The theory goes like this: Controversy sparks attention, attention provokes conversation, and conversation embeds previously unknown or marginalized ideas in the public consciousness," wrote Garrett. "This happens, Plouffe theorizes, even when—and sometimes especially when—the White House appears defensive, besieged, or off-guard."[13]

At the time he wrote about it, Garrett was describing a "gender pay gap" controversy that the White House was dealing with. Or, put in the new "stray voltage" context, it was a controversy that the Obama White House was actively courting, and creating. At its core, the strategy was put into place to manipulate both the media and the public—and it was extremely effective. By introducing an idea into the information ecosystem designed to elicit a controversy or a distraction, it presented the Obama White House an opportunity. The diversion was planted, and the subservient press was happy to participate—consciously or subconsciously.

In truth, the Obama White House treated the Acela Media very poorly, and the masochistic press ate it up while continuing to deify the commander-in-chief. The Obama administration used the Espionage Act to target reporters and sources for doing the job of journalism more than all other administrations combined—including the Trump administration.[14] The Department of Justice under Obama secretly obtained the phone records of AP reporters.[15] They spied on Fox News reporter James Rosen.[16]

Another reporter, *New York Times*'s James Risen, was

pressured to reveal his confidential sources by the DOJ and Eric Holder. He concluded that the Obama administration was "the greatest enemy of press freedom in a generation,"[17] and later, before Trump took office, wrote a column in the *Times* on why "If Donald Trump Targets Journalists, Thank Obama."[18]

In a *New York Times Magazine* profile of Obama's top aide Ben Rhodes, Rhodes bragged about how "we created an echo chamber" in the media by building personal relationships with journalists and pundits. "They were saying things that validated what we had given them to say," said Rhodes.[19]

I go through these examples to illustrate a few points. First, it's good to remember that the stories we see in the press, and about the press, are nuanced—nothing is black-and-white. Also, while the Trump administration did not treat the press well, and the media was outraged by the relationship (in some cases, members went a little crazy because of it), the poor treatment of the press didn't begin with Trump either. And most importantly, the issues in the media that were exacerbated during the Trump Era didn't begin with the election of Trump. They existed to some extent already.

But ultimately they are just examples—they are symptoms. We need to address the underlying problems at the root of what's ailing our American press.

CHAPTER 2

Geographic Bias

O NE OF THE MOST COMMON misconceptions that exists about the media is the idea that politics, or a political bias in favor of the left over the right, is what informs media mistakes, or drives media malpractice. "Politics" is too easy an out for the press—and it only scratches the surface of what's at the core of the matter.

There's no denying that much of the media leans left. The mainstream, establishment press is made up of liberals who often vote for Democrats.[1] But there are deeper issues at play, and allowing politics to envelop what ails the industry ignores so many other factors.

As I'll detail later in the book, how can a political bias explain what happened with Bernie Sanders when he ran for president in 2016 or 2020? How can it explain the stories the media gets wrong or ignores that have absolutely nothing to do with politics at all?

There's an overriding bias that is far more pervasive in the corporate media today, and it is one of geography.

A geographic bias brings with it a level of blind spots and ignorance. And while the corporate media today holds tremendous power, it is powerful in a very specific and isolated way. It's why it's the first major problem with the modern media.

The entertainment power center in America, and perhaps the world, exists almost exclusively in Los Angeles. The tech power center in America is largely based in and around San Francisco and Silicon Valley. Similarly, the media power centers are almost exclusively based in New York City and Washington, DC.

While DC provides a powerful outlet for media to liaise and engage with government officials, New York City is the home to the corporate headquarters of almost every major media outlet outside of the ones specifically based in DC, like the *Washington Post*. And for those who are unfamiliar with New York City, I want to walk you through just how isolated it actually is. Let's say you wanted to visit the offices where the top media executives in America worked. You could start your journey at CNN, currently located on 33rd Street and Eleventh Avenue. Then hop north and east a bit to the *New York Times*, on 41st Street and Eighth Avenue. Go north and east a bit farther, and you'll hit NBC News and MSNBC on 48th Street and Sixth Avenue, and then for good measure go literally across the street to Fox News and the *Wall Street Journal*. Then take a brisk walk north to ABC News, on 66th Street and Columbus Avenue (roughly Ninth Avenue). And finally go west and south a bit to CBS News, on 57th and Tenth Avenue.

If you're efficient, you could hit each of these locations in the span of approximately ninety minutes. And now you've visited the offices where a large portion of the top decision-makers in the media work each day. These buildings in New York City, like so many in NYC, are full of transplants from all over the country and all over the world. But they have arrived at a single geographic destination, and are far away from the bulk of the population that consumes their content.

When so much of our media is geographically isolated in one city, in a short thirty-block stretch of a small but densely packed island on the far east coast of America, bias is inevitably going to creep in. Perhaps it does so subconsciously. But it can be very noticeable to those who consume the media, and it manifests in several damaging ways.

The audience often doesn't have much choice in the matter but to consume a geographically biased national press. Salena Zito has spent the past few years traversing America and covering politics and policy by actually embedding in the communities themselves. She was one of the few who correctly saw the Trump phenomenon coming, and she wrote about it in her excellent 2018 book, *The Great Revolt.*

"We have massive newsroom deserts across the country," Zito told me. "Local news is evaporating. When local news evaporates, you go to a larger entity to get your news. And the more that [happened,] people sort of gravitated towards the national news...What they didn't understand is that people in the newsrooms that were their local news reporters, the reason why you didn't hear like fake news or bias or whatever, was because those people were geographically rooted to where they worked. Not only did they work in the newsroom, they lived in the community. They coached their kids' softball, they were an usher at your church, you know, they were in the Rotary Club. They were invested in that community. It doesn't matter if they were left or right. They were rooted."

Some of the geographic bias is created by decisions made at the executive level, based on the business model of the industry. Joel Cheatwood was a longtime executive at CNN, Fox News, and throughout local news. While the national media may hope on some level to cover the full country, the incentives are not necessarily there. "The national media, the legacy media, is sticking true to that formula," he told me. "It's been around forever, which is the ratings come from New York, LA, Chicago, and Houston and Dallas, and that's basically where we're going to put our focus."

When Cheatwood was at CNN, he recalls pitching a plan to develop a show for Anderson Cooper that would put Cooper on a bus going throughout the country, avoiding the power centers like New York, DC, and LA. "It was all for the purpose of getting out of that ivory tower syndrome of 'we have to be in the major markets because that's where the ratings were,'" he said. "And they just didn't quite get it. You know, it'd be like, 'yeah, but we have to do well in New York, we have to do well in Washington.' And I don't think they're by any stretch of the imagination out of that mindset, because that's still how the financial metric is situated."

It's worth noting that during Cheatwood's time at CNN, the network's headquarters was actually based outside the Acela Media, in Atlanta. But the shift away from Atlanta as the network's hub began during my time at the network—so while primary election nights in 2012 were held in Atlanta,

the general election coverage was held in DC, and trips to
Atlanta became fewer and fewer. By the time I left CNN
the next year, nearly every hour of programming originated
from New York or DC.

Ali Velshi has traveled around the country as a host on
CNN and then MSNBC. He says there's an appetite for a
sort of dialogue that we don't normally see modeled in our
corporate media. "It's going to be a series of little conversations," he told me. "We in the media have to model them
for the public. And when the public starts to do that, politicians will say you know what? My answer lies in modeling
discourse, dialogue and debate, not in modeling extremist
views. I'm gonna shed the extremists on either side of the
spectrum in favor of the broad middle, who really is curious
and wants a discussion…I think the road is there."

Of course, being isolated by geography will inevitably lead to biases beyond just geography. "Where are your
major networks headquartered? New York and California,
and then they have big bureaus in DC," said John Roberts.
"Those are all three very Democratic places. If you had a
news network that was headquartered in Orlando, you
probably would have a really interesting mix of political
backgrounds. Because Orlando is a very purple area of the
country. The I-4 corridor is one of the biggest swing districts
in America. And so you get a lot of Republicans, you get a lot
of Democrats, and you get a tremendous number of independents. And those political ideologies would fit into the mix
of whatever that news organization was doing. But when
you have a news network, it's headquartered in New York,
and then its biggest bureau is in DC and then Los Angeles,

three Democratic strongholds, you can probably surmise that the majority of people's political leanings are going to be Democratic."

At the core of geographic bias is a lack of trust that the elite Acela Media has toward its own audience. That lack of trust stems from ignorance, and ignorance plus arrogance can be a deadly combination.

We're going to spend a lot of time on the COVID-19 pandemic later this chapter and throughout the book, which both served as a media story on its own and became a slate to graft so many problems that already existed in the media onto one of the most serious stories of our lifetime. But shortly before the pandemic kicked off in earnest in America, a viral tweet told a story that's important to spend some time on. On February 28, 2020, CNN tweeted to its tens of millions of followers the following results of a poll: "38 percent of Americans wouldn't buy Corona beer 'under any circumstances' because of the coronavirus, according to a recent survey. Just to be abundantly clear: There is no link between the virus and the beer."[2] This has been retweeted more than 40,000 times and liked more than 60,000 times. The most liked reply to the tweet has hundreds of retweets and another 10,000 likes, and concludes: "38 percent of Americans like trump. Think there's a connection?"[3]

The problem with this tweet and the corresponding article is it's absolutely false. First of all, the poll is not scientific in any way. A PR company put out a press release saying they surveyed 700 or so "beer drinkers," and found that the coronavirus pandemic could be bad for the brand Corona.[4] But the 38 percent figure actually refers to the percentage of "beer-drinking Americans" who would not buy Corona—not those who would not buy it, as the CNN tweet says, "because of the coronavirus." That number is actually represented in the survey, though—of those who actually drink Corona, a measly 4 percent said they would now stop drinking Corona because of coronavirus.

Yes, this is a stupid poll and a stupid story. But it's representative of the sort of elite disdain media outlets have for the population at large. Did not a single person pause to think that perhaps 40 percent of "beer-drinkers" aren't as dense as the tweet and article ultimately imply? No, because they don't trust their audience. Because they spend their time isolated from large swaths of their own consumers.

But trust goes both ways.

Concept: The Temperature Test

Imagine you're in a foreign location—somewhere very unlike where you live and where you're comfortable. This location has an unfamiliar climate and terrain, and you feel very much out of your element. Now for the sake of this hypothetical, you step outside of a house in this location where you are staying. You survey the landscape, and then you re-enter the house and turn on the TV, which happens to be playing a news broadcast. In this news broadcast, you watch as the weather report comes on. In a strange twist of fate, the weather report happens to be giving the temperature for the exact location where you currently are staying.

Having just been outside, you make a guess what the forecaster will say the temperature is. Let's say you think it's

74 degrees Fahrenheit. If the meteorologist says the temperature is 71 degrees, or 77 degrees, it wouldn't give you much pause at all. We all have a general feeling about temperature, but no one can perfectly determine the exact temperature.

What if he relayed a further deviation, though? What if the meteorologist said it was, say, 67 degrees, or 81 degrees? Could you get to 62 degrees, or 86 degrees, and still believe him? That's a bit more off than you would think, but you could easily give him the benefit of the doubt still. You're in a foreign location. Perhaps the climate is messing with you a bit. It's unfamiliar to you, and after all, the guy on TV is the expert.

Now imagine you're watching this broadcast, making a guess that it's 74 degrees, and instead the forecaster says it's 38 degrees. You double check. Is he talking about Fahrenheit? Yes. 38 degrees Fahrenheit.

It would be logical at this point that you'd simply think it was a mistake. That sort of discrepancy would make no sense. Sure, it's a place you've never been before, but you know what 38 degrees feels like, and this is not that.

Suddenly your whole philosophy changes. This meteorologist is wrong. He surely must not be an expert after all. In fact, it's also easy to see how suddenly you're even more confident in your original projection of 74 degrees. Suddenly, the flexibility you once had to believe in the deviation outside your perceived temperature is evaporating. No, it's 74 degrees. Not 77. Not 75. 74.

You dig your heels in. And you certainly lose confidence in the man on TV.

This is what I call "The Temperature Test," and it's a

good corollary for the cause and effect in a corporate media that exhibits traits of geographic bias (among other problems). Audiences are willing to have some flexibility, and deference, when it comes to their media outlets. The press are the experts, and audiences don't have the time or resources to study up on every issue. They rely on the experts in the media to distill for them what matters, and, most importantly, what's accurate.

And so, yes, perhaps the media will give them an impression about an issue, or about an entire country, that feels unfamiliar. An audience may begin to be skeptical but will go along cautiously to a point. But that can only go so far.

At some point, a media that insists on telling a story in a way that is entirely unfamiliar to the audience will lead to a backlash. This certainly is the case with Donald Trump, which we'll dive into much more in later chapters. But it's also more broadly the case with the Trump Era, and the divisiveness displayed on cable news panels or through op-eds tailor-made for a Twitter audience over-indexing in NYC and DC.

And the reason this is so deleterious to the corporate press is because when it loses the trust of the audience, it makes the audience skeptical of everything—even when the press is telling the story straight. Suddenly an audience of Americans outside this Acela Media bubble will dig their heels in and dispute whatever storyline they're being fed. And then in instances where the press is actually more accurate than an audience is giving it credit for, the audience's distrust of the "expert" leads them to believe their own feel for the temperature of the moment.

The Temperature Test can be applied to every story. Does it *feel* right? And at what temperature will a willing audience suddenly turn against the man on the TV?

So how does this geographic bias get solved? It's not just about hiring a bunch of journalists from places outside the Acela corridor and flying them into the same newsrooms. "I do think it's entirely too New York City, Washington DC, Los Angeles–centric, and it's not that they only hire people from those areas," said Will Cain, who is from outside of Dallas, Texas. "But the people that leave Middle America and join this industry are often people that hate where they came from."

Salena Zito points out the way to balance these national newsrooms is through culture, not politics. Cultural diversity can be a big differentiator. "They didn't go to a community college. They don't own a gun, they don't know how to operate a gun. They would never consider being pro-life," she said of the general crop of legacy media journalists in national newsrooms. "And yet that's what the people are that are covering them, even if they are a Democrat or Republican. They have no cultural tissue, no connection to them. There's a geographic bias because they don't know anybody like them. When they cover something they don't know, it tends to be an oddity, tends to be a freak, because they didn't grow up with anyone like that, that they live in these sort of super zip codes that are oftentimes the center of wealth and power, like Washington, DC, New York, and Silicon Valley.

Everyone went to the same kinds of schools. Everyone goes to the same kinds of place to eat or drink and the people that they hang out with share their worldview. And they're covering people who do not share their worldview and they're looked at as odd."

Amy Chozick of the *New York Times*, who grew up in Texas, has seen this sort of cultural dissonance within newsrooms in the Acela Media firsthand. "It's about finding journalists who have family in the military, who go to church every Sunday or are religious Jews," she said of the need for certain kinds of cultural diversity in national newsrooms. "Journalists who have different experiences, journalists who have shot a gun. I mean, it was small things, but just being from Texas, I have a cousin in the Air Force, I've shot a gun. Like all of these things, you didn't meet anyone else in the newsroom, or very rarely did you meet anyone with those experiences in the newsroom. This predates the *Times*. When I was just starting at the *Wall Street Journal*, I was going home to Texas and the business editor was like, 'Oh, that's so interesting. You should check out a Walmart while you're there.' I was like, 'Where do you think we shopped?'...But I think it's very important. And it's hard. Like it's easy to hire people who went to Dalton and Harvard and worked at the *New York Times*, it's very hard to find a really cool reporter at the *Detroit Free Press*, or the columnist in St. Louis."

When you have a geographic bias and are tasked with covering a country that's unfamiliar to you, journalism becomes more like anthropology. You're on a mission to explore new cultures and report back about the strange locals you're encountering. We get helicopter journalism—touching down in a community, hitting a diner or two to grab some local colorful quotes, and jetting back to the NYC newsroom to file the report. The story doesn't delve beyond the surface or, worse, misses the story entirely.

We saw a lot of problems with COVID reporting, but the hypocrisy that came from geographically biased COVID coverage was some of the most glaring of the past several years.

Case Study: COVID Hypocrisy

It's always important to read beyond a headline. Headlines in mainstream media are largely not the work of the author of the piece (a point that will lead to a major issue a few chapters from now). But headlines are powerful—they can stick with you, in ways a really juicy passage of a lengthy, nuanced article can't. I'll always remember a headline from *The Atlantic* in April of 2020, a few weeks after the COVID pandemic really began: "Georgia's Experiment in Human Sacrifice."[5]

The article was a reference to some slight pandemic restrictions being eased by the southern state. People were scared in the early days of the pandemic—I get it. But the ominous prediction from *The Atlantic*'s Amanda Mull never came to be. Sure, cases, and hospitalizations and deaths, in Georgia and throughout the country—in every single state—eventually did rise. But the "experiment" described in the headline proved the media's hypothesis entirely wrong. In a rare case of media accountability, NBC News looked at the experiment a month later and found there was "no major spike in cases" due to the slight easing of restrictions.[6]

The Georgia story early in the pandemic was a precursor to the type of coverage we were about to get from the geographically isolated media—even more isolated than ever before thanks to the COVID lockdown. Suddenly the New York–based media was dealing with a state health crisis that was very real. Hospitals were filling up, and New York was finding it challenging to get the pandemic under control. That extended to the whole tri-state area, New Jersey and Connecticut, north to New England and south to Washington, DC. The northeast was hit hard at a time when we didn't have any real treatment options available.

At the same time, the Acela Media began adapting to the pandemic new normal by working from home and broadcasting remotely. If they barely ventured out of the Acela corridor before, 2020 and 2021 only exacerbated that. And so it's in this context of ignorance we got the sort of hypocritical coverage we saw about the rest of the country. It started with Georgia, but it extended to a few very select states. Florida and Texas were the most favored targets of the media—largely thanks to their high-profile Republican governors, Ron DeSantis and Greg Abbott respectively.

This geographic bias played out in a lot of different ways, but here are two specifics. First, we saw it in coverage of outdoor cases. Now, mind you, early on in the pandemic we learned that in fact outdoor spread was very rare. By May 2020 we had a study out of China that found that out of more than 7,000 cases, only a single case could be traced to outdoor transmission.[7]

But that didn't stop the Acela Media from COVID-shaming anyone who dared step outside unmasked. And they didn't spend their focus on beaches in their backyards—in New York or New Jersey. No, they hopped over to their favorite targets instead. CNN covered the first Memorial Day weekend of the pandemic like it was a mass criminal event. "As death toll nears 100,000, some Americans break from social distancing during holiday weekend," blared one headline.[8]

On TV there was practically wall-to-wall coverage, with the lower-third chyron on the screen noting Americans in these often red states were "flocking" to the beaches—largely unmasked (while pictures and videos did not show a particularly high amount of "flocking"). CNN's Gary Tuchman got nearly nine minutes on *Anderson Cooper 360°* for his report from Alabama, highlighting an outdoor bar that was, apparently, dangerously "jammed." The segment was full of southern accents and finger-wagging reporting from the east coast–based Tuchman.[9]

You would think that a year of the pandemic would be enough time for the mainstream media to learn from some of the mistakes they made, like about the actual lack of danger of outdoor transmission, but by the next year, the same tone was continuing. In March 2021, NBC News headed down to Florida for a report on "spring break superspreaders."[10]

Another issue with the COVID hypocrisy related to a favored, almost religious, symbol of the left and the media, the mask. Let's put aside for the moment the actual effectiveness of masks when it comes to stopping the spread of COVID—a particularly nuanced discussion that has evolved greatly during the length of the pandemic (although we can't ignore that some of the biggest mask advocates audiences saw in the press have changed their specific recommendations, like Dr. Leana Wen, who would say at the end of 2021 that cloth masks are "little more than facial decorations"[11]).

The geographic bias kicks in with masks when it comes to what the media believes red state citizens are actually doing. And perhaps it most stems from an intentional or unintentional misunderstanding about what "mask mandates" actually mean. In March 2021, Texas relaxed its mask mandate and allowed businesses to make their own decisions about whether patrons had to be masked. CNN began one report looking at the state by declaring, "Texas has been mask-free since the beginning of March."[12]

Do these reporters believe Texas actually had eliminated masks from existence? No—in fact they quote quite favorably throughout the article a diner owner who is still requiring masks. But this casual, shorthand misinformation is prevalent throughout when talking about states outside the bubble.

It's the same for schools too. On NBC's *Meet the Press* in August 2021, a graphic showed the states where masks in schools were "banned," including in Texas, Florida, and Arizona.[13] Masks, of course, were never banned in schools—any parent who chose to have their student wear a mask could continue to do so. Instead, mask mandates were banned, and masks were not required.

Dr. Marty Makary is a professor at Johns Hopkins and health expert who later became a medical contributor to Fox News during the pandemic. I spoke with Makary about the way the media misrepresented so many of the core elements of the pandemic to its audience, and some of the root causes behind this problem. We also talked about the hypocrisy of the coverage—specifically honing in on the way the media covered large gatherings of a political nature. The media condemned Trump rallies, even outdoor rallies, as potential superspreader events, while the social justice protests that came after the killing of George Floyd were deemed acceptable because of the subject matter. Said Makary:

> People want nonpolitical doctors because they want to know that their doctor is being scientifically objective. And when the medical and public health community beclowns themselves by saying that a Trump rally is a significant public health concern, but a BLM close gathering is important because of its overall benefits to health, these were mixed messages that, separate from whether or not it was good medical advice, it exposes the sort of politicization of medical recommendations. And the reality is, these questions could have been answered in a brief period of time with good definitive studies. We have a culture in the medical establishment that what really matters is laboratory medicine. Give us a drug, go to the bench lab, and have the real scientists give us a solution to our problems. And that's a broader problem in healthcare. It's a pill-popping culture where "give us a drug to fix our problems. Don't tell us about exercise and food, to manage obesity, give us an obesity drug." So when COVID hit us, it was the same thing. "Go to

the lab, and give us a drug, have the scientists produce something that we can take," and that's important. It's always an important endeavor. And it was with COVID vaccines. But also the basic clinical questions went unfunded, and one of those was where does it spread, and how does it spread. So I believe patients want to see an objective physician. And when I look at the community of physicians that I respect the most and have bonded the most with nationally and internationally on COVID, they come from a broad range of political ends of the spectrum—liberal, conservative—the reason I respect them is I believe they have retained their scientific objectivity, in front of any political perspectives they might have.

So where did this come from? "It was driven by the medical establishment having a very cozy relationship with certain media outlets, certain mainstream media outlets, and as you know, many of us physicians that had the privilege of going on Fox were able to speak freely, and give a counter perspective to the narrative on things like natural immunity as an effective form of immunity that offers protection against COVID," said Makary. "Not perfect, but better than the vaccines in the final analysis. And the data has finally caught up with the medical establishment. And many of us who have offered different points of view have essentially now been vindicated through data and science that has come out showing that many of these things we were talking about and challenging were not based on data, instead, it was dogma. And when the science caught up with these individuals promoting the dogma, it turns out that it was not what they had put out."

Natural immunity was almost exclusively ignored by the Acela Media as a topic—but just because it wasn't making it on air and to the eyes and ears of the public didn't mean it was being ignored in the scientific community. But the distrust the media and the elite consensus shapers had for the public was behind the relative silence. "I can tell you in my private conversations with public health officials, they believed one of the reasons we should not be talking about natural immunity as much as they privately acknowledged that it was effective was that people may misinterpret what we're saying," said Makary. "...This intense paternalism we've seen in healthcare before. My philosophy has always been to be honest with the data and let people make their own decision."

Makary notes the way COVID studies have been selectively covered by the media. "It has exposed these tremendous biases, not only in the media, but in the medical profession as well," he said. "And what you see is that selective outrage, the all heaven and earth comes down to scrutinize a study that may suggest a point of view that has been sort of sidelined. Whereas when a completely flawed study on natural immunity or masks and kids comes out of the CDC, journalists seem to have no bones to pick, there's almost no criticism whatsoever."

And then, of course, there was the Trump factor, which we'll get more into in later chapters. "It was sort of the Trump retaliation phenomenon," said Makary. "If he had done something that the medical establishment didn't support, then it was sort of this disproportionate outrage that this is the main problem in society. We have massive arguments about things that barely matter. They are peripheral issues like cloth masks and toddlers... Meanwhile, we're not talking about obesity, the number one common risk factor after advanced age for COVID mortality, we don't talk about therapeutics... You saw this immense backlash over Trump refusing to wear a cloth mask, as if cloth masks were going to really change the trajectory of the pandemic. So it was this sort of retaliation, and you could see those doctors who had lost their scientific objectivity, their rage was disproportionate to the rage that we should have had about the lack of clinical studies to challenge surface transmission, ignoring natural immunity, school closures, boosters in young healthy people."

Overall, the certainty and arrogance of the press when it came to COVID, mixed with the hypocrisy of geographic bias, exposed some of our biggest media problems. "When you're in a fast-moving news environment, to reflexively call things 'wrong' or 'misinformation' when we really don't know, and then to have zero, and I'm talking zero, self-reflection about the fact that we didn't know, I think it's really arrogant, and it's really contributing to the distrust of news," Amy Chozick told me.

That lack of introspection is a huge problem—as in the bias toward "doom"—both of which we'll get to later in the book. But with COVID in particular, we see the glaring geographic bias in the selective outrage, and the total lack of accountability and nuance in coverage.

CHAPTER 3

Laziness and Incompetence vs. Conspiracy

So we've established one problem; what does that look like in practice? And more importantly, what's the underlying reason why we see geographic bias—or, frankly, pick your bias. What's the reason we see bias in general in Acela Media reporting?

One of the biggest misconceptions among those critical of the press is that this is all a grand conspiracy. Certainly there is a level of coziness between the press and power that is both real and insidious, and we'll dig into that in later chapters. But it's too simplistic to use a conspiracy as an explanation for the problems in the media. In fact, it also gives the corporate media too much credit.

Instead, there are other factors at play. There is incompetence, for one. Many individuals who make up the media simply are not particularly good at their jobs. If they were plumbers, or lawyers, perhaps those individuals would receive bad Yelp reviews, and their businesses would be harmed. But incompetence in the media doesn't translate the same way. The incentive structure is different—and the reward mechanism is different too.

But beyond incompetence is something more boring, but realistic—many in the media are simply lazy. Sometimes it's a willful disinterest in stories—avoiding certain topics that are more challenging to cover in favor of those that are easier. Do you ever notice how when a topic is easy to understand, there are thousands of media reports on it, but when the topic is challenging and complicated, it barely gets covered? Think of an election year. How often do we get the horse race coverage—who's up and who's down, what do the polls say? These stories are ubiquitous because they are easy—they can be crafted while the journalists sit in their living rooms, tapping away on their laptops. But the issues—especially thorny, complicated issues like abortion or immigration, where opinion varies wildly and doesn't fit a neat and tidy narrative, and requires actually talking to voters—those often get short shrift. In theory, it should be the opposite, and yet the press, like other occupations, is full of people who are there to do a job and get home to their family. But the information supply and demand is surely out of whack.

In other instances, the establishment media avoids certain storylines because they may not fit into the preferred narrative. But it's not always willful either. Sometimes the best explanation for why a story is improperly covered is a general, more subtle laziness that manifests itself in biases like source bias or confirmation bias.

Let's stick with the COVID pandemic and explore one particular area. Dr. Anthony Fauci has been a prominent public figure for decades in America, and is undoubtably a creature of Washington. As the longtime head of the National Institute of Allergy and Infectious Diseases department (NIAID) within the National Institutes of Health (NIH), he has a variety of previously established relationships with "important" figures throughout the corporate press and other levers of power. Perhaps you had never heard of Fauci before March 2020, but he was certainly known in the world of the DC elite and had been for a very long time.

When the pandemic hit, the media was scrambling to understand it and properly cover it. The mistakes were not made on purpose, but rather out of a lack of understanding of what was truly happening. But the geographic bias comes in because the person whom the media establishment turned to as the singular source of information was Dr. Fauci—because he was familiar to them in an unfamiliar time.

As such, Fauci exerted tremendous power in the early days of the pandemic, when it really mattered—and that power was ingrained into the consciousness of the audience for years to come. He was among a very small group of doctors who became the voices of science for a scared audience.

"We saw so many mistakes by public health officials that could have been challenged with some basic journalism. We saw many media outlets sourcing the same establishment doctors, the same doctors from the government, the same doctors who were party loyalists to that government narrative," Dr. Marty Makary told me. "And so you saw this small group of people making all the decisions, and then another group of people in the normal healthy spirit of scientific dialogue, who had impeccable academic credentials sidelined, and they were canceled."

In practice, this had disastrous effects. Dr. Makary: "When surface transmission was put out there by Dr. Fauci as the mechanism by which COVID-19 spreads and fomites, you had so many people pouring gallons of alcohol-based solutions on their mail and grocery bags. And you saw so many media outlets basically just give Dr. Fauci this enormous platform, crowning him with the title 'the nation's top infectious diseases physician,' even though he is not an infectious diseases–trained physician. He never did an infectious disease fellowship. He did a rheumatology fellowship. Now I still have a lot of respect for him. But when we put our entire faith and trust in one individual without asking any questions, because you know, this must be Moses, coming down with the Ten Commandments. Then guess what, we get burned."

The Fauci love in the media was proportional to the Trump hate—a point we'll get into more later in the book. Josh Rogin is a columnist for the *Washington Post* who has done excellent reporting on COVID. "Anthony Fauci can be a good man who has flaws and there can also be good-faith attacks on him and bad-faith attacks on him," Rogin told me. "But the point is once he became the anti-Trump, criticizing him became supporting Trump and vice versa, and good-faith criticisms of him were not given any oxygen."

One of those good-faith critiques of Dr. Fauci's COVID pandemic philosophy came from the three expert doctors behind a document known as the Great Barrington

Declaration (GBD). The three who created it—Dr. Jay Bhattacharya of Stanford, Dr. Sonali Gupta of Oxford, and
Dr. Martin Kulldorff of Harvard—argued the lockdown
strategy could have a disastrous effect. The document was
published in October 2020, and very quickly the trio were
treated like scientific pariahs, in the science community but
also in the media.

As we would later learn, there was a coordinated effort
by Fauci and Dr. Francis Collins, then the head of the NIH,
to shut down and silence this storyline. In an email later
obtained through a Freedom of Information Act (FOIA)
request, we know Collins emailed Fauci shortly after the
GBD publication to warn about the attention these "fringe
epidemiologists" were getting. "There needs to be a quick
and devastating published takedown," Collins wrote Fauci.

Following up on the request, Fauci forwarded Collins a
report in *Wired* magazine knocking down the strategy.[1] Collins and Fauci got exactly what they wanted—most in the
corporate press treated the GBD like it was published by a
bunch of kooks, and dangerous ones at that. And that was
when it got covered at all—it mostly just got ignored.

I talked to Dr. Jay Bhattacharya about the experience and
the way the media deferred to its preferred "experts" like
Fauci rather than providing a nuanced look at the important
issue.

"The head of the NIH called for, effectively, a coordinated media campaign to destroy us as scientists," Bhattacharya told me. "And the media agreed. I started getting
calls from the *New York Times* and all these other media
sources asking me why I wanted to let the virus rip through

society. The words 'let it rip' do not appear in the Great Barrington Declaration. The thought never crossed my mind. My argument was to protect the vulnerable. That was the main purpose. We were doing these lockdowns that were hurting kids without actually protecting anybody, while we were failing to protect the vulnerable."

But the media had made its decision—its uninformed, or at least underinformed, decision. It lazily focused on a single strategy, which was being propagated by Fauci. "The media essentially decided I was a bad guy," said Bhattacharya. "I had a whole bunch of hostile media trying to mischaracterize what I actually was arguing for."

The reason for the anti-lockdown messaging boils down to a distrust of the public and an overreliance on a single perspective. "Instead of encouraging and engaging in a real science and policy discussion, they decided that they were going to use their power to stop it from happening. And the media helped," Bhattacharya told me.

At the center of it? The guy the DC elite were comfortable with all along, fed by a geographic bias against looking outside of the most convenient messenger. "Tony Fauci was using his absolute command of the media environment to stoke this," Bhattacharya told me. "The lab leak he did this, on the lockdowns he's done this, he did this with the possibility of early treatment. He's using this incredible—he's like a genius for this—absolute control of how to get the media to do what he wants."

And the media was more than happy to comply. It was easy, after all. It would help to not confuse the audience by daring to introduce alternate ideas into the ecosystem. But

why is it important to assess the mistakes when it comes to
the sort of incompetent, lazy media coverage we got during
the pandemic? As Rogin told me, the future of our country
depends on better, more accurate reporting. "All of our institutions, not just in our government, but in our society, made
huge mistakes during the pandemic, especially in those early
months," he told me. "It was a catastrophic, unprecedented,
worldwide catastrophe, affected every human being on the
planet. None of our institutions were prepared for that.
None of them handled it perfectly. All of them made huge,
huge grievous errors in one way or the other. Government,
the media, our national security system, our educational system, our health system. This is not to say these are staffed by
bad people. It's just that these institutions are not designed
for this. So I offer these gentle criticisms of my own industry, the media industry, in the spirit of learning from those
mistakes. It's not to bash on the media. It's just to say that if
we don't talk honestly about what those mistakes were, then
how can we hope to learn from those so that we don't make
them again?"

I concur. Critiquing media mistakes is about fixing the
mistakes, not wallowing in, or celebrating, media decline.
But take a simple example—what the COVID-19 virus was
called. Originally, many in the establishment press called it
the "Wuhan Coronavirus," which was a reference to where
the strain of coronavirus was originally identified. But suddenly the term became anathema—a symbol of "racism" or
anti-Asian hate. CNN hosts described it as the "Wuhan coronavirus" on air for weeks before the pandemic really became
an issue in America, but by mid-March had determined the

term was racist and only being used because Trump was "looking for someone to blame."[2]

This was not some grand conspiracy. It was a reactive, lazy overreach. But it brings us to another element of the problem.

There's another form of laziness or practical indifference that's at play, especially in the current world of journalism. Because of a variety of factors, the incentive structure is massively warped when it comes to reporting what is true and what isn't.

Concept: Pascal's Wager of Woke Journalism

Journalism has always been a cost-benefit analysis. Not to get all philosophical, but I suppose all of life is. And since we're getting philosophical, let's dig into a term known as "Pascal's Wager."

Pascal's Wager was coined in the 1600s by French philosopher Blaise Pascal, and it's a somewhat cynical argument in favor of the belief in God. Pascal argues that the belief in God is essentially a cost-benefit analysis. If you believe in God, and when you die there's an afterlife, you "win"—you go to heaven. If you believe in God, and when you die there is no afterlife, you "lose." But ultimately, what do you really lose? Nothing much—it's a minor loss. You wasted some time on earth believing in something that turned out not to be real.

If you don't believe in God, and when you die there is no afterlife, you "win." What do you win? Nothing much—it's a small victory, but a victory nonetheless. You can pat yourself on the back knowing you got it right on earth, although you'll be dead, so what will it really matter at that point anyway? But if you don't believe in God and there is in fact an afterlife, then you "lose"—and you lose big. Eternal damnation kind of big.

Pascal concluded that it's ultimately better to believe in God because the cost-benefit analysis favors it.

I've used this idea of Pascal's Wager to bring us to present-day journalism and the current "woke" environment media members find themselves in. Instead of believe/don't believe and afterlife/no afterlife as the equation, we have two separate but related elements of the current landscape. For journalists, it used to be the cost-benefit analysis that was most important was whether a story is true or not true. If you cover a story as true and it turns out to be false, that's a big loss. If you avoid a story that turns out to be true, that's a loss too. But there's another important element that has been introduced now—whether the thought is "acceptable" or "unacceptable."

How do we know what's an example of "Acceptable Thought" vs. "Unacceptable Thought"? This is determined largely by the very insular and insidious world of Twitter, a topic we'll dive much more into later in the book. There is a small number of "blue check" journalists, politicians, and other supposed "influencers" who determine what is acceptable or not based on a very narrow, woke, progressive point of view. Cross them, and face the wrath.

If you cover a story that's true, and it's from an angle that is deemed "acceptable," that's a win for you and your organization. But it's not a huge win, necessarily—you probably aren't going to get any awards for covering a true, acceptable, story. If you cover a story in a way that's incorrect, or false, but in a way that's acceptable, that's a loss for you in one sense. In the old days—like B.T. (Before Twitter), way back, say, twenty years ago—it would be a huge loss. You've gotten a story wrong, trust in your organization has been eroded. But for outlets today, coming from an acceptable point of view is more important. They'll grant you the benefit of the doubt.

If you cover a story that's true, but it's from an angle that's deemed "unacceptable" by the Twitterati, that's perhaps a small win, but by coming from an "unacceptable" point of view, you'll face backlash anyway. If you cover a story incorrectly—the story turns out to be false—*and* it's coming from an "unacceptable" angle, that's a huge loss. You'll lose the trust of the public for the incorrect coverage, and you'll face the backlash for coming at it in an unacceptable way.

	Acceptable	Unacceptable
Correct	**WIN**	Lose/Win
Incorrect	Win/Lose	**LOSE**

For the current media, the cost-benefit analysis means it's better to cover a story in an acceptable way, even if that coverage turns out to be false, than risk covering a story in an unacceptable way. That's a huge problem, because the American audience loses in this new equation—they don't anchor their lives around what is Acceptable and Unacceptable Thought. They largely don't know, and don't care. They want the truth—whatever perspective it comes from. In this sense, this is another extension of the media's geographic bias. They are biased against their own audience, because they are more beholden to the whims of the Twitter mob than to the larger American public.

And it is in this warped press environment of Pascal's Wager of Woke Journalism where we start to see an increase in media mistakes, inevitably coming from a single direction.

Case Study: Jussie Smollett

There are two shining examples of Pascal's Wager of Woke Journalism at work—and how it can combine with geographic bias (and a built-in anti-Trump bias too). The first is what took place in January 2019, when a brief video went viral depicting a high school student standing with a slight smile on his face while an older Native American man beat on his drum in front of him. The confrontation took place in Washington, DC, at a pro-life march. The boy, who we later learned was Nicholas Sandmann of Covington Catholic High School in Kentucky, was wearing a MAGA hat.

The condemnation was swift, despite the lack of context or further investigation. Perhaps no segment was more glaring than from CNN's S. E. Cupp, who argued that "there's no place for this in our society," and went on to attack the school, the students, and the parents.[3]

A couple days later, Cupp issued an apology, after she had seen "additional video," and noted that she regretted "reacting too quickly."[4]

She was hardly alone. And to prove just how damaging it was to Sandmann, Sandmann later sued CNN and other outlets who smeared him unfairly, and they settled with him for an undisclosed sum of money. What was the real cost for these networks, though? They signaled the acceptable thought, and even though they got the story woefully wrong, they were not pilloried by their peers on social media. Instead, it was just their credibility with the larger public that took the hit.

Just days after the Covington incident, another even more perfect encapsulation of Pascal's Wager of Woke Journalism took place—and again, it involved "MAGA." TMZ broke the news on January 29, 2019, that Jussie Smollett, an actor on the FOX show *Empire*, had been the victim of a brutal attack in Chicago. According to the initial report, Smollett went to Subway to get a sandwich at 2 a.m., and then while walking home he heard someone yell, as TMZ reported it, "Aren't you that f***ot *Empire* n*****?" Then, "the 2 men—both white and wearing ski masks—viciously attacked Jussie as he fought back, but they beat him badly and fractured a rib. They put a rope around his neck, poured bleach on him, and as they left they yelled, 'This is MAGA country.' "[5]

It was racism and homophobia. It was Trump-related.

And the media instantly pounced, without giving it a second thought. And certainly the police did investigate the story as a hate crime at first, as they should. But while that investigation was taking place, the broader media apparatus treated it like it was absolutely true. And how could it not? It *sounded* true to them. If you spend the bulk of your time in newsrooms in NYC and DC, and don't know anyone who voted for Trump, then it might be believable that a couple of Trump supporters noticed an obscure actor from a TV show, identified him as Black and gay, and because of those characteristics immediately attacked him, and even put a noose around his neck (oh, and happened to have some bleach too that they poured on him).

The TMZ story was definitive. "Jussie Smollett was brutally attacked by 2 men who beat him up," it started. And TMZ often gets stories correct, but it is by no means a reputable news outlet that has to uphold a journalistic standard of ethics and integrity. But it was with that same definitiveness that the rest of the media reported the story too. "Smollett attacked in possible hate crime" was the CNN headline. "Smollett attacked in Chicago by men hurling homophobic and racial slurs," read NBC's headline.[6]

One of the big issues with the story early on was the reliance on, and mischaracterization of, what the police were telling us. It allowed reports to cite the police as describing what definitively happened, rather than what Smollett told the police in that moment. Even outlets that initially inserted caveats like "alleged" abandoned them by the time the next-day stories came. "Celebrities Rally Behind Jussie Smollett after Brutal Attack," read BuzzFeed's headline.[7]

You got the efforts almost immediately from the press to tie this to a larger issue in the country. "This is America in 2019," said CNN's Brooke Baldwin in one report, after one of many segments about the details of the "assault."[8]

Yamiche Alcindor, then a supposedly objective White House reporter and host at PBS, tweeted the story, with a message to her followers: "We have to do better as a country. This is disgusting."[9]

When it was time for Jussie Smollett to speak out publicly a couple weeks later, he sat down with ABC News's Robin Roberts, who is Black and gay herself. What transpired was an embarrassing series of softballs, allowing Smollett to continue the false narrative and smear an entire half of the country. When asked by Roberts why he thought he was targeted, Smollett said it was his criticism of Trump. "I come really, really hard against '45.' I come really, really hard against his administration," he said.[10]

On one hand, it is almost incomprehensible how the story ultimately played out. Yes, we hear about hoaxes all the time, but a semi-famous person, who made up the entire ordeal, paid some Black acquaintances of his to fake the attack? It's so ridiculous. And yet, it's what happened—Smollett was ultimately sentenced to jail time for the scam.

But for the media outlets who covered the story so incompetently, so lazily, there were never any real repercussions in the moment. Sure, long-term, their credibility took a hit— but they don't see it that way. If they did, perhaps they would have made a bigger effort to set the record straight. Instead, those who actually tried to report it accurately saw a negative impact in the moment. *Entertainment Tonight* was one of a few outlets that couched their coverage in accurate reporting—not even skepticism, just reality. "Smollett has been hospitalized in Chicago after a possible homophobic and racially charged attack," they tweeted.

What did they get for this by-the-book reporting? Alexandria Ocasio-Cortez, congresswoman from New York and a prolific tweeter to her millions of followers, quoted the tweet and added her own response: "There is no such thing as 'racially charged.' The attack was not 'possibly' homophobic. It was a racist and homophobic attack. If you don't like what is happening to our country, then work to change it. It is no one's job to water-down or sugar-coat the rise in hate crimes."[11]

The tweet from AOC received more than 33,000 retweets and more than 144,000 likes. For its alleged crimes of wokeness, *Entertainment Tonight* learned a valuable lesson. In the short term, it's better to be acceptable than to be correct.

This idea that the corporate media is driven not by a grand conspiracy but by lower-stakes incompetence and laziness is illustrated in digging into how our media sausage is made. In February 2020, the media was outraged about something Trump did, as they usually were. We'll get into why in a minute, but what was interesting was how the co-author of a book that was published several years before, and was sitting around 18,000th on Amazon, suddenly appeared on CNN, MSNBC, and was mentioned in another appearance on CNN—all on a single Sunday morning. The author, Steven Levitsky, had written a book called *How Democracies Die*, in January 2018, and now, here he was all over cable news, discussing the exact subject.

Levitsky's journey to cable news prominence that week-end began several days earlier. While President Trump was getting himself involved with ongoing Department of Justice criminal investigations, the *Washington Post* quoted former Obama administration attorney Joyce White Vance on the matter. "If a president can meddle in a criminal case to help a friend, then there's nothing that keeps him from meddling to harm someone he thinks is his enemy. That means that a president is fully above the law in the most dangerous kind of way. This is how democracies die," she said in part.[12]

The phrase rocketed around Twitter and the liberal blogosphere. The next day on CNN, during an interview with host Alisyn Camerota, Senator Tim Kaine was asked specifically, twice, whether Trump's actions were an example of "how democracies die," citing Vance's quote.[13]

A couple days after that, *Washington Post* columnist Max Boot had the quote as the headline of his column: "This is how democracies die—in full view of a public that couldn't care less." While he repeated that exact line as the hammer to his column, he didn't cite Vance in the piece.[14]

To be honest, the whole excitement around "democracy" and "dying" actually started with the *Washington Post* more broadly, a couple years earlier as the Trump Era kicked off. Their new slogan, "Democracy Dies in Darkness," was introduced in February 2017. But this particular framing about exactly how democracies die began that week with Vance, and continued for days, culminating with a series of cable news appearances for Levitsky, who had written a book that happened to perfectly match the talking point of the week.

Again: not a big grand conspiracy. In fact, I asked CNN's Brian Stelter at the time how it came to be that he, MSNBC's Joy Reid, and Amara Walker of CNN all happened to stumble on the exact same book that Sunday. "It wasn't pitched to me or my show. I came across the book in my research," he told me. "Complete coincidence re: the author being booked on other shows. But obviously Democratic backsliding is in the news so he would be an obvious person to book." Stelter told me that implying there was some "groupthink collusion" is "bullshit."

No, instead, what appears to have been the case was you had cable news bookers and hosts likely Googling "how democracy dies" and finding that there's a book with that exact name, then moving to get the author on as a guest. But you also inevitably get a narrative spun originally by a former Obama administration official giving a sticky quote in a *Washington Post* story about the Trump outrage of the day, and then the point about "how democracies die" being grafted onto the action.

Labeling some of the practical issues with the media as symptoms of incompetence or carelessness is not to excuse these problems or mistakes. Rather it's an attempt to contextualize the reality of the situation within a fast-moving media ecosystem, with a variety of forces at play beyond simply getting the story right.

A knowledgeable media consumer should be armed with the facts about the current state of those whom they rely on for news and information. And being clear-eyed about what's behind the flaws can make us all more discerning—and better hold those we entrust with informing us accountable.

CHAPTER 4

Lack of Introspection

THERE'S A KNEEJERK INSTINCT AMONG certain parts of the corporate media to meet every bad-faith attack with an instantaneous, pretentious rebuke. Even beyond personal slights, the instinct extends to the coverage of stories they deem to be beneath them. Think a story that Fox News is devoting massive time and energy to is being misrepresented? The press swings the pendulum back the other direction without any second thought about what the actual messy truth may be.

I talked about this "contamination" quandary with Ben Smith, formerly of the *New York Times* and Buzz-Feed, now the co-founder of a new media company, Sema-for. "[There'll] be some incident where allegedly an illegal immigrant committed a crime or something, or a caravan that's headed for the United States, that has this real ideological charge, and they'll cover it as an absolutely simple story about how it proves exactly whatever a conservative viewer thought," Smith told me. "And the reaction of the American

mainstream media typically is to be like 'this whole story is
toxically contaminated by the presence of ideological journalism. And so we're just not going to enter the Contain-
ment Zone. We're just going to ignore it totally...We're not
going to debunk it. We're not going to say actually this is
true. We're not going to say actually, there's a much more
interesting, more complicated story here. We're just going to
stay away because it's so contaminated.' I think it's a terrible
instinct. Often the best stories are weird and complicated."

It's a good thought-starter for another major problem
with the modern American press. In an era where there
are relentless attacks from the right, where the media has
become a popular punching bag, where the labels of "fake
news" and "enemy of the people" became pervasive, the
instinct among the media to dig their heels in and never give
an inch became even more severe.

Elite institutions in America never really were particularly adept at admitting faults, apologizing, correcting the
record. But the lack of introspection among the press has
actually gotten significantly worse in recent years, and it's
the second major problem with the modern media. There are
a couple reasons for it. Certainly the attacks from the right
have played a factor—there's an inclination not to allow the
other side to get a "win." But it's so self-defeating. Admitting mistakes would actually ingratiate the press to a generally forgiving public far more than acting like mistakes never
really occur.

Another reason for this is how fast the news cycle has
evolved. Cable news accelerated the news cycle to twenty-
four hours—a story that was hot one day could be old news

the next. But with social media, and particularly Twitter, the news cycle moves on in mere hours. If you've never used Twitter, it's hard to describe the feeling of logging on after you haven't used it for a few days. There are characters and storylines and trending terms and phrases that are suddenly completely foreign to you. In this environment, it's easy for the press to hold out, wait for the cycle to rapidly move on, and never have to say sorry.

But a final reason for the lack of introspection is more ingrained in the industry and has been for years—although perhaps it has gotten worse for reasons we'll get to toward the end of the book. Humility is simply a character trait that is in short supply in our modern society, and in particular within the elite, geographically isolated media establishment. But a lack of introspection exacerbates mistakes. It begets further mistakes. And it brings with it its own set of challenges and problems.

Case Study: Steele Dossier

"It's one of the most egregious journalistic errors in modern history, and the media's response to its own mistakes has so far been tepid," wrote Axios's Sara Fischer, an excellent reporter within the larger Acela Media, in November 2021.[1]

What Fischer was describing was the fallout from the Steele dossier, and the overarching "Russiagate" story that began shortly before Trump's inauguration and continued for the duration of his presidency.

The entire Steele dossier saga kicked off on January 10, 2017, as CNN published its first report, a quadruple-bylined story, including former Watergate reporter Carl Bernstein and top anchor Jake Tapper. "Intel chiefs presented Trump with claims of Russian efforts to compromise him" was the headline, with the story detailing the "two-page synopsis that was appended to a report on Russian interference in the 2016 election."[2]

The words "Steele dossier" were not mentioned in the CNN report, and the contents of the "synopsis" were largely just nodded to rather than divulged. But later that day, the story was blown wide open by BuzzFeed, which published the entire contents of the dossier for all to read. Even in BuzzFeed's original article, it noted "the allegations are unverified, and the report contains errors."[3] (I talked to Ben Smith, who was the editor of BuzzFeed at the time, about the decision to publish the dossier—a decision he stands by.)

But the saga of the dossier actually goes back further than the original report. These allegations were circulating in media circles for a while. "I remember I was with CNN at President Barack Obama's farewell address," former CNN contributor turned White House press secretary turned Fox News host Kayleigh McEnany told me. "There was this temptation and CNN avoided it. They did not report the contents of the dossier, but I definitely saw and heard rumblings among other commentators wanting to talk about this dossier that BuzzFeed had published, and there was that flirtation with doing so, and covering the allegations. That evening CNN did not cover it, but I think it gave me a sense, that was a moment where I thought this is going to be all-out resistance, if this dossier is even entertained among my colleagues and commentators as something that should be reported on. This is just a taste or a prelude to what CNN and the liberal media will be like under President Trump."

The dossier started the conversation about all the most salacious aspects of how Trump was supposedly compromised by Russia—all the way through the alleged pee tape. This was the beginning of it all, what became the dominant media storyline of the next four years.

As Axios noted, the dossier allegations were always disputed, but it all came to a head in 2021 when the key source was charged with lying to the FBI. The news about the dossier's veracity called into question so much of the media's Russia-based fear-mongering over the past few years. But it was hard for members of the press to accept. "It Wasn't a Hoax" was the headline to David Frum's column in *The Atlantic*.[4] Anne Applebaum, who was one of the journalists who made her career on Russiagate/Dossier–related "scoops," held strong, tweeting, "Even if every single word in the Steele dossier was wrong, that would not change the fact that the Russians sought to manipulate the US election using hacked material and a disinformation campaign. Nor would it change the fact that the Trump family welcomed this intervention."[5]

If you have to start your argument with "even if every single word in the Steele dossier was wrong," you know you're not arguing from a place of power and reason. An introspective media would use the opportunity to think critically about how they so cavalierly spread these mistruths. For example, a March 2017 CNN article headlined "FBI used dossier allegations to bolster Trump-Russia investigation" details just how key the dossier allegations were to the larger efforts by the FBI. What does the news now say about the FBI and James Comey? Or about the media's sources on all these stories—whether in the intelligence community, like from cable news regulars John Brennan and James Clapper, or from those in Congress, like Rep. Adam Schiff, one of the biggest pushers of the Russiagate narrative?

An accounting of how the media got spun by its sources would be appropriate. But that would take a level of introspection we simply aren't likely to see.

Erik Wemple of the *Washington Post* has done excellent reporting on the lack of introspection when it comes to false stories related to Trump, Russia, and the dossier. He cited some of the worst offenders of these storylines as CNN, MSNBC (and Rachel Maddow in particular), *Mother Jones*, and McClatchy. "The degree to which these outlets have gotten away with it is a measure of the fact that I [and] others were unable to get the critical mass required to move these organizations to do corrections. It is my firmly held belief that when editors say, 'when we get it wrong we correct it,' that's bullshit. I don't believe that anymore. And I think that I came into journalism, basically believing that," Wemple told me. "…It's depressing how this whole thing was handled."

One of the media members who covered the dossier story, and the Russiagate narrative, more than perhaps anyone was Maria Bartiromo of Fox News and Fox Business Network. She told me after covering "balance sheets, capital markets, globalization," at CNBC for decades and then at FBN, she "wasn't aware that these kinds of dirty tricks were used" in politics.

"I tripped over the story very soon into it. And when I figured out what had happened and when I had all of this evidence...I wanted to shout it from the rooftops. I mean I couldn't believe it," she told me. "...And I think that was one of the first media failures that I have witnessed in this last eight years."

So what did Bartiromo think was behind the media failure? "I think my speculation is that Trump came on the scene and just came too close to the fire—the fire of corruption—and he just called it out," she said. "Some of the people in the establishment said, 'You know what, this guy's dangerous, we got to get him out of here,' and others said, 'Because of the personality, I don't want to be anywhere near that.'"

Of course, the Trump angle added another wrinkle to the media malpractice—one we'll get into in the next chapter. But the media, which so monumentally screwed up the Steele dossier story, refused to display a real dose of introspection after it was proven false. And that sort of hard-headedness, that arrogance, is what helps lead to distrust among the American people for the press.

Concept: Consensus versus Counter-Consensus

Back in the 1970s and 1980s, our famous actors and comedians used to be part of the counterculture. *SNL* was populated with people who pushed the envelope, who made the establishment, and sometimes viewers, uncomfortable. Actors were respected, but there was an air of mystery to them. Think Jack Nicholson—can you imagine Nicholson having an Instagram account? Athletes, while revered, were not building themselves into sanitized brands. Charles Barkley famously said, "I am not a role model," in a Nike commercial. Today, our NBA stars are carefully cultivating their image through social media campaigns.

Over time, our most famous comedians, actors, late night hosts, and athletes became part of the culture, rather than the counterculture. They were accessible to audiences and developed large followings. The definition of "edgy" was pushed to what were the societal fringes, rather than what was viewed as popular.

In the new landscape, comedians like Dave Chappelle shifted from part of the counterculture, to the culture, back to the counterculture again—simply by continuing to be himself. Chappelle is brilliant—a perceptive social commentator. He's nowhere close to a Republican or conservative. But his brand of comedy has now been deemed dangerous not by the right but by the left, putting him back into the countercultural space.

In fact, you could make the argument that the culture has become what is liberal, and the counterculture is what exists outside those liberal bounds—which is now actually more "conservative," with a small "c." Those who push the envelope and are purveyors of "unacceptable" thought are now in the counterculture.

In the same way, the media has become more ingrained into the establishment than ever before. As a result, we have a media that pushes the acceptable narrative over the unacceptable one. A press that was supposed to question authority, push those in charge, and hold power to account is instead more subservient and in service to those in power.

Just as there's the culture and the counterculture, there's the "consensus" and the "counter-consensus." The consensus is what you see represented throughout most of the corporate media. It's the prevailing opinion of the regulars on cable news, pundits who hang out in green rooms, or, in the age of COVID, make sure their Zoom background is perfectly symmetrical. These consensus pushers, it's worth noting, exist on both ends of the political spectrum. The consensus throughout the Acela Media is mostly uniform.

But the consensus, in recent years, is losing. No story has harmed the perception of the consensus more in America than COVID. And it is through this failure of the consensus that we see the counter-consensus emerging, and thriving. The counter-consensus is not always right. But when the consensus fails with such frequency, and refuses to practice a level of introspection, it opens a lane for counter-consensus purveyors to become even more powerful.

The American people are not naturally supporters of the counter-consensus. We want to feel like we can go to a trusted, bedrock institution. But with the growing distrust of institutions, the counter-consensus becomes a growing force—and one with true staying power.

Case Study: Rogan vs. Gupta

One of the most powerful counter-consensus—and, likewise, countercultural—figures in America today is Joe Rogan. His podcast is consumed by millions, making him arguably the most powerful voice in the modern media. And he's been able to accrue this audience outside of the mainstream, corporate structure. His more than $100 million deal with Spotify has brought him to even more eyes and ears in America and around the world, but he is an example of a true independent who built his platform from the ground up.

Rogan certainly has his detractors—success has brought the inevitable critiques. But Rogan has largely been able to weather the storm because his media model is so transparent. He puts out entire three-hour long conversations. It's uncut and raw. It's clear who Joe Rogan is—he's relentlessly curious, nonjudgmental.

His style of passive interviewing does open him up to claims of "misinformation" propagation. "Misinformation" and "disinformation" have become buzzwords that the media loves to throw around, and we'll get to that toward the end of the book, but Rogan's interviews often let the guest go where they want, and while he has his producer Google to instant fact-check, he can have on somewhat controversial figures who will put their opinions out into the world—even if they're false.

Rogan's style is the antithesis of the current corporate media's. In the spirit of free speech, Rogan gives his audience a variety of points of view that are both in the consensus and far outside of it, and inevitably some untrue information (or "misinformation") will be part of the mix. The corporate media is so afraid of putting out untrue information that in some circumstances the true information gets silenced too as a result. Put me in the Rogan camp. I believe audiences can handle it and should be able to make up their own minds. Rogan is an information maximalist, while the modern corporate press is full of information minimalists.

One of the biggest consensus versus counter-consensus showdowns came when Dr. Sanjay Gupta of CNN went on Rogan's show during his book tour. Gupta has been a mainstay on CNN for decades and is also a practicing neurosurgeon. During the COVID pandemic, particularly in the early days, I thought he did a good job giving staid, objective analysis—especially in the face of his colleagues often speculating wildly all around him.

The context of Gupta's three-hour October 2021 appearance is important.[6] A month earlier, Rogan, who had been vocally unvaccinated for months, announced that he had contracted COVID. During the Instagram announcement, he ran through the laundry list of treatments he was undergoing to counter the disease, including monoclonal antibodies. But the big treatment that stuck with the media was when he mentioned ivermectin.

Ivermectin had been a hot-button issue in the world of COVID coverage, and multiple studies have not conclusively found it helps COVID. But the response to Rogan's announcement was not to simply say he was taking a drug that wouldn't help him recover from COVID. It went much further. NPR's report described ivermectin as "a deworming veterinary drug that is formulated for use in cows and horses"—as if it were not also designed for use in humans.[7]

But CNN, which had previously made Rogan's interviews with controversial scientists like Dr. Robert Malone a big talking point in its relentless "misinformation" focus, went even further. One chyron on Don Lemon's show described the drug as a "horse dewormer," while another on Erin Burnett's show described it as a "livestock drug."[8]

While ivermectin can be used for horses and livestock, it most certainly is used for humans as well. In fact, two scientists who discovered its use in treating malaria and other parasitic diseases won the 2015 Nobel Prize. It has helped literally hundreds of millions if not billions of humans.[9] Our own CDC recommends ivermectin for all refugees arriving in America.[10]

The ivermectin topic was a major one when Gupta sat down with Rogan, and it did eventually lead Gupta to agree that the CNN anchors who implied Rogan had taken horse pills "shouldn't have said that." There was also an extended discussion and debate about whether young, healthy individuals needed to get vaccinated—especially young males, related to the potential risk of myocarditis. There were substantive exchanges on masks, on the COVID lab leak theory (more on that later), and more.

It was an intellectual exercise, and ultimately the audience won. (Also, if I'm scoring the intellectual battle, I'd say Rogan won somewhere around eight rounds to four.)

Josh Rogin of the *Washington Post* agreed that it was good to hear the dialogue. "I went on Joe Rogan. I found him to be very curious, and very open to hearing from people and that's what makes him so listenable," Rogin told me. "...I thought he and Sanjay, it wasn't perfect, but that was a constructive exchange...If Joe Rogan and Sanjay Gupta can sit down for three hours and not agree on everything, but have a smart conversation, connecting two worlds that need to be connected, bravo."

Piers Morgan agreed. "I think that Rogan scored some points and Sanjay made some good points. And it was a very robust and interesting exchange of views about a pandemic where frankly nobody has all the answers," Morgan told me. "Anyone who pretends that they do or sticks rigidly to their original thoughts about everything has been made to look very stupid...What that interview did was very enlightening, because it was two people with different views about some of these issues, exploring them in a very big, public way. I think CNN felt uncomfortable about it, which I wouldn't have been if I was them, I would have embraced it."

The health experts I talked to were less favorable to Gupta, though. "He basically was out of his comfort zone and got some hard questions. And it was embarrassing," Dr. Marty Makary told me. "It exposed a lot of the dogma that we're hearing. For example, he was asked by Joe Rogan, doesn't a vaccinated adult still have a higher risk than an unvaccinated child? And he acknowledged that's true. That is mathematically true. And then he was told, 'Well, you just said, you, Dr. Gupta, since you're vaccinated, and you're an adult, you're not worried about COVID for yourself, you're living your life, you're not worried, you're doing stuff. Can you see how a parent is not worried about COVID in their unvaccinated child?' And he was totally stumped. He tried to change the question, change the topic five or six times. Joe Rogan, in his classic way, held him to it, but it's that sort of journalism, if you will, that is the line of questioning that is piercing, that many of these folks have never gotten."

Dr. Jay Bhattacharya agreed. "I thought Sanjay Gupta came off really poorly from that whole exchange," Bhattacharya told me, citing the ivermectin waffling from Gupta in the interview. "...I think it was deeply irresponsible for

CNN to do, and for Gupta, he really had no defense. I mean, I watched that exchange, and I could see he was struggling because there really wasn't a good argument for what CNN did."

The ivermectin exchange was important, because it included an assurance from Gupta to Rogan that "I will talk to them" about his colleague's previous false framing of the story. And Gupta had that chance when he appeared on various CNN programs to debrief after his Rogan appearance. But as refreshing as it was to see consensus and counter-consensus collide in intellectual discourse on Rogan's podcast, it was immensely disappointing—but also telling—to see how Gupta handled the post-interview experience.

Gupta went on Don Lemon's program, and Lemon defended his original smear—arguing that ivermectin can be "used" as a horse dewormer, and that it's not approved for COVID. That's not actually what Lemon originally said, though, which was that Rogan *took* a drug meant for deworming livestock. Gupta had a chance to "talk to them" on the air, and he didn't (although he was cut off by Lemon when it seemed he might bring up the inconsistency he agreed was an issue when he was talking to Rogan).[11]

But it was Gupta's appearance on Erin Burnett's show that was most disturbing. Their discussion was largely based on the vaccine part of the interview, and Gupta said of Rogan that "when you're convincing yourself of a particular narrative, in this case no vaccine, you find whatever sort of argument you can to support it."

With that context, he then proceeded to theoretically

recount the exchange he had with Rogan about whether the risk of myocarditis was higher for those who had COVID versus those who got the vaccine. Rogan cited a study— which was an actual scientific study—that was very specific. It said a study found that boys between the ages of twelve and fifteen years old "are four to six times more likely to be diagnosed with vaccine-related myocarditis than ending up in the hospital with Covid."[12]

In an attempt to compare "apples to apples," Gupta told Erin Burnett's CNN audience about a study out of Israel that compared myocarditis risk after vaccination and after COVID—but only for adults. In fact, the sub-headline in the *New York Times* write-up of this study made the distinction very clear: "The research did not assess the risks specifically for young males, who are the most likely to develop the rare side effect."[13]

Gupta's decision to either willfully or accidentally mislead CNN's audience and misrepresent Rogan's point was glaring. As Rogan made clear in the interview, the options for young boys are not "get vaccinated" or "get COVID." The risk equation for parents is a real one, and Gupta's lie about the exchange made CNN's viewers less informed.

When faced with the counter-consensus, Gupta initially had a thoughtful and respectful exchange of ideas. But back home in the corporate media consensus, he displayed the same lack of introspection so many in the press have these days— unwilling to engage in good faith, and unwilling to budge when it comes to having an ounce of humility. Instead, it's just another example of why the counter-consensus is winning.

Concept: Doom Bias

"Anytime I looked at CNN or MSNBC, there was a death tracker, where they would track the number of COVID-19 deaths. And we'd repeatedly be contacted by the press, 'what are you going to do to commemorate 50,000 deaths? What are you going to do to commemorate 100,000 deaths?'" Kayleigh McEnany told me in March of 2022 about her time in the White House as the press secretary during 2020. "For us, we didn't want one death from COVID-19. But what strikes me is the contrast of the way it was treated as milestones, markers, in a way that now we've had more deaths under Joe Biden... You no longer have the death trackers. I doubt Jen Psaki has many emails, 'What are you going to do to commemorate as we approach a million deaths from COVID-19?' We've already reached 900,000. That element is gone—a dramatization of COVID-19, which I'm sure scared a lot of people."

That particular element of COVID might be gone, but the instinct toward coverage that scares the audience isn't—and it's another element that was exacerbated during COVID, but existed long before the pandemic within the media too. I describe it as a "doom bias"—a bias toward the worst possible outcome, or the scariest one.

The New York Times published a performative front page on May 24, 2020, listing the names and some biographical details of 1,000 of the nearly 100,000 people who had died of COVID up until that point. It was a style over substance choice—with a hearty dose of doom bias. Never mind that one of the names was actually someone who had been murdered.[14] And now? It's a collector's item—you can buy that front section in the *New York Times* store.[15]

You had ridiculous segments about scary new variants of COVID, like ABC's *Good Morning America* warning about the perilous dangers of the "double mutant" variant that was identified in America in April 2021, signaling what could be a "fourth wave."[16]

But one of the most glaring and damaging examples of doom bias manifested over the issue of kids and schools— and there are real consequences. In July of 2020, Anderson Cooper was interviewing an expert from the Institute for Health Metrics and Evaluation about the upcoming school year. "Kids going back to school, if that happens, that means more people will die?" asked Anderson Cooper.[17] To his credit, the guest did not say yes.

The Associated Press later added to the fear-mongering over a return to school with an absurd article highlighting the death of four teachers shortly after the school year began in September 2020. "Teacher deaths raise alarms as new school year begins," read the headline, which then went on to tell the story of four teachers who had died after bouts with COVID.[18]

Buried far down the story were the circumstances for each of the tragic deaths. Notably, the fact that all the teachers had contracted COVID outside of the school—some even before school was back in session—was an afterthought. Yes, these tragic deaths could have been any profession. But if you group four COVID deaths together as the occupation most meant to spin the most scary version of doom bias about kids and schools, you get this poor piece of reporting.

"It's so emotional, school closures. In my opinion, the most catastrophic of all the failures by our public health officials," Dr. Marty Makary told me. "...Many of us talked until we were blue in the face at every platform that we were privileged to have about the importance of keeping kids in school. Urging outlets like the *New York Times*, which was dangling fear to young people inappropriately throughout the entire pandemic, to send one reporter over to Europe and do a story on the schools that were open, free and clear, without masks, with strong recommendations from the WHO and the European CDC not to mask children in primary schools because of developmental delays, and the quote unquote 'psycho- and socio-impact,' which is exactly what was described in that guidance from their medical authorities...What you had was a bi-coastal elite that were in charge of public health policy, whose kids were with private tutors and $10,000 Zoom suites in their second homes. And they saw their, say, high school kid, or almost all of them had older kids, and they thought, 'You know, they're doing fine for now.'"

A doom bias only affects *some* people.

But even without COVID, the media's doom bias isn't going to go away. And an introspection-free media elite that doesn't have to deal with the consequences—or ultimately correct the record—and knows that fear can be a valuable part of the business model means it's only going to get worse.

CHAPTER 5

The Trump Addiction

YES, DONALD TRUMP HAS ALREADY been mentioned more than a dozen times in this book, but it's time we devote a larger chapter to the phenomenon around the 45th president. There have always been points to critique the media about, but for various reasons, when Donald Trump burst onto the scene in 2015, it changed the corporate press in significant ways—mostly for the worse.

Trump's startling rise through the primary and then the general election, followed by his tumultuous presidency, was a shock to the system for an industry that believed it had a handle on how these sorts of stories were supposed to go. Trump was the wrecking ball to the establishment that the mainstream media never saw coming. And he threw their equilibrium off so significantly they were not able to recalibrate in a meaningful way. So much of what happened over the past five years can be traced to Trump's surprise victory over Hillary Clinton—even if it doesn't seem that way on the surface.

I have heard from several people that media members began having trouble sleeping during the Trump presidency— that they'd have to take pills to be able to fall asleep, or to help with depression, caused by their perceived existential fight with the man in the White House. These journalists and other media members were sick—and addicted. They had a Trump addiction.

Much has been written about Trump, but I'll try to tackle it in a different way—by getting to the core of how the media lost its path and how the addiction bled into so many other practical problems with the press over this last era.

So what happened? Here are some thoughts from those I interviewed.

"Really with the emergence of Trump in 2015, I began to realize, wait a second, the whole point of the system is self-preservation and self-enrichment, and I was right in the middle of it still," Tucker Carlson told me about Trump, and the response to Trump from the media elite. "...Hunter Biden lived right down the street. Our wives were very close. You know, I'm like part of the city. And my views are different from most people. I'm conservative. I was never like a secret liberal or something, I was always sincere. But I never thought like this whole thing is actually scary, but when Trump arose, the reaction was beyond belief. People were so upset, like genuinely upset like, walk your dog at night. 'I can't believe this, it's a fascist takeover!' And I was like, 'You know, I know Trump. First of all, he's not conservative in the way that you're afraid of, you hate evangelicals, you hate the religious people.' He's not like that. He's liberal on social issues, which I am not, but my neighbors were. So I was like, 'Don't worry.' They didn't care."

So then what was really at the core of the Trump hate? "The reason they hated Trump, and I watched it forensically, was because they were afraid he would say something he wasn't allowed to say," Carlson said. "They couldn't control what he was going to say. Someone like that might tell the truth about what's actually going on. And as someone who had never really questioned what was actually going on, I began asking myself, 'Why are they so afraid that he might say something out of turn?' Well, because they know that the system is essentially illegitimate. Like its goals are not consistent with the goals of the majority of the population at all, or their interests."

More from Carlson: "I just dismissed Trump. You know, he's hilarious, but he's an idiot or whatever, he's a showman, he works for NBC on some entertainment show I've never seen. To this day I never saw, I'm not interested in that stuff. You know, I don't have TV. I don't care. So I didn't get it at first. It was only the reaction—watching Trump reflected in the faces of my neighbors. Very highly educated, interesting, worldly, super sophisticated people. It was watching their panic that just changed my life. It really did. Ultimately we left the city over it."

Carlson happened to be at Fox News—and not one of his previous stops of MSNBC or CNN—when the Trump phenomenon hit. "That's when I realized there's a lot at stake here, this was not what I thought it was at all, and I have to make a decision—am I going to go the Jon Karl route?

Jon Karl's a nice guy actually, and a smart guy, but he's just a fifty-five-year-old white guy like me," Carlson said of the ABC White House correspondent during the Trump years. "He's like 'oh man, do I go along with this and save my job, or do I tell the truth and get fired?' And, of course, he's taken the first route. I just by accident found myself working for a family who's committed to free speech. I don't know if they agree with me or not. Who knows? But they're totally committed to letting their anchors say what they want."

The way Trump changed the media was almost immediate. "There was no social penalty for reporting critically on Donald Trump or anyone in the Trump administration, nor on anything happening in the Trump administration, and if anything, there were considerable rewards socially, I think, for people who were willing to be really bold, or be really theatrical, and play along with the campy aspects of that White House," Olivia Nuzzi of *New York* magazine told me, contrasting that with coverage of the current Biden administration. "I think there's something to the fact that a lot of the people in the current White House are creatures of Washington, and a lot of the people who cover them and cover Joe Biden are also creatures of Washington, and they have long histories. And that's not to say like everyone's having Thanksgiving dinner together or anything. But I think it changes the way you interact with people when you've been chitchatting with them at cocktail parties for like the last fifteen years."

The reaction the press got over how they covered Trump was something Tara Palmeri, previously of Politico and now of Puck news, told me she noticed. Suddenly the news was the culture—and everyone was engaged. "You're covering Trump, and anything that you write about him, it's going to be celebrated by one side or the other," said Palmeri. "If you're going to be a journalist that wants to get stories with teeth, not just putting out what the administration wants, it's probably going to be critical, and it's probably going to be celebrated by the left. I've seen it go both ways. When people are like, 'Oh my God, you broke this huge story about Trump, and you're a rock star.' Then you have another story that's maybe like less critical about Trump, maybe it's critical of Biden in some way. It doesn't even mention the word 'Trump' in it. And you're the ire of the left and the hero of the right."

Kayleigh McEnany saw the Trump addiction from a variety of perspectives—both sitting on CNN panels in the run-up to the 2016 election, and then later from the other side of the podium as the press secretary. Of her time at CNN, McEnany remembers something then-president Jeff Zucker said about her and Jeffrey Lord, another Trump-supporting contributor. "He analogized us to characters in a play. And I think that may have been what to Jeff Zucker things initially were, you know, Trump was bringing them good ratings," McEnany told me. "They brought on Trump surrogates, they brought on conservatives. We were characters in a play, I suppose. And then all of a sudden, I think that there was a lot of pointing of the fingers at CNN in particular. And I don't agree with this, but they were accused of paving the way for Donald Trump, for making him the nominee, for, in some ways, making him the president by giving voice to conservatism in the form of Jeffrey Lord and myself. I believe

Trump would have won without CNN. But that was the prevailing liberal narrative. And I certainly think Zucker and others felt pressure to distance themselves from that."

From the other side of the podium, facing the press during 2020 White House briefings, McEnany noticed a different side of the media. "I think that televised element adds a different dynamic. There were some incredible reporters—Steve Holland of Reuters is one who always stands out to me as an excellent reporter. Zeke Miller was a pretty straight shooter over at the Associated Press. But if you notice the names I'm giving you, Philip Wegmann at RealClearPolitics, I'm giving you print publications. These are publications that—apart from the *New York Times* and *Washington Post*, which have gone totally off the deep end—these are old school, print reporters," McEnany told me. "...One unnamed journalist said to me, there's old school journalism, and then there's new school journalism. And it occurred to me that person was suggesting there's kind of a different tone in the briefing room. And to me, it's the televised element of it, and the social media aspect, where a lot of these journalists are in search of their own shows, like Jim Acosta now has one, or publishing books, Jon Karl, for instance."

Piers Morgan won the first season of *Celebrity Apprentice*—hosted by Donald Trump, and under the leadership of Jeff Zucker when he was running NBC's entertainment division. He knows both well. "I think Jeff felt a bit like Dr. Frankenstein, having created the monster of Trump, TV superstar, and then backed him with massive amounts of airtime when he was running for president, when he was a candidate, and CNN basically became the Trump News Network for months on end, fueling Trump's appeal across America and helping to get him elected," Morgan told me. "I think the realization that this guy that they were giving so much airtime to suddenly went from being a political joke to someone who might win was a bit of a shocking wake-up moment for them. And I think that if you look back on the whole thing, I think Trump won the 2016 election because he was very different to any other politician and the way he spoke and behaved, but also because he was a massive TV star. And the person responsible for that was Jeff Zucker. So there is an irony that Jeff then presided over this sort of desperate attempt to destroy Trump, having created him."

Rick Sanchez spent decades in local news before joining CNN in 2004, and rising up the ranks to become one of its top anchors, before leaving in 2010. He recalls the way Trump was treated as a candidate on CNN, but also on MSNBC with Joe Scarborough and Mika Brzezinski. "There's no better example than Mika and Joe. They literally had him call in from his toilet," Sanchez told me. "And they'd laugh and they'd chuckle. Like they're old friends. And then all of a sudden, as soon as the guy becomes president, he's a pariah. They hate him. You kind of can't have it both ways."

For John Roberts, who covered past administrations at CBS and CNN before moving over to Fox News in 2011 before the Trump years, the Trump phenomenon was familiar to anyone who covered the New York mainstay in his previous iterations before running for office. "Donald Trump has always used the media and the media has gleefully been used, because it gets what it needs out of Donald Trump,

Donald Trump gets what he needs out of the news media," Roberts told me. "It was this weird, symbiotic relationship that at times was destructive, and Trump would call certain networks 'fake news.' And I think the definition became broader and broader as time went on. So that served his purposes. At the same time some networks would be called 'fake news,' that served their purposes because they said, 'Look, the president doesn't like the fact that we're holding his feet to the fire and this is how he reacts.' So again, it was the same symbiotic relationship. It was just a little more twisted than it was in years past."

Roberts saw firsthand in the briefing room how the Trump-obsessed press benefited from their sparring with the administration. "It goes a little further and initially, you're like, 'Oh, maybe that went a little bit too far, strayed outside of the boundaries of what we normally do. But hey, it got this great reaction. And so maybe we should keep going down this road.' And then it just keeps feeding on itself to the point where every interaction with the president becomes a confrontation," Roberts said, relating what he witnessed with other reporters. "And it's a confrontation that makes news and that's why you saw a lot of White House correspondents using cutaways of their question to the president in their nightly reports on the big newscasts. It didn't become, 'the president said this.' It became 'our correspondent got up in the president's face and said this,' and so it's not necessarily what the president said that becomes news. It's the way the correspondent asked the question of the president and the reaction that the correspondent got to the question that they were asking. So it's not necessarily some big policy announcement. It's the fury of the interaction that becomes news. And I think people became almost addicted to that. It was who got the biggest and the best reaction out of the president, not who broke the most news."

Was it performance or authentic? Was it business or personal? Was it a combination? I don't think it's an easy answer. Undoubtedly, Trump was good for the financial aspects of media companies from 2015 through 2020. He brought in viewers, who saw politics as a prime cultural activity. He brought page views and subscribers. But it's too simple to say it was just about money. No matter how it started, some reporters who covered Trump truly felt they were fighting for democracy in fighting against Trump—however misguided that looks to an outsider. Some in the press believed Trump was a unique threat to America, and they finally could do the important work they'd always dreamed of—their own Watergate, every single day.

I also think we need to sit back and assess the early days of the Trump candidacy. I'll get into my time at CNN next chapter, and my time working with Jeff Zucker, whom I enjoyed working with quite a bit. I don't fault Zucker for how he covered Trump in the primary. Perhaps some empty podium minutes could have been spent on other stories. But the Trump presidential run was the most interesting political story in decades, and CNN was right to give it a lot of airtime.

Similarly, while CNN and MSNBC didn't treat Trump like they did when he ran in the general election or during his presidency, there's also some revisionist history about how those networks covered him during the primaries. Sure, there were much less contentious exchanges than what was to come, but they weren't all softballs either. Sure, Trump got the "call-in" treatment from *Morning Joe*, but when he appeared in studio for one June 2015 interview, it was substantive and objective.[1]

Trump gave a variety of interviews to primetime hosts at CNN during the primary, including Don Lemon—who went on to be one of his fiercest and most hysterical critics. In one December 2015 interview, the two had a respectful back-and-forth on serious topics, and viewers were given a fair representation of the man who would ultimately win the nomination and the presidency.[2]

It's a great little artifact, the Don Lemon–Donald Trump primary interviews (there were quite a few). Especially for what was to come at CNN during the Trump presidency. One representative exchange that stood out to me was one of the old "handoffs" Lemon and his former colleague Chris Cuomo had between their shows.

"It's a scary time," Lemon said in the February 2020 exchange, with Cuomo joking at first, then appearing to get serious, about Trump potentially throwing each of them in jail.

"What's to stop him?" asked Cuomo. "You're right about that," Lemon responded. "But we can't allow that to stop us from doing our jobs."[3]

They were chuckling during this bizarre exchange, but they also seemed serious. Perhaps just a side effect of the Trump addiction.

Concept: Hypocritical Corrective

Let's pause for a minute and just note that the media is not all bad and in need of fixing. Or, to be more precise, "the media" is not even really the media—critiques of certain aspects of the media are not indictments of the whole. Look, you'll hear from more than two dozen individuals who make up "the media" in this book, and they are people whose perspectives I value greatly (although they are also not without any criticism).

But it's not just them; there is so much that is good in the current media environment—in fact, the good often is even better because of how it contrasts with the larger portion of not-quite-good. On the pandemic, besides Josh Rogin, who has been quoted here, Nate Silver of FiveThirtyEight, David Leonhardt of the *New York Times*, David Wallace-Wells of *New York* magazine, David Zweig of *The Atlantic* and *New York* magazine, and Alec MacGillis of ProPublica stand out for their excellent (and early) coverage of everything from kids and schools, to lockdowns, to masks, to the problem with statistics like "cases."

There are excellent journalists at every media outlet that I critique in here—including the ones I seem to go back to quite a bit, like CNN. Jim Acosta was corrosive to the CNN brand, but Kaitlan Collins, who took over his position of chief White House correspondent, is a far superior and more objective journalist. And this is just scratching the surface.

I preface this concept section with that little interlude to note that sometimes when a media establishment has covered a story poorly, and then they adjust what they do and cover the story or a similar story properly, it's worth pointing that out. It doesn't invalidate the forces who got it wrong in the first place from being criticized for the way it was handled—but it also doesn't preclude us from applauding the change in the right direction.

Often when the change occurs, the reasons for it are clearly not because of some great new journalistic standard—an introspective look, and arriving at the new place with a level of humility and transparency. No, it's usually because the circumstances change—the story is suddenly easier to get right. It's what I call a "hypocritical corrective." Sure, the coverage has been a corrective from what came before, but it doesn't invalidate the hypocrisy it now exposes.

Like Dr. Makary mentioned when it came to the coverage of outdoor activities early in the pandemic, the media treated red state beachgoers in May 2020 like they were spreading the plague—and also castigated the anti-lockdown protests that developed around the same time. But when it came to the social justice protests a short time later after the killing of George Floyd, the idea that these outdoor protests would be massive superspreader events was ignored. Now, as we know, outdoor transmission is very low with COVID. So the media was wrong to finger-wag the spring break partiers in their coverage, and they were right to leave that aspect of the coverage out when it came to the social justice protests. But we can at least acknowledge the hypocrisy at play here. When the cause is more celebrated by the media, the coverage shifted.

Hypocritical correctives can be identified beyond COVID,

and in many stories. Large portions of the press treated Sarah Palin in 2008 with a disdainful sort of sexism when she was running as John McCain's vice presidential candidate. When it came to Kamala Harris after her selection by Joe Biden, there was a blatant effort to stop any sort of coverage that could be perceived as sexist—including a letter from various contributors and other Democratic operatives warning the media to avoid sexism as soon as she got picked as the nominee. The corrective to sexist Palin coverage—like former MSNBC host Ed Schultz calling her a "bimbo"—was to not get sexist Harris coverage.[4]

The media was making the corrective in the proper direction. But it's still hypocritical.

Case Study: Lab Leak

One area in which the hypocritical corrective related to COVID coverage was the possibility COVID came from the Wuhan lab researching infectious diseases under dubious safety protocols, rather than from a wet market.

There are two clear points we should make about the "lab leak theory" at the forefront. First, we still don't know how COVID originated. It could have come from the lab; it could have come from the wet market. We don't know, and that's part of the problem. Second, it's clear the story got muddled almost immediately because of the existence of Donald Trump—the Trump factor turned the story from a scientific one to a political one.

And perhaps most concerningly, by President Trump pushing the lab leak theory as his preferred origin story, it likely squashed the curiosity of a press that instinctively turned against any Trump point—and set us back months, if not years, in finding a crucial truth. And that's an important point too—some stories I've written about in this book, and will write about later, are noteworthy for one reason or another, but they aren't critical to our lives. How COVID started, and ensuring a massive global pandemic doesn't start again, is actually an exception. It's imperative we get to the bottom of it. And for far too long, the press was actively uninterested in the topic.

There were two parallel path problems with the coverage of the lab leak theory. First, Dr. Anthony Fauci and Dr. Francis Collins from the NIH were working behind the scenes to suppress it. We know thanks to emails obtained by BuzzFeed via the FOIA that scientists whom Fauci respected were indicating in private emails in early February 2020 that COVID-19 had "unusual features" that "potentially look engineered."[5] We also know from an email a couple weeks later that Fauci said to "please handle" a note from a professor who outright said "we think that there is a possibility that the virus was released from a lab in wuhan, the biotech area of china."[6] By April 2020, Fauci was publicly rejecting this possibility from the White House podium.

"You have Tony Fauci and Francis Collins spend February 2020 essentially organizing a cover-up of this, of the possibility that it's a lab leak," Dr. Jay Bhattacharya, one of the key experts behind the Great Barrington Declaration, told me. "Creating this idea that it is a conspiracy theory to say that it might be a lab leak."

We know the media's deference for Fauci in particular. So it's not surprising the media would then buy whatever Fauci is saying. But it's not just rejecting the possibility—it's *how* the media went about rejecting it that's so notable. They made it toxic, an unacceptable thought. "Dr. Fauci throws cold water on conspiracy theory that coronavirus was created in a Chinese lab," read one April 2020 Business Insider headline.[7]

But the implication that the lab leak was unacceptably toxic to even discuss began even earlier. In February 2020, Senator Tom Cotton, a Trump-associated GOP senator from Arkansas (whom we'll discuss much more in a later chapter), went on Maria Bartiromo's Fox show and raised the possibility that COVID-19 started in the lab. He didn't say it definitively, he simply said that was one possible option. And he was careful to distinguish between different possibilities— that it leaked accidentally from the lab, or that it was engineered in the lab and released on purpose.

He was treated like a lunatic by the compliant press. The *Washington Post* described it as a "debunked conspiracy theory."[8] Vox, which purports to be the "explainer" news site, gave their explainer on "the conspiracy theories about the origins of the coronavirus, debunked."[9] Chris Cillizza of CNN wrote that Cotton was "playing a dangerous game with his coronavirus speculation," as if asking questions on the topic should be disallowed.[10]

"Tom Cotton comes on the show. He is on all of these committees in the Senate, he's getting his information, and he says it's likely the lab leak," Bartiromo told me. "And at that time there was this body of people who were just attacking. Peter Daszak came after me on Twitter. And you're right—no accountability."

Tech companies, in another elite censorship collusion racket moment, worked with the media and government forces to shut down any discussion of the possibility and ban the speculation about the origins of COVID if it pointed to the lab leak. It couldn't be that this theory was just incorrect—it had to be dangerous. And racist.

The *New York Times*'s COVID reporter Apoorva Mandavilli was, as late as May 2021, tweeting about the theory as if it was both wrong and racist. "Someday we will stop talking about the lab leak theory and maybe even admit its racist roots. But alas, that day is not yet here," she wrote, in a since-deleted tweet.[11]

But by then, reporters at other publications had been doing the work to look into the very real possibility of the lab leak. Josh Rogin of the *Washington Post* was one of them. As early as April 2020, Rogin was writing in the *Post* about "state department cables" that warned of "safety issues at Wuhan lab studying bat coronaviruses."[12]

"If you're an honest, unbiased person, looking at the circumstantial evidence on either side of the debate, you would have to admit that either one is a possibility. You would have to admit, if you're being honest, that either it could have spilled over from nature, or it could have been connected to the labs in Wuhan doing all the bat coronavirus research in some way," Rogin told me. "And we just don't know. And if you're not willing to admit that, then you're not being honest in the debate."

So what does he see as at the core of the media malpractice in this story? Trump, yes—but it goes deeper. Said Rogin:

The reason that the media got this so wrong is complicated, but it involves two institutional biases. One was among the science writers. When the pandemic hit, of course, we relied on those science writers; there's a whole field of journalism dedicated to science writing, they must know the most about it, this is their moment to shine. It's a once-in-a-lifetime pandemic, and these are the people who are smartest on this issue. And what a lot of people in political journalism and national security journalism didn't realize was that, oh, the science writers were totally, totally misled by their main sources, who were the leaders of the scientific institutions like the NIH and NIAID and USAID and all these institutions that, if you're covering them as an independent journalist that you're supposed to be overseeing, in a sense, you're supposed to be looking at with a skeptical eye, but the science writers were all captured, because these were their best sources, and in the world of science writing, that's actually fairly common. Of course, it's common in the world of national security writing and political writing, too. But for some reason, a lot of people thought all the science writers were above all that, turns out they're not.

So what about Trump's involvement? "This became super politicized because of Trump," Rogin said. "My view on that is well established, that the broken clock is right twice every day."

The reactive media apparatus kicked into high gear at that point too—as Ben Smith discussed related to stories in which the legacy media treats topics as contaminated by the right-wing press, and thus instinctively ignores any evidence they might be onto something. "It becomes a confirmation bias, and the mainstream media guys don't want to get caught being wrong by the right-wing media guys. So they have to constantly find reasons to confirm their own story, regardless of whether or not that had anything to do with the outbreak," Rogin said. "And all of those things going on at the same time was just too confusing, especially in that crazy environment for our media ecosystem to really process. But luckily, I was in the middle of it all with no biases except to report out the truth and writing a book on this very subject with really good sourcing."

Rogin's book, *Chaos Under Heaven*, gets at the China connection to the story—and the media's reluctance to cover it properly. "I don't think there was a conspiracy in the media. I think it's basically a mix of source bias, confirmation bias, anti-Trump bias, 'fighting the right-wing attacks on us' bias, and general incompetence. I've worked in eight different newsrooms in eighteen years and I've seen all of that in one degree or another, in different mixtures over different circumstances," Rogin told me. "…The right-wing media has been transparent about its opinions, and the mainstream media is pretending to be objective, and then betraying that to their readers. And that's because we hold the mainstream media up to a higher-level standard, we're claiming that standard. So I believe that, I agree with that, the mainstream media should be held up to that higher standard. At the same time, it's full of human beings, human beings aren't perfect, and they make mistakes. And the integrity is admitting the mistakes when you make them. The integrity is not dodging the correction."

Rogin told me a story of the tech suppression of his reporting that he's never revealed publicly before. He published an excerpt of his book in *Politico* magazine telling the "behind-the-scenes story of the Wuhan cables," which have been attacked by the Chinese Communist Party. Suddenly Facebook "banned" the link. "That was the first time that had ever happened to me because it's like, 'I'm a mainstream columnist, writing for a mainstream DC publication, *Politico*. It's not on the list of things that people are usually banning.' I put up a stink and they unbanned it," he told me. "And the next day, they banned it again, and then I put up another stink and they unbanned it again. And I was like, 'Wait a second, if they didn't care about me, because maybe I have a little mainstream media power to shame them…But what is a regular person supposed to do?' If you didn't have that connection or that ability to appeal all of this—because it was just totally crazy…That was the moment when I was like 'wait a second.' It's not that the tech companies shouldn't be arbitrating what's free speech and what's not free speech, it's that they don't know what they're doing. They're not good at it. They don't know what they're talking about, especially on these very complex issues. And that's why they can't be trusted to do it. One, because it's not a power that they should have, and two, because they suck at it."

The *Washington Post* went on to change its February 2020 headline and remove "debunked" and "conspiracy theory," instead going with "fringe theory that scientists have disputed," because, according to the correction, there has been "no determination about the origins of the virus." A corrective—albeit a hypocritical one.

What would have happened if Trump hadn't pushed the lab leak theory at all? We'll never know, but it's a good thought experiment. Nate Silver of FiveThirtyEight made a great point about the competing theories. "When the evidence is murky and there are plenty of experts lining up on both sides, but one side is excessively concerned with policing the discourse...I tend to think that side is more likely than not to be wrong," he tweeted.[13]

An important lesson—that goes beyond the lab leak theory.

Concept: Glance Journalism

There's a negative sort of journalistic mistake that bubbles up occasionally which can combine the Trump addiction, the speed of the news cycle, and a general laziness—I call it "Glance Journalism."

Glance Journalism is loosely when a media outlet glances at a story, often one that confirms its prior convictions, puts it out into the world, and when it's proven false or ultimately becomes clear that it wasn't true, the correction never gets a particularly high amount of attention.

It could be ignorance, and a passive interest in accuracy. Or perhaps it's more insidious—an active disinterest in the truth. Or maybe it's just the press is moving too damn fast to slow down and get the story right.

It's damaging to the credibility of the press, but that's almost secondary. Glance Journalism most harms the audience, who don't have time to fact-check and double-source every story they consume, and rely on the media to distill for them the truth. Americans are also not conditioned to go back and make sure they've read all the updates to a story that has been corrected, and they shouldn't be forced to. The media owes the public the decency of looking at a story with more than a glance—really discerning the truth—before putting it out into the world.

Do you remember the deadly shooting at the Pulse nightclub in Orlando, Florida, in June 2016? The man responsible, Omar Mateen, walked into the gay nightclub and opened fire, killing nearly 50 people and injuring another 50, before killing himself. It was unspeakably tragic.

At the time, it was almost universally reported that the act was one of LGBT hate—that Mateen had targeted these individuals and the Pulse nightclub because of his hatred of the gay community. "Let's say it plainly: This was a mass slaying aimed at LGBT people," wrote Daily Beast senior editor Tim Teeman at the time, in a piece headlined "Omar Mateen Committed LGBT Mass Murder. We Must Confront That."[14]

And at a glance, I suppose that storyline makes sense. But not every story is so neat and tidy and easily explainable. In an excellent 2018 HuffPost piece entitled "Everyone Got the Pulse Massacre Story Completely Wrong," reporter Melissa Jeltsen looked back at the truth about the case. As it turned out, Omar Mateen may have hated gay people, and he certainly committed a mass murder of what turned out to be gay clubgoers. But there was more to the story.

"Mateen may very well have been homophobic. He supported ISIS, after all, and his father, an FBI informant currently under criminal investigation, told NBC that his son once got angry after seeing two men kissing. But whatever his personal feelings, the overwhelming evidence suggests his attack was not motivated by it," reported Jeltsen. "As far as investigators could tell, Mateen had never been to Pulse before, whether as a patron or to case the nightclub. Even prosecutors acknowledged in their closing statement that Pulse was not his original target; it was the Disney Springs shopping and entertainment complex. They presented evidence demonstrating that Mateen chose Pulse randomly less than an hour before the attack. It is not clear he even knew it was a gay bar. A security guard recalled Mateen asking where all the women were, apparently in earnest, in the minutes before he began his slaughter."[15]

It was an anti-American terror attack, from an Islamic extremist. But with Glance Journalism, media members around the industry got the story wrong in the moment when it happened. It seemed so obvious—of course he targeted the gay nightclub. But in the end, how many in the audience are left with a false impression because they consumed the story back when it happened, never saw the follow-up reporting by HuffPost and others, and simply still believe it was a hate crime against gay Americans? Maybe you still believe that— and it's important to know the truth.

Glance Journalism can show up in more silly and less consequential stories too. About a week after the January 6 riot at the Capitol, CNN published a quadruple-bylined story about "how a swift impeachment was born under siege." It tracked some of the media's favorite members of Congress, like Democratic representative Ted Lieu, and his efforts to avoid the mob that had entered the Capitol unlawfully. Lieu is a frequent on-air guest at outlets like CNN, so it's no surprise Lieu would also be a source behind the scenes, on background, too. The story described what Lieu's actions were in that moment, which had to be relayed by either Lieu or a member of his staff. "Grabbing a crowbar in his office, Lieu said he and his chief of staff called the top aide to Rhode Island representative David Cicilline while wandering the halls and asked if they could hunker down in Cicilline's office," it said.[16]

Imagine reading this story—what impression do you have? Ted Lieu is about to beat up some Trump supporters with his crowbar, like he's fighting zombies on *The Walking Dead* or something?

A short time after publication, the article was corrected. "Grabbing a ProBar energy bar in his office..." the sentence now read.

Crowbar...ProBar...same difference, right? None of these four journalists caught the mistake—and no editor did before it went up on the website. Because with Glance Journalism, the combination of speed, laziness, incompetence, lack of introspection, and a sprinkling of Trump addiction, it never got beyond the glance.

Before we get to the third problem with the modern media, I want to stay on the Trump addiction and dive deeper into the outlet that was arguably most addled with the ailment: CNN. The next chapter takes a brief diversion into the network, a lengthy case study in where the media was, how it changed, and where it is today.

CHAPTER 6

This Was CNN

"KRAK, HOW WE LOOKING?"

That's how I remember many of my interactions with Jeff Zucker starting, as the CNN president walked up behind my desk on the seventh floor of the CNN center to glance at the large screen in front of me.

During Zucker's first year as president of CNN in 2013, I was the senior executive for the US TV channel in charge of how television content would live on social media and the website. Often at my desk there would be two windows open simultaneously: The first, Twitter.com logged into the CNN Twitter account, which I ran for two years during my time there. The second would be Chartbeat, the tool to see how many people were on each individual CNN.com story in real time. I'd send a tweet from the CNN account, and we could watch it shoot up the Chartbeat chart, as people migrated over to the link.

My experience at CNN was largely positive—but it also feels like an entirely different era. The changes that would come to the network within a few short years of my exit in August 2013 would both mirror large portions of the Acela Media and singularly epitomize the moment in the industry.

And while the problems in the press accelerated rapidly beginning around 2015, it's not that there were zero signs of the erosion to come during my time at the network either. Each of the five problems *Uncovered* lays out are emblematic of this particular period of time, but seeds of each were evident for years before, if not decades.

Here's one example. It was August 2013, and I was nearing the end of my four years at CNN. I was finishing an eighteen-month run where I was at every primary debate, every election night in Atlanta and DC, and then was in the room working closely with Jeff Zucker and a small group of executives to launch shows like *New Day* and the revamped *Crossfire*.

But a secondary aspect of my role was running the team behind the CNN Twitter account, with more than 10 million followers at the time. There were several individuals that I oversaw, so content could go out from the account twenty-four hours a day, seven days a week. But between 9 a.m. and 5 p.m. Eastern Time Monday through Friday, just about every tweet that was sent from @CNN came from me personally.

Beginning in September 2012, CNN was one of the few media outlets covering the truth about Benghazi. Arwa Damon was the journalist who found Ambassador Christopher Stevens's diary in an unsecured compound, and CNN reported on the contents, which included repeated calls for more security, which were not granted (and the reporting was barely covered by the larger media, and pushed back against hard by the administration).

In August 2013, CNN exclusively reported that dozens of CIA operatives were on the ground in Benghazi during the attack and had not been dispatched to help. The CNN story also found that the CIA was going through an "unprecedented attempt" to keep the information secret from the public.[1] It was a blockbuster report. At the very next White House press briefing, I remember watching with anticipation to see how the press secretary would spin the information—with the CNN Twitter account open, ready to tweet the White House's response to CNN's scoop.

Instead, Jay Carney wasn't asked a single question about the report—not even by CNN's reporter in the briefing room. The story simply died, and the media moved on. It was a sad sign of what would come, and be exacerbated beyond my wildest imagination, in the Trump Era.

That afternoon I emailed a very high-profile journalist, asking what the hell was going on. Because that email was not for publication when it happened in 2013, this will be the only time I give anonymity to someone in this book. "Don't look for courage in that room," he told me. Of the White House press corps, he said, "They're a bunch of cowed pussies."

One of the most recognizable shifts in the media during the Trump Era was with CNN. And it also happens to be the news outlet I'm personally most familiar with.

I joined the network in 2010 as a digital producer for *Piers Morgan Tonight*. I was promoted to senior digital producer in 2011 and oversaw TV as it related to digital. And I loved my time at CNN. I met my wife at CNN. A bunch of CNN employees were at my wedding.

But the CNN I was at was different from the CNN it became after Trump. I spent every primary election night at CNN headquarters—first in Atlanta, then in DC—during the 2012 election. I was on site for every CNN debate—and there were a lot of debates. I was in the rooms with the top executives while the biggest political coverage decisions were being made. I did not see anyone put their thumbs on the scale in favor of Obama over Romney. Did more people in that building want Obama to win? Sure. Were there more Obama voters? Undoubtedly. (I didn't vote in 2012—I felt too close to the situation. I know some other journalists feel that way too.)

Back during 2012, the CNN election coverage was largely led by the DC bureau. I worked closely with Sam Feist, the bureau chief, as well as other executives like Michelle Jaconi, who were great journalists. The staff I worked with in DC believed strongly in putting a fair and objective product out to the public—in the CNN mission that Ted Turner crafted from day one. In fact, most executives I interacted with at CNN—both as a reporter before I joined the network and after—were focused on journalism above all else.

Jon Klein was president until 2010; he is a fantastic executive whom I interviewed many times as a reporter, who steered the network toward down-the-middle coverage (even at the expense of ratings—which ultimately led to his eventual exit). After he left, Ken Jautz, another CNN main-stay with great journalistic acumen, took over as president, but Mark Whitaker, formerly of NBC News, took on the main day-to-day editorial oversight and direction. I enjoyed working with both. But Whitaker's role meant he led the 9 a.m. morning calls each day and allowed the journalists and executives at the network to get insight into what he believed were the important stories of the day.

More often than not, these were unremarkable meetings. Occasionally, a bizarre sort of insinuation would make its way into the discussion. I remember one call about the Tray-von Martin shooting, as the trial of George Zimmerman was set to begin. The self-defense argument was accompanied by the report that Zimmerman had two black eyes. Whitaker floated the theory that perhaps Zimmerman punched himself in the face in order to make it look like there was a struggle. Thankfully, no CNN show ran with this on air or online.

Whitaker eventually left CNN as Zucker stepped in as president in early 2013. And the changes Zucker brought would be significant, for many reasons. But before we get to what happened, let's look back—because it's important. In 2007, the New York Observer published a fascinating profile of Zucker, then the thirty-nine-year-old head of NBC. The headline was "The Apprentice's Sorcerer," and it tracked Zucker's tremendous success at the network and massive rise to the position he held. Buried down in that piece is an anec-dote that's worth revisiting. "Now Mr. Zucker could get down to business: hammering home the brand, making Don-ald Trump into—for his NBC—what Milton Berle, Sid Cae-sar, Jack Paar, Johnny Carson, Bill Cosby, and Jerry Seinfeld had been for earlier versions of the network: the emblem, the spokesman. Somehow, this big, cheesy, unscripted megahit, *The Apprentice*, had become the savior of NBC's Thursday nights," wrote Joe Hagan.[2]

Trump and Zucker were intertwined for more than a decade. We would see in September 2020 the casual way Zucker and Michael Cohen talked about "the boss," in an audio recording from 2016 obtained by Tucker Carlson.[3]

But there was another side to Jeff Zucker. I worked closely with him during the nine months we overlapped. I was one of a dozen or so executives who worked hand-in-hand with Zucker to launch the new morning show *New Day*, brainstorming names, dissecting the set design, culling promos and focus group reactions. We would later do the same for the relaunch of *Crossfire*, a concept that was ultimately far less successful.

What I saw in my interactions with Zucker was a person who listened to ideas in the room. Someone who wasn't afraid to try, and fail, and try again. Zucker was eminently accessible—far more than anyone else of his position. His office was a tiny, nondescript spot in the middle of the newsroom. He often floated between shows and desks and control rooms, giving his two cents but also taking in feedback.

And something else stood out to me. He was obsessed with winning—winning each little moment, and winning on a big scale. And ratings, for better or worse, represented winning. Sometimes that obsession would manifest in the types of journalism that would get him criticized—the "poop cruise" coverage, or the massive time and resources devoted to covering the "missing plane." (On a totally separate point—I defend that missing plane coverage! It's a fascinating story, and still is. Maybe my next book will be on MH370, but until then go read *The Atlantic*'s excellent report from 2019 called "What Really Happened to Malaysia's Missing Airplane" and you'll find out it was probably the captain who purposely killed everyone on board and then dunked it into the deepest part of the Australian Ocean. It's fascinating! Okay, moving on.[4])

But other times that obsession would equate to real, fantastic, journalism. He and I would coordinate closely during the week of the Boston bombing in April 2013, tracking each individual twist and turn to the story. There would be details hitting at two in the morning, and I'd be sitting there tweeting out from @CNN while coordinating over email with various teams. When the "Boston bomber" was finally caught, I emailed Zucker to say we had achieved something I'd never seen before—one million concurrent visitors to the CNN website.

The obsession with winning—with ratings, if you will—would ultimately become intertwined with the previous relationship he had with Donald Trump. Initially that was devoting a ton of time to his primary campaign. I think he was mostly right about that. But then Trump became the general election candidate, and then he actually won—and he became, essentially, the network's enemy. Trump, always the showman and never one to turn away from a PR fight, ate it up—and happily embraced the role and the positioning. It was, after all, mutually beneficial.

But that fight would change CNN. It would loosen standards so objective hosts could give their opinion on air—a major change from the way things used to be. In a particularly introspective moment in December 2020, Jake Tapper discussed with Brian Stelter the way his team referred to his opinion monologues off air, calling them "Murrows"—a reference to the celebrated journalist Edward R. Murrow. That should give everyone an idea the weight the network gave to these breaks from objectivity to deliver a very important opinion rant.[5]

We'll get into what happened with the Cuomos in the next chapter. But it went beyond that. It was reported that Tapper was direct messaging a Republican congressional candidate in 2019 to try to convince him to run in a safer district. Even casually, this would have been considered a serious ethical breach mere years before.[6]

It's sad to say, but the guardrails that were once firmly on the network when it came to journalistic integrity had been slipping and then eventually seemed to have been removed altogether. It's not to say that there aren't a lot of great people still at CNN. And great journalists too. But the guardrails being removed will inevitably have real consequences.

What happens when the guardrails are off? You get comments like the one from reporter Leyla Santiago, in July of 2020, ahead of President Trump's July 4 speech at Mount Rushmore. In her report from Washington, DC, rather than, you know, Mount Rushmore (I mean—she wouldn't dare go *there*, would she!), she described one of the most recognizable American landmarks as "a monument of two slave owners and on land wrestled away from Native Americans."[7]

This isn't a Democratic pundit or a commentator. It's not even an opinion host masquerading as a journalist. It's someone who is being positioned as an objective reporter, doing her job at what was, at one time, "the most trusted name in news." Something went seriously off the rails there.

In May 2022, Chris Licht took over as president of CNN, shortly after the sale of WarnerMedia to Discovery. Licht and the head of Discovery, David Zaslav, had a different plan for CNN—one based in news and journalism, and not preening and signaling to a specific sector of a specific party. I have high hopes for the new CNN. In many ways, it feels like the CNN I remember from when I was there—less than ten years ago. But it feels like a lifetime.

I talked to a variety of the media members for this book about CNN—those who have worked at the network and those who are just observers in the industry. Salena Zito joined CNN shortly after the 2016 election. She was specifically sought after by Zucker because of her excellent and unique reporting from the rust belt to the heartland. She saw Trump's shock victory coming in a way few else did inside Acela Media newsrooms, including at CNN.

"I sat down with Jeff Zucker in a very informal way, [he said] 'we really admire what you did, and we really want to pay attention to these voters.' Like we really missed this," Zito told me of her conversation with Zucker. "And then they had me speak in front of the entire company in an auditorium about how I covered things, with Alisyn Camerota. She was asking the questions. And for a while it was great. In the beginning, it was like 'well, why would someone who voted for Trump feel that way?' But it quickly evolved into 'why are they still like that,' 'explain the racism.' They quickly evolved back into being oddities for the people that were producing the shows. More importantly, the people that were the journalists that I would be on with."

Zito told me about one incident in particular that stood out to her. "I remember I was on Don Lemon one time, and he said, 'Why can't you tell these voters not to think this?' and I'm like, 'That's not my job. I'm supposed to be here to tell you what they think, not to tell them what to think,'" she told me. "I'm a journalist. And I remember one time Zucker told me I needed to yell more, and I'm like, I don't do that. I mean, my kids would argue against that. By [2018], I was barely on. My contract ended in January of 2021. But I can't remember the last time I was on after 2018."

So what happened to the sentiment after November 2016—to the town hall in which there seemed to be real curiosity? "It was gone by one month after the inauguration," Zito told me. "It really was, and it was very disappointing, because I was really—if anyone says you have a bias, I would say my bias would be geographical, and probably because I was born and raised in western Pennsylvania. But I understand because I've seen so many things come and go in this area. And a lot more go than come. And all lost from a lot of promises from a lot of people in what I call cultural curators, not just politicians but academia and unions and institutions and corporations. They promised all these things, and they walked away."

The issue predates 2016 and Donald Trump, though. "There's this idea that if it's a Democrat, unless they're doing something really bad, sort of leave them alone, but if it's a Republican, you jump all over them," John Roberts, who previously worked at CNN and CBS News before Fox News, told me. "And I think that's an idea that's firmly ingrained in the culture of American news, that all Democrats are people to be listened to and taken seriously, and all Republicans are crazy people that you beat up on them every time you have them on the air. I know, because that's the attitude that there was at CNN when I was there doing the morning show. You would interview a Democrat, you would ask them about policy questions. When you interviewed a Republican, you would hold their feet to the fire. That's just kind of the way that the producers saw things going. And I was resistant to that notion."

Legendary ESPN anchor Bob Ley hasn't worked at CNN, but as a longtime viewer, he sees the connection to the new CNN and some of the programs on his old home. "I mean, here's a guy, and he said it in the *New York Times* Sunday magazine, was programming CNN with an eye towards First Take and Steven A. Smith, was casting his news network," Ley told me about Zucker. "Listen, a master showman and is beloved by all who worked with him, but in the long view, if Donald Trump is not, every time he stepped in front of a live camera in 2015 and early 2016, was not on CNN like that, I mean, where would Trump's candidacy have been? I think in a far different place."

Rick Sanchez was at CNN from 2006 to 2010. But he was a consumer during the Trump shift. "The Trump story was easy. I mean, CNN saw an opportunity to make ratings so they put this clown on TV every opportunity they possibly [could]," Sanchez told me. "And I don't say 'clown' to disparage Donald Trump. Donald Trump is brilliant. He was literally doing a clown show. And he knew he was doing a clown show, because he knew by doing a clown show he would get a lot of eyeballs. In America, you don't get live coverage on CNN or Fox or MSNBC or any other damn network if you go out there and read a policy speech."

Sanchez said once the ratings started growing, he imagined it was all in: "They never once thought, 'Is this the right thing to do? Is this good for our democracy?' That 'this person is running for president and he's essentially using us. And he knows he's using us. And we know he's using us, but we're going to continue this charade, because you know what? No one's really gonna vote for him. There's no way he can really become president. In the meantime, we'll get some good ratings out of this,' and that was basically the decision. Unfortunately, after it happened, after they literally put him there by maximizing his visibility to an extent that's never been seen before, probably in the history of the United States, with anybody running for president. Then they said, 'Oh shit. Now what do we do?'"

I see where Ley and Sanchez are coming from, but I don't believe CNN putting Trump speeches out there a lot during the primaries led to his primary and eventually general election victories. If anything, doing so did more for the perception of CNN than it did Trump—because of the whiplash that came when Trump became the network's antagonist. What is obvious, though, is that for CNN—like other networks—Trump was a ratings machine, and ratings were enormously important.

Maria Bartiromo previously worked for Jeff Zucker when she worked at CNBC. "At a time, Jeff Zucker loved

Trump because he was giving him the ratings in the show, and I think they both had a partnership. They both liked each other, but when Trump ran for president, Zucker probably didn't think it was possible [to win]," Bartiromo said.

Will Cain worked at CNN before moving to ESPN, and later to Fox. He left CNN in 2014, and he, as I do, knows many people who are still at the network. He told me:

CNN, in my estimation, traveled the path from bias to agenda to propaganda. When I was at CNN, which was in roughly the range from 2010 to 2014–15, the pre–Donald Trump CNN, I would describe CNN as biased...The objective journalists who held themselves out as nothing more than objective and failed miserably at that ideal, I attributed to bias. I look down and I'm like, you just have internal opinions. You can't reconcile or you can't hide and you're not good at seeing objectively the issue from any side but your own. I think that as Donald Trump took over, and I left CNN, and I've spoken to several people who were at CNN at that time, it traveled the path to agenda, meaning they no longer simply were 'oops, my opinion made its way into the program.' They had a mission. They had a mission and the mission was to attack Donald Trump. And by extension, attack anything on the right. Any opinion, any ideology, any news story from the right. And then I think that over the last two to three years, they've evolved even from the agenda into what I would describe as simply propaganda.

I asked Will about what "bias" examples he remembers from the "old CNN," and he brought up his time on the *Starting Point* morning show set, hosted by Soledad O'Brien, where he was a regular contributor. "Sandra Fluke was the guest, and she was receiving very favorable treatment. The questions were softballs," he said. "...Soledad O'Brien is actually a very, very good interviewer and cross-examiner. But she was incredibly biased. She might be something different today. But I don't wish to trash Soledad O'Brien or anyone else. But Sandra Fluke was not the subject of a rigorous hard interview. And I got one question, and I asked Sandra Fluke whether or not gym membership should be covered under healthcare as well, or whether or not special diets, I think, or something like that, should be covered under healthcare as well. And she stumbled and she fumbled and she didn't understand the logic and the point was, is anything related to health an injustice if it's not covered by your employer's health insurance? And I remember the tension on set. And I remember people covering for Sandra Fluke helping her answer and telling me why my question was off—on air. But the most obvious example of a lack of objectivity to me was Trayvon Martin, George Zimmerman. And that was early and that was the beginning of racial conversations that coincide and clash with the criminal justice system, where people didn't care about proof beyond a reasonable doubt, due process. They didn't move forward with any sense of curiosity. They fill gaps, literal gaps in that story, because I believe, if I remember correctly, was about ninety seconds of lost audio where the tragedy, and it was a tragedy of a killing, took place. But in that ninety seconds, we would find out whether or not it was an act of self-defense or a murder. But I just remember everybody on set with a complete lack of objectivity filling all the gaps in their knowledge, filling in and showing no curiosity and operating from a place of conclusion."

Piers Morgan worked at CNN from 2011 through 2014. He saw the evolution of the network—from the inside and the outside—but he also has a unique perspective on the man who ran CNN, Jeff Zucker, and his foil, Donald Trump. Morgan won the first season of *Celebrity Apprentice*. "I liked Jeff Zucker, always got on very well with Jeff, and I worked with him at NBC with *America's Got Talent* and then again at CNN. So I've got nothing against Jeff Zucker. I think he's a brilliant television executive and was a brilliant producer. But I do think he made a strategic error in going so in the tank anti-Trump," Morgan told me. "I think they did it for commercial reasons, they were making tons of money from the surging ratings from bashing Trump 24/7. But I do think some of the anchors like Don Lemon, Anderson Cooper, and others drank the anti-Trump Kool-Aid to the extent they became indistinguishable from MSNBC. And that's not what I always thought CNN was supposed to be. When I worked there and you worked there, the standards and practices were enforced very strictly. You were not allowed to even give the impression of being remotely partisan about any political issue where it could be skewed left or right. And I think that they were quite unashamed about it. And they spent two years telling everybody that the Trump election was fixed by Russian collusion, that turned out to be nonsense. And then they did all they could to not report on a story which could have influenced the election against Joe Biden."

Morgan cited Wolf Blitzer, Erin Burnett, John King, and Tapper as some who have remained "down the line," and pointed to CNN's reporting on the war in Ukraine as an example of the old CNN. "Ted Turner, who created CNN, once said to me, 'The day you lose that at CNN, the business model dies,' because the whole business model is predicated not on chasing ratings in the way that other cable news organizations may be quite happy to do. It's about actually being the network of record. Where if something important happens, people come to you because they trust what you're saying, to be completely unbiased and impartial," he said. "And I think CNN has lost that."

Joel Cheatwood was a former CNN executive who left in 2007 to move to Fox News. "I remember being in so many different meetings with the senior executives of CNN, and number one on the agenda was 'How do we go forward in the changing environment? What's our place? What's the niche that we're going to occupy?' And there would be lively debate back and forth," he told me. "…Roger [Ailes] has mapped out the right, MSNBC is going to take the left, and we'll be left in the middle. And there was a faction that would say, well, that's where we should be. There was a faction that would say, nobody's going to watch the middle. You know, that's no fun. And every single meeting would end up the same thing. We've got to figure this out. We just got to figure this out. But with no resolution. It was amazing to see this, not a bunch of chumps—these were senior executives of a major media company—who really could not come to grips with an answer, and not even a good idea. So you started to get a sense, and I was there for three years, we started to get a sense that this is a real issue...Most of this was during Jim Walton's time, a little bit Jon Klein's. And for the most part, there was this sort of just hanging on to 'we are journalists, we can't give in to this sort of lean one way or the other even if it means our ratings aren't gonna be what we want them to be.' But of course, we've morphed into a situation where journalism has changed dramatically. We've become this sort of institution now that is controlled by profit and ratings, and it was never set up to be that way."

And into that void came Trump. "I honestly think the majority of it was, 'My God, he's great TV. People just respond.' And if you're CNN, it was sort of the best of both worlds because already during that time they were ignored by the conservative side of the equation, had been labeled specifically a left-leaning organization by those guys," Cheatwood told me. "And Trump comes in and as he's developing into the darling of the right, you know, he's also just great TV, so their hardcore left audience love to friggin' hate it. They loved it. You know, it's like watching the villain and hissing at the villain and guffawing at all the incredible things that he would say. And I think, from their standpoint, never believing he would ever be taken seriously. But for CNN, we could all see the ratings, right? It's just when he was on the ratings were high, when he was not they were not. And I think they tapped into something that they saw as a phenomenon. A real character experience. It drove their ratings, and I hate to say this, but I think that's the primary motivation."

John Roberts broke down the eternal CNN conundrum. "CNN for the longest time suffered this huge dilemma, and that was that people used it as a utility, and when there was breaking news, people would go to CNN for the breaking news. And when there wasn't breaking news, people would turn off CNN," he told me. "...They did all kinds of audience surveys. They did demographic breakdowns. They tried to figure out how you hang on to people when there wasn't breaking news, and they could never figure out how to do it. So the numbers would always spike and drop, spike and drop. They finally figured out how to hang on to the audience. And that was Donald Trump. And so when Trump came in, CNN went all out in terms of being the channel that was going to be a foil to Donald Trump, and their ratings went through the roof. And I said to people that I knew from CNN and other people at Fox that they had better be careful because the day that Donald Trump leaves office, their ratings are going to start to go into decline. And they did, and clearly, because of the war in Ukraine, they got their bump for a little while, but that bump is waning again. So now they're back to the same old dilemma that they had since they started. And that is how do you hang on to the breaking news audience when there isn't breaking news. And with rare exception, they haven't figured out how to do that. So it's the same old problem."

It's the same old problem. But the context is new—a CNN that has forever changed its ethos and lost the credibility and trust it once cherished as paramount.

Will it be able to regain it? The stated mission now is to infuse the old journalistic sensibility back into the network.

But the problems that shifted the focus away from the editorial core have not subsided either. And it's certainly much bigger than CNN.

These problems are systemic in the media ecosystem. And identifying each issue—breaking it apart, examining it, diagnosing it—is the only way to fix what's ailing the industry.

CHAPTER 7

Coziness with Power

The 2005 WEDDING WAS A "magical merger," according to *People* magazine—a gathering of 450 family and friends, brought together to celebrate the nuptials of Donald Trump and Melania Knauss.[1]

In the grand scheme of life, the wedding wasn't particularly long ago—a mere ten years before Trump would ultimately announce his candidacy for president. Of course, it felt like a lifetime ago in the culture—especially when you take a look at the guest list.

Two wedding guests in particular stood out—former president Bill Clinton and the woman who would be Trump's 2016 general election opponent, Hillary Clinton. What were the Clintons doing there, exactly? "I happened to be planning to be in Florida and I thought it would be fun to go to his wedding because it is always entertaining," Hillary Clinton said later when asked about it during the campaign.

Trump remembered it differently. During a primary debate, he said, "She had no choice," claiming he had been a donor to the couple's Clinton Foundation, and so they felt an obligation to come. That sort of blunt transparency about the transactional nature of the elite was part of what helped Trump ultimately win the presidency.[2]

But there were many other notable names in attendance, and they tell a different story. Jeff Zucker, then the president of NBC Universal and who would ultimately become one of Trump's biggest foils as president of CNN, was there. In fact, news personalities from across the dial were among the 450 guests. Katie Couric was in attendance, a year before she would jump to CBS from the *Today* show, and her co-host Matt Lauer was there as well. Gayle King was at the wedding—who would later go on to anchor the CBS News morning show. Barbara Walters and Kelly Ripa of ABC joined in the festivities. Chris Matthews of MSNBC was there too.

You could go down the list of celebrities—Anna Wintour of *Vogue* magazine, music mogul Russell Simmons, Heidi Klum, Shaquille O'Neal, Billy Joel, who performed. But what really was most notable were the media personalities, especially in light of the "fake news" battle Trump would wage with the press a decade later—a battle they were more than happy to join in on.

This illustrates a few key points. First, Donald Trump ran with the elite crowd that would eventually turn on him, and vice versa—he was a turncoat to his class. Perhaps that was some of the motivation behind the hate that was to come. But it also is just one of countless examples about how the corporate media structure has become more aligned with the powerful than with the people. Journalists are celebrities.

Those who are on TV or who have achieved success in their field are often very wealthy. They inevitably have begun a sort of natural coziness with those in elite positions, within government, finance, national security, and more.

Being friends with powerful people doesn't invalidate your reporting. You can't help it if you end up standing on the soccer field with rich and powerful figures who happen to have kids who go to the same school as yours. But that sort of coziness can ultimately bleed into the day job—whether consciously or subconsciously. It affects the stories that get covered and how they get covered. And the innocent bystanders in all this are the people, the American public, who rely on the Fourth Estate to be their conduit and representative, and a check on the powerful, not buddies with them. And that's the third major problem with the modern media.

"I think at some point the higher-up people are in the media business and the more successful they are—they're running a network, or running organizations, or are the top talent—they become enmeshed in a world that they're covering," Tara Palmeri of Puck news told me. "...I could see for some journalists, if you're coming from those upper echelons of society, you might end up writing about people that were your family friends, or you grew up with, heads of banks, heads of media organizations, and I'm sure that gets complicated, because we are people ultimately and we have pre-existing relationships or existing relationships. I respect people and we all try to do this where we separate our personal life from our professional life. That's life, but it can get really sticky for journalists. In some ways, the best journalists are often outcasts in a way because they can't get too close to anybody without really doing their job [with] 100 percent integrity. That's not to say, 'oh, wealthy people can't be journalists.' That's not what I'm saying. I'm just saying that it's harder, it's truly harder."

This ultimately plays out in very real ways, whether through active protection or passive disinterest in powerful figures possibly doing something wrong. Rich McHugh spent decades working in TV news at ABC and NBC. When he was working with Ronan Farrow at NBC on an exposé of powerful film mogul Harvey Weinstein's history of sexual assault, he described roadblocks being put into place to stop him from doing the work. I talked to McHugh about his specific experience with what happens when a news organization becomes too cozy with the powerful.

"I was a bit naïve to have this all-out trust for news organizations. I thought that the mandates of news organizations would supersede everything else. In 2017, I learned that was not the case," McHugh told me.

McHugh said he and Ronan Farrow had the Weinstein story, but were told by NBC to "shut down" the reporting. He later learned that NBC executives were communicating with Weinstein directly as they squashed the journalism.

"I look at my experience with Weinstein in the media. There's two parts of it, and there's two stories," he told me. "There's the story that we were trying to get Weinstein, trying to expose him, and we have the story. And then we're being told to shut it down here at NBC. How do we get it out? So we were able to find a way to get it to the *New Yorker*. Fortunately, Ronan, who was not a staffer, could take it there.

That's one. But the bigger thing that was a punch in the gut for me was my actual news organization was all of a sudden a story, and it was kind of crushing to know that people were lying to my face. And I think the most troubling part of this whole thing is that they were lying to us throughout, and then they lied after when I tried to set the record straight, and Ronan did."

McHugh said the experience was an eye-opener for him. "It took me a while to kind of rebound from that. Honestly, I feel like I was in a daze for a while," said McHugh. "...Looking back, and now looking forward, my trust levels with media have changed. I don't view news organizations the same way that I used to view them. I view them as businesses. Very cold and calculating. And there's conflicts all over the place."

McHugh described NBC as having several conflicts with the Weinstein story. But a big one was the almost-blackmail that Weinstein had on them, stopping them from going forward with publication—because Matt Lauer was still working at the network, and hadn't been exposed for the alleged sexual assault claims against him, which were reported by Farrow in his book Catch and Kill.[3] As much as Weinstein's misconduct was an open secret within the industry—although not among the broader general public—so were Lauer's. And Weinstein knew it. "Knowing that, here you have a major news organization, one of the main networks, making agreements with a predator not to cover them, because what? They were afraid of their own in-house predator, who they were protecting, and all these other agreements? Yes, I do think it was an inflection point. And I think everybody has taken a step back and looked at the media and how to cover serious stories like this," said McHugh. "...There were people in the food chain above us who had their own, let's call them inappropriate experiences, HR files and whatnot. And so I think Weinstein exploited the fact that NBC was conflicted all over. And he was smart, and found their Achilles' heel."

Lauer was as powerful as anyone at NBC, and seeing him exposed would have been disastrous for the network. Of course, it would all come out anyway. Lauer would be fired as the *New York Times* exposed that story just a mere month later. "It's the confluence of money and power," McHugh told me. "At NBC, Lauer was basically the de facto president, because he had this massive salary and he had ratings and was on the top show."

Sharon Waxman is the founder of TheWrap and previously spent decades at the *New York Times* and other outlets. She knew Harvey Weinstein—personally, and, as she later wrote, she knew of some of the allegations against him. After the news broke about Weinstein in October 2017, she went on to write about Weinstein's enablers—and named the *New York Times* as one, for killing a story she had been preparing more than a decade earlier.[4]

"By the time the story broke about Harvey, Harvey was already on the decline as a locus of power in Hollywood. His power had already significantly declined," Waxman told me, pointing to that as one reason the thaw in Weinstein coverage was broken. "It's much easier to hit somebody when they're on their way down. And, secondarily, the women who spoke out were willing to go on the record. And that was my biggest challenge at the time. I couldn't get anybody to go on the record. So it wasn't that I wasn't interested in telling the story. I couldn't go and step into a controversy, like accusing Harvey Weinstein."

Waxman notes that what Farrow and McHugh had, which Farrow ultimately published in the *New Yorker*, was separate from what she had—in Farrow's story were on-the-record accusations of rape, which even the initial *New York Times* story that broke the Weinstein dam did not include.

"I spoke to Harvey Weinstein the day the story came out in the *New York Times*, because he used to call me. We had a very long-standing relationship, as he did with many people in the media. But I believe on that date he spoke to two people...and he was already going out there and swinging and threatening to sue the *New York Times*," Waxman said. "...The story that I had in 2005 was a story of him procuring women with Disney money at film festivals in Europe." (Disney owned Miramax, the company Weinstein headed for many years.)

More from Waxman: "That's not the same as coercion. And the *New York Times* didn't have the stones to publish the reporting that I had. And that's why I called them out, because when you have one person who really didn't know what he was talking about saying everybody knew, this is a very easy thing for people to say. I don't think it's true that everybody knew. I think people knew that Harvey fucked around on his wife, and he might have done it flagrantly, and he might have done it with prostitutes. But he's not the only person who did that. And he might have done it in a more obnoxious way. But I think you needed people who would go on the record. It's easy to say everybody knew; it is not easy to publish a story that is clearly defamatory, without somebody's name attached to it. And he's a very powerful person who's very litigious."

So there are a few factors of note with the Weinstein story. There's NBC's conflict and the subtle blackmail Weinstein was able to hold over the news network to stop them from publishing. There's the coziness Weinstein had with journalists through the years, to gently nudge them away from the story. And then there was a third point: the timing. Is it any coincidence the #MeToo era began shortly after Donald Trump entered office? Waxman says no. "I think it was very, very profoundly impacted by Donald Trump's election. I think women everywhere who were involved in society, involved in media, involved in politics, involved in business. I think they were so deeply offended by Donald Trump, by the allegations against him, that were completely swept aside and ignored during the campaign ahead of the 2016 election, that I think that significantly contributed to a certain tipping point and women being willing to step forward and say 'no more of this shit,'" Waxman told me.

The Weinstein story was one example of the ramifications of an Acela Media coziness with power. This next case study is an even more glaring one.

Case Study: Jeffrey Epstein

It's a jarring, almost incomprehensible, article to read in the *New York Times*, from July 2008. In retrospect, it's obviously outrageous, but even in the moment it's shocking to think how this made it past editors. At least Twitter barely existed then, so it wasn't trending all day.

"Financier Starts Sentence in Prostitution Case" was the fairly understated headline by Landon Thomas Jr. The article tells the story of Jeffrey Epstein about to turn himself in to Florida police, and of his conversation with Thomas via phone from his private island, Little St. James. But the article also delves into what appears to be an earlier conversation, in person on the "palm-fringed Xanadu in the Caribbean," between the reporter and Epstein.[5]

Here's how Thomas describes the encounter: "Sitting on his patio on 'Little St. Jeff's' in the Virgin Islands several months ago, as his legal troubles deepened, Mr. Epstein gazed at the azure sea and the lush hills of St. Thomas in the distance, poked at a lunch of crab and rare steak prepared by his personal chef, and tried to explain how his life had taken such a turn. He likened himself to Gulliver shipwrecked among the diminutive denizens of Lilliput."

Then Thomas quotes Epstein: "Gulliver's playfulness had unintended consequences...That is what happens with wealth. There are unexpected burdens as well as benefits."

The massive article, which doubles as a form of reputation laundering, spends a few paragraphs on what exactly Epstein had been accused of. It started when a "young woman who gave Mr. Epstein massages" told police she was fourteen years old at the time. That led others to allege similar crimes of underage...massaging—and Epstein's crack legal team, including former Clinton impeachment special counsel Ken Starr and legal titan Alan Dershowitz, was able to get him out of jail time thanks to a reduced sentence for "soliciting prostitution."

But that didn't stick, according to the article, and he ultimately had to "plead guilty to a charge that would require him to register as a sex offender."

Between in-depth descriptions of Epstein's library, bathhouse, and future "villa" being built on the island, Thomas tries to explore a little about what exactly it is Epstein actually does. "As Mr. Epstein explains it, he provides a specialized form of superelite financial advice," writes Thomas. "He counsels people on everything from taxes and trusts to prenuptial agreements and paternity suits, and even provides interior decorating tips for private jets. Industry sources say he charges flat annual fees ranging from $25 million to more than $100 million."

This, again, is something that ran in the *New York Times* in 2008. "It's one of the most embarrassing pieces of journalism in any major outlet, in a competition for which there are many viable contenders," NPR's David Folkenflik, who is one of the few mainstream reporters to cover the Epstein story, told me. "Like what a dipshit piece to put out there. Even in the moment."

What Folkenflik found reporting the story was the true icing on the cake: Landon Thomas had kept up a cordial relationship with Epstein over the years. In 2017, he solicited and secured a $30,000 donation from Epstein to a personal charity. Thomas was pushed out of the *New York Times* in early 2019.[6]

Epstein pled guilty to a lesser charge of solicitation of prostitution with a minor. He also settled at least a dozen civil lawsuits alleging Epstein molested women when they were underage. He ultimately did go to prison—or, rather, "prison." He spent six days in a "work release" program at a cushy office, where he was once again accused of sex crimes. He registered as a sex offender, and after finishing his probation in Florida, he went up to New York City.

A short time after his probation ended, in December 2010, power publicist Peggy Siegal arranged a party at Epstein's gigantic nine-story townhouse. In attendance were George Stephanopoulos of ABC, CBS Evening News anchor Katie Couric, late night host Chelsea Handler, actor Woody Allen, and more—a party in theory for Epstein's friend, Prince Andrew. "Despite the pedophile mogul's conviction for soliciting underage prostitution, his circle is standing by their man" was the sub-headline to the Daily Beast story from 2011 that broke this news.[7]

All those in attendance have since distanced themselves from it—saying it was the only time they had met Epstein and claiming to be unaware of his past crimes.

Eventually, in the post–#MeToo era, the dam broke on Epstein too, largely thanks to some excellent reporting by Julie K. Brown in the *Miami Herald*. Epstein was charged with horrific crimes, and then, while awaiting trial, he died of a suspected suicide. We may never know the full extent of what he did. But we also know the reason it took as long as it did to eventually expose his crimes was the reluctance in the media to give it attention.

Rich McHugh said he was told NBC was working the story too, but had been "waved off." "My understanding is that interviews had been shot and it had progressed to a level that was approaching reportable. I think that the Epstein victims who had sat down for interviews felt that they weren't served well by NBC," he said.

ABC also had the story—as we know thanks to a leaked video put out by Project Veritas in 2019. Anchor Amy Robach could be seen on set with cameras rolling, talking privately about how she had the Epstein story years earlier. "I've had the story for three years," Robach said. "I tried for three years to get it out to no avail, and now these new revelations and—I freaking had all of it...I'm so pissed right now. Like, every day I get more and more pissed."[8]

In the video, Robach implied part of the reason the interview didn't air was because "the palace found out" about allegations against Prince Andrew that were going to air, and "threatened us a million different ways." She ultimately put out a statement corroborating ABC's position that it had not yet met the "editorial standards" of ABC.

Tara Palmeri, now of Puck news, hosted a podcast, "Broken: Seeking Justice," about Epstein and his victims. She is very familiar with the story—and the challenges of reporting out any story when the source at the center is a powerful figure, which the broader corporate media is in some ways intertwined with.

"Suddenly people cared about the way women were being treated, and suddenly you've got Trump in the White House," Palmeri told me. "...It needed to happen. But it festered for ten years. And he was probably allowed to continue to abuse girls because of that."

Palmeri said some of it came from a fear of litigation. "First of all, Alan Dershowitz is extremely litigious," she said. "He's a lawyer, he represented Epstein, but Virginia Roberts," one of the Epstein accusers, "and others have said that he also took part in a sexual abuse against these girls." (Dershowitz has denied wrongdoing.) Of Epstein, Palmeri said: "He's also technically protected by the non-prosecution agreement. There were really powerful forces...So I think for a lot of these news organizations, it becomes really costly. It's a tough story to prove, because the sexual encounters, there aren't often many people there. You've got people with a lot of money willing to go to bat and then you've got the threats of losing access, which obviously is not something that we in a business should be so concerned about, but truly television news is a lot about booking interviews and having access to powerful people."

Palmeri specifically cited the Prince Andrew connection, and the royal pipeline for TV networks that's so important to keep active—what would the royal family do to a network that put a Prince Andrew accuser on the air? The network likely would be cut off.

Meanwhile Epstein stayed highly connected to powerful people, outside the media world too. Epstein was said to be a close confidant to Bill Gates, whom he counseled on marriage and on how he could potentially win a Nobel Prize. Gates, who consistently gets favorable interviews across the establishment media dial, is rarely asked about his association with Epstein.[9]

There's still so much we don't know about the Jeffrey Epstein story. A hungry, curious media would continue to pursue it and not let his untimely death kill the truth about what happened. Among the creepy art pieces displayed at Epstein's giant New York townhouse was a huge painting of Bill Clinton, wearing a blue dress that mimics the infamous "Monica" one. It was prominently displayed, for all to see. Clinton, as we know, spent some time with Epstein.[10]

What was the significance of the painting and the way Epstein displayed it? Was it about power? Was it just a sick joke? A threat? Was it blackmail? Like he was telling all those who entered his townhouse, "Cross me and I'll emasculate you on my wall—I did it to one of the most powerful people in the world, and I can do it to you too"?

We don't know. But a corporate media not corrupted by coziness with power would be interested in finding out.

———

There's another side to coziness with power.

In 2013, Jeff Bezos, one of the richest men in the world, bought the *Washington Post*. It was a relative drop in the bucket for Bezos—just $250 million for the multibillionaire. In the years since, Bezos has poured money into the *Post* and made it profitable.

But let's be honest: Bezos isn't in the media business now for the money. Instead, it's a vanity project. It's a status symbol. He has the yachts. Some billionaires buy sports teams. He bought a newspaper. And it happens to be one of the most powerful newspapers, located in arguably *the* power center of the world.

Bezos isn't alone in following this path. Billionaire Marc Benioff bought *Time* magazine. Billionaire Elon Musk explored buying Twitter—a social platform, instead of a media outlet, but a property that would put Musk on the media map nonetheless.

So what should we make of Bezos's pet project? Is it a good thing or a bad thing for the industry?

Sharon Waxman thinks it's "not a coincidence" that Bezos would want a media property in Washington. "Amazon has lots and lots of policy interests in Washington, DC, and that is a good way for Jeff to build goodwill and relationships, in a place that can deeply impact his core business, Amazon," she said. "But he's also done, I think, a good job of standing up for journalistic credibility and also pouring resources into the *Washington Post*. The *Washington Post* was a sinking ship when Jeff bought it."

Tucker Carlson sees it more negatively. "This is like a nightmare scenario. This actually is the end of democracy," he told me. "Amazon is not really a company at this point. It's, you know, it's a country. It's that big. And so to give an oligarch like Jeff Bezos control over the main information source to the federal government, and not even acknowledge it, and watch him take an aggressively partisan position on behalf of the party that awards him the largest share of his contracts for Amazon Web Services, which would be the Democratic Party, the federal government. No one says anything about it. You're kind of like, 'This is what Upton Sinclair warned us about.' "

Carlson says this is an inflection point. "I was always a

conservative. I grew up that way. I am now a conservative. But the assumption that corporate power is better than federal power—I'm not sure where we got that assumption," he said. "It's not. It's less accountable, actually. And when the two of them converge and align against the interests of the American middle class—you know, I grew up in an affluent world, so it's not like I'm the voice of the people or something. But I'm watching this and like, who's speaking for the guy who makes fifty grand? I'm not that guy. You know, I'm at the top end, but I'm an American—I still care. And those people are being completely, not just screwed, but like, marked for destruction."

Katie Rosman of the *New York Times* sees the Bezos move as an influence play. "The *Washington Post* is a publicly traded company, but the value of media to Wall Street, it's not paying off. So that then changes the value proposition of a media property, instead of being a moneymaker, mainly to being a prestige conveyor," she said. "It used to be you got a yacht, and now you buy a media property. I mean, that's sort of a crass way to put it, but it might not be wrong. It is a status symbol, and it does confer a lot of influence. But let's look individually. My sense is that Jeff Bezos has been good, he's pumped a lot of blood and oxygen and money into the *Washington Post*. It feels vital to me."

Bezos's influence in DC will certainly be growing, as is Amazon's generally in the world. And it will make it more complicated for those at the *Washington Post*. So far, Bezos has stayed out of any active editorial control—but what sort of passive influence might he have?

Concept: Information Hostage-Taking

One of the trickier forms of bias that exists in the media world is a bias of omission. What *doesn't* get covered is sometimes as important as what does. But unless you're a discerning media consumer, how could you even know what doesn't get covered?

And as tricky as a bias of omission could be, there's an even trickier variation, and in some ways it relates to the sort of coziness with power that can come with the modern corporate media. I call it "information hostage-taking."

It's a tactic that happens when a media organization works with another entity it should be skeptical of, but instead is essentially working together with. This often comes into play with sources within the intelligence community.

Essentially the press's job is to disseminate information to the public. But by holding certain information hostage, the true picture is locked away. In its place—innuendo, speculation. And then, when a "ransom" is paid—sometimes the hostage can be released.

Here's an example. In June 2020, the *New York Times* published a bombshell article about the war in Afghanistan and Russia's alleged covert involvement.

"American intelligence officials have concluded that a Russian military intelligence unit secretly offered bounties to Taliban-linked militants for killing coalition forces in Afghanistan—including targeting American troops—amid the peace talks to end the long-running war there, according to officials briefed on the matter," read the piece. "The

United States concluded months ago that the Russian unit, which has been linked to assassination attempts and other covert operations in Europe intended to destabilize the West or take revenge on turncoats, had covertly offered rewards for successful attacks last year."[11]

The piece rocketed around the internet. The next day, one of the reporters of the article, Charlie Savage, was a guest on Joy Reid's MSNBC show. "This whole response to this apparently solid, at least believed to be solid within the US government, intelligence finding has been strangely lethargic," he said, alluding to perceived coziness between President Trump and Russia that stopped the government from having someone go to Russia and saying "We know you're doing this and knock it off, at a minimum."[12]

In fact, what Trump knew and didn't know would become a core piece of the story. The MSNBC.com title of the Reid segment with Savage was "Trump knew of Russian bounty on troops before late March: report."

Approximately a month later, the Trump-specific hook was the topic of another *New York Times* story. Savage, along with two other reporters, published a piece on Trump's recent conversation with Russian president Vladimir Putin. "Trump Says He Did Not Ask Putin about Suspected Bounties to Kill U.S. Troops" was the headline.[13]

This was July 2020, and the presidential election was mere months away. A story about Trump being soft on Russia, and soft on defending US troops, certainly could have had some sway when it came to November.

In April 2021, the Daily Beast published a massive scoop.

That Russian bounty story? Maybe there wasn't much to it after all. Under the headline "U.S. Intel Walks Back Claim Russians Put Bounties on American Troops," the outlet revealed how the whole story was shaky to begin with, despite getting attention throughout the *New York Times*, cable news, and Twitter.[14]

So how did the story take off in the first place? The Daily Beast found the rumor originated from "detainee reporting," or "someone told their US-aligned Afghan jailers what they thought was necessary to get out of a cage."

From jailhouse rumor... to the *New York Times*.

Meanwhile the White House would only confirm the intel community now has "low to moderate confidence" in the authenticity of the original story. Or, as the Daily Beast translates "from the jargon of spyworld"... unproven at best, and, plausibly untrue altogether.

That didn't stop Trump's general election opponent Joe Biden from speaking definitively on the matter back when it was first reported. "His entire presidency has been a gift to Putin, but this is beyond the pale," Biden said at the time. "It's a betrayal of the most sacred duty we bear as a nation to protect and equip our troops when we send them into harm's way. It's a betrayal of every single American family with a loved one serving in Afghanistan or anywhere overseas."[15]

The information that would have turned the story into a far more nuanced portrayal—that it was coming from an overtly shaky source—stayed far away from the audience. Taken hostage. By whom, though? Did the *Times* know and just avoid printing that? Or were they spun and left out to dry by their intel sources? It happens when coziness with those sources allows them the protection to get their partial stories out into the information ecosystem.

Either way, it fit the information hostage-taking formula. The ransom—Trump lost. And then the truth being held hostage can be released.

Like this, and the Hunter Biden laptop truth, what other stories from the Trump Era will we get to find out the truth about—now that it's no longer useful to keep the truth hostage?

CHAPTER 8

The Interconnected Mess

THE CONSOLIDATION OF THE MEDIA is poison for the free flow of information in the United States," Rick Sanchez, former CNN anchor, told me. "And we've seen that happening and it's a really, really horrible thing which makes us want to question whether the news we're getting is really news or if it's being influenced by some higher power, only because it's so much easier for that higher power to now influence it. The second part of it is the fact that there's this thing called interlocking, and interlocking is essentially a word that defines when people from one corporation are able to influence another corporation. And what happens plainly is that you get board members from, let's say, a company like Raytheon, or any other weapons manufacturer, or a tech company, or these companies that are good companies. I have nothing against these companies, they do good things, in many ways, but I don't want a company that makes bombs to have influence over the company that controls the message."

Sanchez's point about "interlocking," or "interlocking directorates," is an interesting one. Essentially what Sanchez is pointing to is how these media companies, which are growing larger as we see consolidation of the biggest brands, have boards of directors, and those directors are directors on other boards for other companies. Whether there's active influence is unclear, but could there be passive influence?

Let's take an example. The board of the Walt Disney Corporation includes directors who are also on the boards of Oracle, a software company; Proctor & Gamble, a consumer goods company; Illumina, a biotechnology company; Nike, a sporting goods company; and Carlyle, an investment company. That's just to name a few. I couldn't find any Raytheon board members on there, but this is just a single example.

The point isn't necessarily that these board members are going to get ABC News to do a positive story about Nike or kill a negative story about Proctor & Gamble. It's not even really an argument that these board members have much to do with what's happening at ABC News to begin with. But what's obvious is the more these giant corporations that deliver us the news get even more gigantic, it's going to be an interconnected mess.

Let's get even more practical. During the Obama years, you had real or perceived conflicts all over the place. Jay Carney, the White House press secretary, was married to Claire Shipman of ABC News. Top advisor to the president Ben Rhodes's brother was the head of CBS News, David Rhodes. Across the dial, Ben Sherwood was then running ABC News—and his sister is Elizabeth Sherwood-Randall, who was a top national security advisor to Obama. CNN's deputy Washington bureau chief Virginia Moseley was married to Tom Nides, who served as deputy secretary of state to Hillary Clinton. Ari Shapiro, the NPR White House correspondent, was married to Michael Gottlieb, who worked in the White House counsel's office.[1]

And we haven't even begun to scratch the surface of which government officials were close friends with which journalists—or who played on each other's softball teams, or in golf foursomes, or just happened to make small talk in the bleachers while their kids played middle school softball.

It's important to recognize how intertwined the media is with the elite and powerful figures they cover, and also not to put too much weight into it either. On the surface, conflicts of interest like this are rampant, and frankly, the ones we know about—the family members, the spouses—are less concerning than the ones we don't, the connections that happen in the dark, away from the public.

And you don't need a familial connection to see the problem with media and governmental power getting too cozy. In December 2017, CNN got a story so mercilessly wrong that the New York Times, in its write-up of the incident, described it as the kind of story that is "fueling claims of 'fake news.'"[2]

The CNN story originally claimed Donald Trump Jr. received an email with an encryption key to access WikiLeaks documents more than a week before the documents were released publicly. The entire premise of the story was this prepublication access, but there was also a notable inclusion. "Trump Jr. told investigators he had no recollection of the September email," the report said. And later: "Trump Jr.

was asked about the WikiLeaks email Wednesday when he was questioned in the House Intelligence Committee behind closed doors, several sources familiar with the exchange told CNN."

As it turns out, whoever CNN's source was got the date wrong. Trump Jr. didn't receive the email on September 4, he received it on September 14—one day after WikiLeaks released the whole archive publicly, and anyone in the world could access it. Thus, the entire point of the article was moot.

CNN was forced to issue a correction to the top of the story, along with corrections and clarifications throughout the entire piece. "This story has been corrected to say the date of the email was September 14, 2016, not September 4, 2016. The story also changed the headline and removed a tweet from Donald Trump Jr., who posted a message about WikiLeaks on September 4, 2016," read the correction, and later, perhaps most embarrassingly, this line was added, "The new information indicates that the communication is less significant than CNN initially reported."[3]

Yeah, I'd say so! But that's not where this story ends. A couple days later Politico published an odd story where Congressman Adam Schiff's office went on the record to dispute that he or his staffers were behind "leaks" related to Donald Trump Jr.'s testimony. "Ranking Member Schiff and his staff do not leak classified or confidential information, and any disclosure of non-public information by the congressional committees undertaking investigations is singularly unhelpful," Schiff's office said.

Adam Schiff is as much a mainstay on cable news as just about anyone who walks the halls of Congress. It would not be at all surprising if he or someone in his office were the source for that botched CNN hit job, which screwed up the email date and the entire premise of the story. And yet, there was never any real reckoning with Adam Schiff, on this story or any others related to Russiagate—many of which turned out to be loose ends and went nowhere, making the media look bad in the process.

No, instead, Adam Schiff released a book in 2021 called *Midnight in Washington*, and his media friends rolled out the red carpet for him. Rachel Maddow devoted nearly half her show to it, including a close to fifteen-minute dramatic reading of the book before she even got to the interview portion. In total, Schiff appeared on MSNBC ten separate times during the first eight days after his book was released. CNN had Schiff on five times during that span, and he was on CBS, ABC, a *New York Times* podcast, and more.

As a result of that public relations boosterism, Schiff's book shot up to number one on the *New York Times* bestseller list, thanks to the same media that didn't seem to mind being the vessel for Russia collusion misinformation for years during the Trump Era.

It's all in the game...and it's all connected.

Case Study: The Bernie Primaries

Sometimes an article drops and it makes you re-evaluate everything you've thought about before. That happened to me in November 2017 when I read the Politico excerpt from Donna Brazile's book *Hacks*. The Politico excerpt was titled "Inside Hillary Clinton's Secret Takeover of the DNC."[4]

Now that's a juicy headline. And it delivered. "I had promised Bernie when I took the helm of the Democratic National Committee after the convention that I would get to the bottom of whether Hillary Clinton's team had rigged the nomination process, as a cache of emails stolen by Russian hackers and posted online had suggested. I'd had my suspicions from the moment I walked in the door of the DNC a month or so earlier, based on the leaked emails. But who knew if some of them might have been forged? I needed to have solid proof, and so did Bernie," began Brazile.

What she ultimately found was a "Joint Fund-Raising Agreement between the DNC, the Hillary Victory Fund, and Hillary for America," which showed Clinton's campaign in 2016 had an agreement long before Clinton was the actual nominee that she would take over the DNC operations, which is customary after the candidate wins the nomination, not before. In that way, the deck was completely stacked against Sanders from the start in 2016, by his own party machine.

Let's pause for a minute. You may not be a Bernie Sanders fan politically, but we should acknowledge that whether you are or not, our democratic system must allow for a fair electoral process. And clearly in 2016, Sanders was screwed over by the Democratic Party and the Clinton campaign. But what happened to Bernie Sanders in 2020 was different, and actually a little more alarming. And it points to something far more all-encompassing and messy.

Yes, there was still the political operation that tried to stop him from winning the nomination. There were two bizarre moments that pointed to the Democratic Party working against Sanders still, four years later. First was the candidacy of Michael Bloomberg. There was no real constituency for Bloomberg—a billionaire financial and media mogul who was a solid New York City mayor but had no real national hook. Yet he jumped in with a massive spend. His appearance in the debates seemed to indicate he was there for one main reason—as a kamikaze mission to take down Sanders. He ultimately was barely even able to register a real hit, instead taking incoming from Elizabeth Warren and others, and fading away.

The other moment was on March 2, 2020, the day before Super Tuesday, when two of the final six competitors in the primary dropped out and endorsed Joe Biden. Pete Buttigieg had won Iowa and, while not necessarily on a path to the nomination, surely would have registered some electors on Super Tuesday and kept in the mix. Amy Klobuchar was not far behind the pack, and also could have performed well in a few states the next day. But instead they met Joe Biden in Texas, took the stage with him, and threw their political capital behind the, at that time, co-frontrunner with Sanders. What was the reason? It was obvious. As the *New York Times* put it in its headline: "Buttigieg and Klobuchar Endorse Biden, Aiming to Slow Sanders."[5]

But the other major factor in 2020 that differed from 2016 was how the media treated Sanders. The Acela Media didn't necessarily want Joe Biden. In fact, they pretty much went through just about every other candidate trying to make them happen before ultimately being forced to settle on Biden as the last man standing not named Bernie. They went through an Elizabeth Warren phase; they liked Mayor

Pete; Kamala Harris got some time in the spotlight; even Beto O'Rourke got a fancy *Vanity Fair* cover. But nothing stuck. And so it was ultimately Biden or Bernie, and there wasn't a single chance they were going to let Bernie happen, if they had anything to do with it.

MSNBC was a big force of anti-Sanders content during the primary campaign. Chris Matthews, still a lead anchor with the network in February 2020, went on a rant against socialism, questioning where Sanders stood. "I remember the Cold War. I have an attitude towards Castro, and I believe if Castro and the Reds had won the Cold War, there would have been executions in Central Park and I might've been one of the ones executed and certain other people would be there cheering. So, I have a problem with people who took the other side," he said to an uncomfortable panel.[6]

Joy Reid went after Sanders's team for their push to eliminate the "superdelegates," pointing to the fact that it took "Black elected officials" out of the game. "It's the only power they had, that was taken away, just to appease the Sanders supporters," she said.[7]

Reid was a frequent critic not just of Sanders himself but of his supporters. A few weeks later, after Sanders won big in Nevada and appeared to be the clear frontrunner, she essentially pled with Democrats to step up to stop him. "The rest of us that sort of look at politics have underestimated the sheer unadulterated rage, the anger, of working-class people," she said. "No one is as hungry, angry, enraged, and determined as Sanders voters. Democrats need to sober up and figure out what the hell they are going to do about it!"[8]

At one point MSNBC was forced to suspend frequent

contributor Jason Johnson, who said during a radio interview that it was "racist white liberals" who supported Sanders, and castigating the Black staffers who worked for the
candidate. "I don't care how many people from the island
of misfit black girls you throw out there to defend you," he
said.[9]

It got so bad that Sanders's campaign manager actually
told *Vanity Fair* that Fox News had been "more fair than
MSNBC...Fox is often yelling about Bernie Sanders's socialism, but they're still giving our campaign the opportunity to
make our case in a fair manner, unlike MSNBC, which has
credibility with the left and is constantly undermining the
Bernie Sanders campaign."[10] (Sanders, smartly, was the first
Democratic candidate in the crowded field to take Fox News
up on its offer of a town hall.)

CNN wasn't much different in its treatment of the Sanders campaign. There was the graphic that made the rounds
on Twitter that showed Sanders up by three percentage
points and the header "No Clear Leader."[11]

But the most noteworthy moment on CNN came from
an oppo dump ahead of a CNN debate, with Elizabeth
Warren's campaign leaking that Bernie Sanders had told his
friend and fellow senator in a private 2018 meeting that "a
woman can't win." The sourcing in the article was interesting, to say the least—showing the leak came from friends of
Warren (or Warren herself), with a vested interest in boost-
ing her campaign: "The description of that meeting is based
on the accounts of four people: two people Warren spoke
with directly soon after the encounter, and two people familiar with the meeting."[12]

This vague description of the sourcing was undoubtedly by design. Sanders immediately and strongly refuted the accusation, and his press secretary Briahna Joy Gray shared a video of Sanders in 1988 saying a woman could win.

Why were the left-wing partisan forces in the corporate media working overtime against Sanders in 2020? Perhaps it was ideological—that they thought he would be bad for the party. Maybe it was strategic—that they thought he couldn't beat Trump. Whatever the reason, through the Democratic party once again galvanizing behind his opponent in the middle of a primary and through the media's actions, Biden took the lead on Super Tuesday and never looked back.

Tucker Carlson has been in and around Washington for a long time, and his perspective on Sanders and Biden is interesting.

"I really believed in the system, I really did, it was totally authentic. Like, I'd never even questioned that. Maybe it's reflected in my low IQ, but I did. Watching Bernie Sanders, man, what happened to him? Really changed my view. I couldn't even believe it," Carlson told me. "...Watching the reaction to him. It was like, 'We just have to stop Bernie Sanders,' and they stole it from him. Then watching them cover it up, with 'the Russian government had hacked the DNC': there's no evidence the Russian government hacked the DNC. All the evidence suggests that the DNC employee leaked that because he was pissed, and he wanted to show that the DNC had their thumb on the scales against Bernie Sanders and in favor of Hillary. So they concocted this enormous lie that changed the course of American history to hide the fact that they have rigged their own primaries. I couldn't believe I was watching this and it actually took me months to sort it out. I'm good at sniffing out bullshit, but it takes me a long time to figure out what actually happened."

And then, it happened again. "You're like, wait a second, the whole party mobilizes against the democratic system, not just against Bernie Sanders, but against the system itself, stops democracy, blames a foreign country. Anyone who says anything about it is accused of being an agent of a foreign country. I was like, this is out of a movie. I can't believe it's happening in my country. And then you see it again" in 2020, he said. "I knew Biden and I knew the family as noted, and talk about a fixture of Washington, someone who everyone sort of likes, he'd always hug you. I've been hugged by Joe Biden many times. That's why whenever they were like, 'Oh, he's a pervert for sniffing girls,' I was like, 'He's sniffed me.' I mean I don't like Joe Biden, it's the worst presidency ever. But he sniffs people, he sniffed me, I don't care. I like sniffing."

"He's a very mean person, a cold person and ruthless person, but at the same time, he's a warm person," Carlson told me about Biden. "And that's his best quality. It's just true. And I've been around the guy for thirty years, so I can vouch for that. But I knew that he was fading. I knew for a fact he was fading because members of his family had said out loud that he had dementia. And his son had died and it was very sad. I knew his son, I knew Beau, he was a good guy. My wife went to the funeral, you know? But anyway, the idea in the Biden family was he's bereft because his son has died and so he's running for president to sort of work it out, work it off, his third run for president. That made total sense to me. No one imagined in a million years he'd be the Democratic nominee. It wasn't even a possibility."

But as Carlson tells it, Biden ultimately became the nominee because the Democratic Party "literally appointed him." From Carlson:

People kind of accepted it and was like, "oh well, that's okay, we're against Trump and the party needs to get behind the guy. It doesn't matter, strength in numbers. We're party people above all." And when I saw that, I was like this is not how democracy is supposed to work. This is the antithesis of democracy, and this is not good, because it suggests that there's something hidden and not at all straightforward going on. People making these decisions are not publicly known. These decisions are not transparent. And you don't want to have a government like that, because it's very creepy and not responsive and it can do all kinds of bad things. So I was very bothered by the Biden thing, and he was obviously senile, it was clear during the debates. I actually did a segment on it once and then I felt guilty because I thought, "Well, I hope I make it to seventy-eight or whatever, I'll probably be senile. I don't want someone making fun of me." I don't make fun of old people. I like old people. I give them a pass. Old people and children, I have a soft spot. But I made fun of him because I'm a dick and I couldn't control myself, but it never occurred to me that that man would be the nominee because it was just so out in the open that he was fading. And they did it anyway. I think it's the most cynical, cruel, reckless thing I've ever seen.

It's interesting to think about Trump versus Bernie in that sense. In some ways, the way Trump was treated early by the Fox Newses of the world—the right-wing sphere—was similar to how Bernie Sanders was treated. Trump was not the preferred 2016 nominee of the Fox News opinion crowd. But he was able to overcome that, and certainly Fox News's opinion hosts got on board after that. Sanders wasn't. What does that tell us? One possibility is the voters on the right were less swayable by the media than those on the left. Another possibility is that the left media's attacks on Sanders were more effective. Or it could be back to the party—that the DNC was able to overcome a Sanders surge and close ranks faster and more successfully than the RNC was against Trump. Another option is that it was more isolated—that Trump ultimately connected more with the GOP voters than Sanders did with the Democratic voters.

Whatever the reason, what happened to Sanders in 2020 shows the power of the corporate press, but it also shows an insurgent candidate what to do next time in 2024—go to the powerful independent media, and bypass the gatekeepers altogether.

Case Study: The Cuomo Show

It's hard to sum up the problems with the Acela Media in a single image, but this one might be close: Chris Cuomo on his primetime CNN show, holding up a giant prop cotton swab, yukking it up with his brother, Gov. Andrew Cuomo, on May 20, 2020.[13]

"See, I said I was going to be nice and sweet," said Governor Cuomo, as Chris implored him to answer whether the giant nasal swab was what was used to administer his PCR test—a joke about his large nose. "I thought I did so well on that nasal test standing up there, she did the swab, I did not flinch, I was a cool dude in a loose mood," Governor Cuomo continued, changing the subject.

"Of course you were, that swab is like a piece of lint going in that thing in your face," said Chris, taking another large nose jab. "How could it have collected anything? It was like throwing a rock around a cave!"

"This is not love," said Governor Cuomo as the pair laughed. As he went to break, Chris teased he'd have more with the governor—"something that everybody wants to know." It won't surprise you that when they returned from break, the interview didn't turn into an actual give-and-take informing the audience of anything serious.

The situation with Chris Cuomo, Andrew Cuomo, and CNN has many layers, and involves a multitude of the problems laid out in this book. "The Cuomo Show" exposed both something unique about this particular incident, and also gave a look, perhaps an extreme look, at the way much of the media operates in this current environment.

We'll start at the beginning, when the very first exception was made, which started a snowball effect of dubious journalistic choices by those on our TV, those behind the scenes, and the politicians they get cozy with in ways that cross ethical lines.

That May 2020 appearance with the giant prop cotton swab was the tenth time Governor Cuomo appeared on his younger brother Chris's CNN show in the span of approximately one month. And before we go through exactly how this massive ethical breach began, it's worth contextualizing the moment we were in. The pandemic was raging, with a scarily high death rate in New York. And the entire experience began under far different circumstances than Chris sitting in his studio with props. The prior month, Chris came down with COVID, and after taking off for a day or two, began to broadcast his show, with COVID, live from his basement. It was emotional and a bit frightening—he'd tell the audience about nights he'd spent shivering, challenges with his health. He was living the story while he was covering it.

Of course, the whole charade became a bit of a reality TV exercise—one that I began calling "Keeping Up with the Cuomos" in my Fourth Watch newsletter. Chris's wife, Cristina, was a bit of a media personality herself, with a health blog called The Purist. On the site, Cristina, who also contracted COVID, described in great detail the treatments she was taking and she was passing along to her husband while he was quarantining in the basement. In a blog post headlined "Cristina Cuomo Corona Protocol, Week 3," she went through the "protocol" for recovering from a case of COVID—at least if you're rich and live in the Hamptons. Cristina's self-treatment included a vitamin drip performed by a doctor in a "full hazmat outfit," a "body charger" suggested by an "energy specialist," and Clorox in her bath.

Meanwhile, the food sounded pretty sweet. "Every day, Chris and I both ate an Ayurveda lunch from Corey de Rosa at Tapovana to-go in Bridgehampton," Cristina wrote.[14]

In her "week 2" blog, she explained how she sent "a sample of Chris' hair" to see what Dr. Linda Lancaster in Santa Fe, the author of *Harmonic Healing*, should prescribe him.

One vitamin prescribed was quinine. Cristina wrote that both Cuomos took quinine daily as part of their recovery. What's quinine? From the NIH website: "Quinine was first recognized as a potent antimalarial agent hundreds of years ago. Since then, the beneficial effects of quinine and its more advanced synthetic forms, chloroquine and hydroxychloroquine, have been increasingly recognized in a myriad of other diseases in addition to malaria." In other words, Chris Cuomo was given a natural form of hydroxychloroquine by his wife to recover from coronavirus.[15]

When his recovery was complete, Chris took viewers on a journey with him when he said he emerged from his basement after fourteen days in quarantine, walking up the stairs and hugging his family in dramatic fashion. Never mind that days earlier, it was reported he got into a heated confrontation with a man who spotted Chris and his family at another property of his—outside, it should be noted. And to be fair, that's the only time we know Chris actually emerged from the basement, without cameras around.[16]

I defended Chris having his brother on his CNN show when he was in his basement with COVID. I thought it was a light, heartwarming moment back in early April, as Chris was struggling with the early stages of the disease. This was also a time when it still appeared Governor Cuomo was doing at least a competent, if not excellent, job during the crisis ravaging his state.

But the circumstances drastically changed by the time the next month came around. By then, we already knew the horror in nursing homes around the country, where COVID was so harmful to the elderly, and the elderly were inside, surrounded by one another. But it was particularly bad in certain states, including New York. In New York—and some other states—nursing homes were directed to take COVID-positive patients and put them back into the nursing homes, rather than keep them in hospitals that were filling up. Cuomo's administration took steps to hide the true numbers of nursing home deaths, but we knew just from available data that it was in the tens of thousands—and likely much higher.

We knew all that information during that May 20 comedy routine, and Governor Cuomo wasn't asked about it. In fact, it never came up during any of his interviews with his brother.[17]

Before those appearances, CNN had a rule in place that barred Chris from interviewing Andrew. And it was dropped by CNN president Jeff Zucker—a lengthy exception was made. Some in the media strongly disagreed with that decision.

"I think Chris Cuomo from day one should have recused himself, he should have never interviewed his brother," John Roberts, now of Fox News, told me. "That right there crosses a journalistic line. Unless you say, 'I am not a journalist. I am an opinion host. My brother was the governor of the state of New York. I love him. I think he's doing a fabulous job. And anytime, full disclosure, you turn in to my program you're going to hear me saying great things about him.' If you say that up front, then I think you're okay. But this was Chris Cuomo saying that he was a journalist, and then throwing all of these softballs. And then eventually the whole thing came home to roost."

"It plays right into the 'we don't trust anybody' narrative. It just does. it's a lack of integrity. It's really a lack of judgment," former CNN and Fox executive Joel Cheatwood told me. "... I mean, there's no way in hell that you let a family member interview another on a serious story, because there can't help but be a bias. And listen, anybody would have a bias. If you were interviewing your wife, or I was interviewing my wife on a story, I would have a bias, right? I wouldn't ask the tough question, most likely. And to allow that to happen on the word of Chris, who can say 'I can do it,' is absurd and ridiculous."

Ben Smith had a different take on it. He had written an early story for the *New York Times* about the interviews. "I wrote about it at the time, and honestly, maybe I was a little too cynical in not saying this is like a crazy, grotesque violation of standards. It just seemed to me as the latest in a totally relentless pursuit of ratings," Smith told me. "And of doing whatever interested people in the moment, and that sort of was what it was in that regard. It's not my type of journalism, but it also didn't totally surprise me based on how cable news works."

And perhaps that would have been the end of the story. The nursing home scandal was not an easy piece of Glance Journalism. It took work, and digging, and what was the incentive to implicate a popular, powerful, vindictive Democratic governor? But what came next for Governor Cuomo was too much for the media to ignore.

In December of 2020, a former aide to Governor Cuomo, Lindsey Boylan, accused him of sexual harassment on Twitter. She wouldn't talk to the press, and Cuomo denied the allegation. Then in February of 2021, Boylan expanded on the allegations of sexual misconduct in a post on the blogging platform Medium.[18]

Initially, the reaction was still somewhat muted. CNN's coverage of it led with the denial, rather than what Boylan said happened: "Cuomo denies former aide's sexual harassment allegations."[19]

But Boylan's column had opened the floodgates. By the next month, another half dozen women had accused Governor Cuomo of some form of sexual misconduct.[20]

At the same time, the *Washington Post* published a massive piece on the toxic workplace Cuomo had created, with one reporter on the story tweeting, "I've been a reporter for a decade now, and I don't think I have ever heard people as fearful to speak about someone as they are about Gov. Andrew Cuomo. Former staffers described his rage & vindictiveness & said they feared he would destroy their careers."[21]

The attorney general of New York began an investigation, and ultimately published a damning report by the end of the year. Cuomo tried to remain in the job despite calls to resign from nearly all the top Democratic politicians. The pressure was too great, and he eventually stepped down.

There was another angle to the Boylan story that involved the media, and it relates to an excellent piece of journalism from Eric Lach of the *New Yorker* in March 2021. Lach dug into who "ordered the smear" of Boylan, which came in the form of "personnel documents" media outlets received after Boylan's initial tweets in December 2020.[22]

As the article makes clear, there was an immediate effort to make Boylan seem like a "bully" and add a subtle racism charge too. One outlet that picked up this storyline was the *New York Post*. In their report, the *Post* detailed how an "internal memo" shows that "three black employees went to state human resources officials accusing Boylan, who is white, of being a 'bully' who 'treats them like children.' "[23]

The immediate pushback would no doubt contribute to the media's reluctance to cover the story at the time. But who put these personal files into the media's hands?

Meanwhile during this entire time, Chris Cuomo was back to being barred from interviewing his brother. Suddenly the standards were back in place. In fact, he wasn't even allowed to talk about Andrew Cuomo or any stories he was involved in. It made for awkward moments, like when Chris would do his "hand-off" with former friend and colleague Don Lemon, followed immediately by Lemon leading his show with calls for Governor Cuomo to step down. And the CNN rules meant the biggest political scandal in the country had to be ignored for one full hour of primetime each night.

"It seemed awfully clownish and off-key for the times that we were going through. I know in retrospect that the CNN people thought that it was a dose of humanity. And there were some people in the media who were saying yes, this is what we need now," *Washington Post*'s Erik Wemple told me. "...I don't think it's very complicated. They wanted ratings, and this is corporate media. They wanted ratings and they had primetime competition, they needed to put up a fight in primetime, more than anything. And this particular show, the Cuomo and Cuomo Show, was what they had...It was one of the most cynical instances of ratings driving editorial decisions that you will find in American media. I mean CNN's standards guide is like 100 pages long, and it covers all this sort of stuff. And I guess they made an exception for this, which is bonkers in its own right."

And then, the walls came tumbling down. In November of 2021, thousands of emails obtained through the Governor Cuomo investigation were released publicly. They showed that Chris had been far more involved in the political activities of his brother than previously known. He was involved in the messaging when it came to pretty much every topic—including the pushback against sexual misconduct accusations. After a brief suspension from CNN, he was abruptly fired.[24]

What happened next was shocking, even for regular media watchers. Cuomo sued CNN, and through that lawsuit—which claimed his boss Jeff Zucker already knew that Cuomo was advising his brother—details emerged that linked Zucker himself to Governor Cuomo. It also implicated the head of marketing at CNN, Allison Gollust, whom Zucker had been covertly having a long-term relationship with. Gollust had previously worked for Governor Cuomo as a communication staffer. By the end of February, both Zucker and Gollust were gone from the network.[25]

"It's really disturbing. I can't say it's all that surprising,"

TheWrap's Sharon Waxman said. "I've had debates about this with journalists I respect, some of whom feel like it's really shocking and upsetting to know that Zucker or whoever else, Gollust, were involved in talking to Cuomo. And then liaising with Chris Cuomo, either about having the governor on or the coverage. To me, it's a little bit like 'there's gambling going on in Casablanca, wow.' It's to be expected... When I first heard about it, I thought, 'We were going through a global pandemic, New York was the epicenter of the pandemic at that time, and the idea of having Cuomo on as a figure who was reassuring people and would get some special status when there's a public health crisis going on. Maybe you cut CNN slack for that reason,' but I have talked to journalists who are like, 'You're completely wrong, and here's why you're wrong. What was going on at the senior citizen centers? And this was all about ratings.'"

"I think it proves a lot of what people have been saying, people have been complaining about CNN, people complain about all the networks, so I don't have a gripe against CNN, but people have been complaining about CNN for years saying, 'It's swung too hard in this one direction,'" Rich McHugh told me. "...This one episode, it's a window into how the heads of these networks can operate, and cozy up to power. And they shouldn't. I think this episode shows that they got caught with their hands in the cookie jar. And it's definitely unethical in journalism. But it happens all the time. And I think viewers know that, and they're disgusted by it."

NPR's David Folkenflik has covered the media industry for decades. He sees this case as a complicated one, but also an instructive one. "I think that affirms the idea of coziness among elites puncturing through the boundaries that are supposed to separate the media and political realms," he told me. "...There was stuff that was happening in public that was clearly problematic, and justified because of the extraordinary times in which we lived in, essentially unprecedented in the television era. And so the pandemic unremittingly gripped time. And so you have, 'Hey it's the Cuomo brothers providing a little levity.' And I understood the desire for that. I didn't watch a lot of it. But it seemed like they were having a good time, and people online, you saw having a good time with it, whatever. But there was always an undercurrent of a problem, in that he was allowed for a few minutes to sort of be America's uncle, the governor, and sort of tell you what you need to do and what we needed to know. And in putting him in that way, he became beyond scrutiny and reproach, certainly on that show, which was an hour-long show, right in the middle of primetime."

And then there was the Zucker side of it all, which came out later—and it wasn't just that Zucker and Gollust helped in the booking process, as was reported. "I make that case to people—that's not an illegitimate thing for TV executives. This seems like more than that. And this seems like there was a blurring of agendas, the idea that somehow they would get Cuomo to schedule his press conferences, which had delighted so many folks who were troubled by the way the Trump administration dealt with the pandemic, so there would be a time of day, that would be in a day slot," said Folkenflik. "...This was in pursuit of ratings, and what you would hear from CNN were things like, 'Well, this is an absolutely unprecedented circumstance. Who can imagine that somebody's brother would be governor?' Journalistic ethics aren't designed to anticipate every possible circumstance. They're designed to offer you values that you then figure out how to navigate these waters. So the fact that there hasn't been a sibling before, which I'm sure there probably has, doesn't matter. What matters is, has it erased your values?"

The whole interconnected mess had come full circle—and was even more interconnected than it appeared at the time.

CHAPTER 9

Broken Financial Incentive Structure

Perhaps nothing I've discussed in this book would have come to fruition if not for an external factor that hangs above all of it—the old way of making money in the media has evaporated forever. If the financial incentive structure that had existed for decades remained in place, there would of course still be media mistakes, instances of bias, and a general coziness among the east coast establishment. But they would be far less prominent because the corporate structure these businesses were built on would still be paramount— and the business would ultimately win out.

Instead, what we've seen over the past fifteen years or so has disrupted the industry to deleterious effect. And this broken financial incentive structure is the fourth major problem of the modern media. The external forces have softened the ground for the sort of issues we've seen with the press. First, the rise of social media platforms as a major factor in the entire media ecosystem (a topic we'll dig into more in a later chapter) has caused many in the press to panic. Some media outlets dove headlong into that world and attached their success to the whims of these tech giants. When Facebook incentivized links to websites, they adjusted their strategy. When Facebook said it was time for video, the publications followed suit. Then when Facebook decided that actually people want to see less of media outlets in their feed, the revenue started drying up.

The rise of social media as a force in the overall media—which can be tracked to the early 2010s—coincides with the general shift from traditional media to digital. Whereas the *New York Times* and the *Washington Post* used to be primarily print products, suddenly the print "newspaper" was a secondary consideration. CNN and ABC News were legacy media TV networks—now, they are as much a digital hub as they are an over-the-top television product.

Naturally, these shifts have meant the possible audience for each traditional platform is, inevitably, getting smaller. There are more media outlets, and they are competing over a decreasing pool of viewers and consumers as market habits shift. If we look at this from the positive perspective, most media outlets no longer need to have as much mass appeal to be successful. The financial incentive structure of today means "success" can be achieved without as much scale.

But this comes with a new set of problems and challenges.

Concept: Structural Polarization

We frequently talk about polarization in America as it relates to our political discourse. I'd argue the polarization is actually a bit overblown when it comes to the bulk of the country, but certainly the Democrat-Republican dynamic in Congress, among TV punditry, and on Twitter has gotten more evident and extreme.

But there's another area where we've seen polarization, and it's a contributing factor to various issues that arise as tangential to it. "Structural polarization" has enveloped a variety of entertainment arenas.

Take the movie industry. A common refrain is that Hollywood no longer makes mid-budget films anymore—everything is either a giant blockbuster or an independent film. The industry has seen massive structural polarization, and the two ends of the spectrum have wildly different incentive structures. They are essentially two completely different businesses, with two different standards for success.

The media has undergone this structural polarization too. For decades, the national media outlets have been large, and the local outlets have struggled to compete when it came to talent, resources, or revenue. But those large national media outlets have only grown more gigantic in recent years. CNN was owned by Time Warner. Then it was owned by the even larger WarnerMedia. Now it's owned by the even larger Warner Brothers Discovery. News outlets are just components of larger behemoths, made up of all sorts of properties. What does ABC News really mean to Disney? Or NBC News mean to Comcast? These all-encompassing blobs have no real defined identity, and, as such, the financial incentive structure for the news properties is harder to define—but excellent journalism certainly isn't at the top of the list. The system is broken.

On the other end of the spectrum in the media ecosystem

are the super small outlets. Progressively smaller. It's not just digital upstarts—now with platforms like Substack, media properties can be literally a single person. Writers can start a news outlet based around their writing, send newsletters directly to their consumers, charge a small monthly fee, and make a comfortable living. Others may choose the video route, like through a YouTube channel, or through audio and podcasts (and generate revenue with ads). The structural polarization in the media means the small outlets are getting smaller, by design.

In many ways, this can be a positive, exciting development. This bypasses the gatekeepers, and the barrier to entry has never been lower. But it does have its drawbacks too. Media outlets have elements that can often come in handy when doing necessary reporting, like legal resources or insurance. Going it alone can leave the tiny media outlet vulnerable.

"I think the Substack model is fascinating," Rich McHugh, formerly of NBC and ABC News, told me. "I've debated it myself, going on it, because I think the media landscape is so fractured right now, and people are trying to find the next iteration. Fifteen years ago the energy in the room was all in morning TV, and I'm not sure that that's the case anymore. I think people, viewers, readers, consumers of news are smart, and they want to be reading the most cutting-edge stuff. And right now, most of that, a lot of it, I should say, is happening on Substack and in places where people are finding new places to report. There is a fear—I've considered doing Substack and I've talked to others who want me to do some investigative journalism with them. And I said, 'Well, what kind of legal resources do you have?' Because, you know, if you go up against somebody like a Weinstein, you need to know that you're protected. And so I'm not assured at this moment that the right venues have been created for that."

But it's hard to argue against the idea that the smaller the outlet is, the closer they are to their audience—by necessity. This presents a challenge to the behemoths and the media blobs. How do giant companies counteract that? As audiences get increasingly fractured, how can the largest properties still cultivate a bond with a specialized audience? There are examples of success. Back in 2009 I interviewed Jimmy Fallon and his two top producers, Mike Shoemaker and Gavin Purcell, about the concept behind *Late Night* shortly after Fallon took over the reins. Shoemaker said one of the main differentiators of their show was "we like to do things that certain people love, as opposed to something everybody likes." They purposely alienated audiences in order to grow a stronger affinity with their fans.[1]

Of course, on an entertainment show, this makes sense. Comedy isn't going to appeal to everyone, so if you can hone in on what works best, or what differentiates the product in the marketplace, you can form a strong bond with those who find it most appealing—even if it's wrapped in a "big media" veneer. But the equation is different when it comes to the news media. What happens when a giant news property no longer cares whether large portions of the country would ever consume it, nor cares whether many Americans trust it?

"I think overall it's not a good thing," Joel Cheatwood, the former CNN and Fox News executive, told me. "I think the large conglomerates that control media, they do so in a very homogenized sort of thirty-five-thousand-foot way. You've lost any sort of sense of personal connection and customization to specific markets or niches. So you get the factory-generated sort of news. And I've always said that's a really dangerous thing because you get a single perspective or you get that generic-templated perspective that has only a modicum of relation to your life. At the other end of the spectrum, I love the startups, I love the various newsletters, but they are never intended to be somebody's source for news. They just don't have the capacity, the bandwidth, and the resources to really provide the depth of coverage...What I fear is we're developing these news deserts, if you will, that are growing massively."

The structural polarization in the media industry means the financial incentive structure is broken. And that broken system allows behavior to be incentivized that does not comport with the stated values of the organization. As you see instances of behavior from the press that seem incomprehensible, it's important to remember the old way of explaining decision-making was that it was financially beneficial. In other words, it was good for business.

But now that the system has been broken, the incentive structure is no longer solely based on the economics of a decision. In fact, decisions will get made that are, simply, bad for business. But the incentives in this now broken structure reward bad decisions in other ways.

Case Study: ESPN's Drift

One of the most glaring examples of the broken financial incentive structure in the press takes us outside of the news media and into the sports media. When it comes to the behemoths, it's hard to argue anyone can compete with ESPN's size and scale. Owned by Disney, ESPN is the prime real estate ABC News never quite was. For years—decades even—its place as a massive revenue generator and untouchable outsized dominant sports entity was a given. The slogan "The Worldwide Leader in Sports" was unquestionably accurate. It was a money-printing, über-relevant machine.

And it's important to remember the role ESPN, and sports in general, plays in our American culture. Jane Coaston is a *New York Times* columnist and podcast host—and a huge sports fan. "This is beyond politics. It is parallel to politics," Coaston told me. "And I think that's why in part I love sports, because I've had conversations with so many people where they would probably hate everything I believe about any number of things, but we could talk about football all day, and probably have talked about football all day. I'm impressed by ESPN's success, and I'm fascinated by how they've continued to build on it."

But even the giants can begin to panic as they feel the quicksand beneath their feet. ESPN had a thriving digital property too, but perhaps no other television channel would be as directly impacted by the consumption habits of an increasingly streaming focused American public as one dependent on live sports. And it wasn't necessarily the live sports themselves that were taking a huge, across-the-board viewing hit. With the Oscars no longer a ratings draw, the final television product to generate consistent ratings in America will no doubt eventually be NFL football games. But the idea that sports consumers needed to tune into a 6 p.m. or 11 p.m. edition of *SportsCenter* to learn about what happened in the world of sports was a relic of the past. And the carriage fees that ESPN relied on from cable providers were drying up—slowly at first, then with an alarming acceleration.

ESPN, for the first time since it became the "worldwide leader," was vulnerable. And it was in that vulnerability decisions start getting made that are not about the business, but about forces outside of it. The financial incentive structure was broken, and now the cultural incentives were playing a role.

A good example of the shift at ESPN is looking at the suspensions. Back in the pre-Trump Era, Bill Simmons got suspended for three weeks for criticizing NFL commissioner Roger Goodell.[2] Keith Olbermann was suspended for tweeting a snide comment about Penn State in the wake of the Joe Paterno–Jerry Sandusky scandal.[3]

In the Trump Era, the suspensions were quite different. In 2017, Jemele Hill was suspended after urging an NFL boycott because Dallas Cowboys owner Jerry Jones urged players to stand for the anthem. That was a second social media "violation," after she had just previously called President Trump a "white supremacist."[4]

After the Trump comment, in September 2017, ESPN

boss John Skipper sent a memo to employees outlining what appeared to be a line in the sand during the Trump Era. "ESPN is not a political organization," he wrote. "When sports and politics intersect, no one is told what view they must express. At the same time, ESPN has values. We are committed to inclusion and an environment of tolerance where everyone in a diverse work force has the equal opportunity to succeed. We consider this human, not political. Consequently, we insist that no one be denigrated for who they are including their gender, ethnicity, religious beliefs or sexual identity."

Of course, the policy didn't really stick. A couple years later, star NBA reporter Adrian Wojnarowski was suspended after he responded to an email from Senator Josh Hawley's office about the NBA and China by simply saying, "Fuck you."[5]

ESPN tried to keep politics out of the channel for years, but ultimately Trump was the wave that broke the dam. But the key point to remember is that the business had shifted, so the financial incentive structure no longer penalized overreach into the political sphere as harshly. These extreme examples that led to suspension were nothing compared to the countless examples that led to no penalty at all. The guardrails were off, because the equation had changed.

Bob Ley joined ESPN three days after it launched in 1979. He won multiple Emmys at the network, and was the longtime host of *Outside the Lines*, one of the most respected television shows not just at ESPN but on all of television. He left the network in June of 2019, after taking a leave of absence the year prior.[6]

No one knew ESPN better—and perhaps no one could be more objective about the shift at the "Worldwide Leader" than Ley. "Going back to '16 and '17, I sat in a meeting that was called, in '17, front-facing folks, some of the front-line folks, with the leadership, including John Skipper, the president at the time, in the wake of the Twitter folderol with Jemele, to basically remind people that this Twitter handle that you have, this is not your soapbox, this is a soapbox that's been built by other people, this megaphone that you have," Ley told me in one of several conversations we've had over the past couple years. "But in the course of that meeting, I mean you talk about an activist workforce in various places, flexing their weight and causing management to wonder, 'Oh, gee, what's going on here?' I saw in one meeting, for example, this workforce rise up, especially among the women, with a nascent deal with Barstool about to take effect, a very small deal like a half hour show per night. But it was in this meeting of about thirty or forty people, one woman, a front-facing personality who shall remain nameless, basically told the room and upper management that 'this is the group of people that called me the c-word on social media.' And I glanced over, and upper management's like they couldn't believe it. And I think in that nanosecond, they realized, 'Oh shit. We have to try and manage that.'"

Like Skipper's memo after Hill called Trump a "white supremacist," Ley shares the sentiment that ESPN had long been a company at the forefront of diversity. "They've walked the walk and talked the talk about diversity, inclusion, etc. And were very outspoken, and John made this a hallmark of his administration, of advancing the cause in the numbers of women. And so to have that as one of your pillars of your administration at the same time—I think that was strictly a cause and effect," said Ley. And then something changed: "Now the Trump thing, Trump's election, and I remember talking to our public ombudsman about this, and telling other people, I mean, I came to work this morning after the election in 2016, and there were people crying in my arms. To the point where we got real close to having to ask a couple of people, 'You might want to think about taking some personal time after three or four days, because we've got a job to do, we are a sports network, and we're dealing with this.' But it sent a ripple that could not be avoided through everything. It was a workforce and a workplace that was as divided as the country, where people right of center were apprehensive about putting Fox News Channel on a TV that could be seen."

Ley said after the 2016 election he personally dug into the political giving of his own company, to get a real sense of the political affiliations at the network. "I did a study in 2016. I think it was 2016. I don't think I've ever told anybody this. I went back three presidential election cycles using the federal election law database and looked at all the political contributions by employees of ESPN, and it took me a long f—ing time, but through congressional and presidential cycles going back twelve years at that point. What do you think the ratio was Democrat to Republican, by number of contributions, not dollar figures?" he asked me. "82 to 18 percent Democrat...I brought this out in a meeting when we got onto this topic at one point. I said this is a liberal network, and there was agreement. Some of it is unavoidable.

We're in the northeast. We have a lot of products of exclusive colleges here. I get that point. For a company that rightly championed and acted well on diversity, I think the greatest challenge was, and it continues to be…diversity of thought, it is the most elusive, because how do you chart that? How do you make a judgment on that, on diversity of thought? You step into a very emotional minefield there."

Diversity of thought would be an admirable goal for all sorts of outlets, and perhaps it would have paid dividends with some of the decision-making happening at ESPN behind the scenes. But as Ley's data shows, it wasn't that ESPN suddenly became a sports network full of liberals and Democrats—it had been that way before. For decades, in fact. Yes, Trump was there now. But the guardrails had shifted too, in a real and tangible way—and it opened the door to embrace left-wing politics openly and publicly.

Ethan Strauss is a former ESPN employee who now writes on Substack (nice symmetry on the whole structural polarization from before!). He puts ESPN's drift on the same track as the rest of the sports world—more broadly—to November 2016.

"Trump's election definitely was a tipping point, certainly not just at ESPN but in the NBA in general," Strauss told me.

Strauss gave me an example of the subtle shifts we've seen in what is acceptable "sports" conversation—when it came to looking at Steve Nash as a white player who maybe got preferential treatment from media members when it came to MVP votes. "Dan Le Batard brought up or theorized that Steve Nash might have won over Shaq because of that, and saying that was very taboo. That was not okay. That was not cool," said Strauss about the kinds of topics that were at one time off limits for the sports network. "But a massive course correction took place in a very short amount of time. And it's one of those things like so many large-scale phenomena, it's little by little and then all at once."

But what was driving the shift? "People often make whatever is expedient into their morality, retroactively, and will convince themselves that what they want to say for career advancement, or at least to avoid social ostracism, is actually the thing they believe," said Strauss. "...I think that there is a huge aspect of just saying whatever you need to say to just move up in your organization, or at least to not be isolated as the wrong thinker. And you can see a lot of that, but it was always difficult for me to know. Something I'm endlessly fascinated by is how many people believe these things versus how many people are pretending. Now that I have a Substack I'm discovering that more and more there are a lot of people who are faking it, and there are a lot of people who DM me and email me as I say, I think, reasonable things. The funny thing in media is that you can be a contrarian by saying stuff 70 percent of people agree with."

But there's another disconnect—and it has to do with the locker room. While the sports media world has grown more overtly liberal, the sports world—the actual athletes that the sports media world covers—are not in adherence to the same type of woke worldview. "The modal sports media person is much more in line with your basic Twitter liberal than the athlete," Strauss told me. The athletes may lean left and vote Democrat, but they aren't what would traditionally be called "woke." Said Strauss: "In the NBA, it's over 70 percent of players are Black and roughly 90 percent of Black voters vote Democrat, but that doesn't mean that for instance, when the NBA is out in front saying we're angry at the bathroom bill, it is a transgender right in North Carolina, how many players in the NBA view that as a priority or even something they would agree with? I'd say not very many. So it creates this funny dissonance where, yes, the average sports writer might be in line with the average blue-check liberal in media and they might feel in their heart of hearts as opposed to our theorizing how some people are faking it, but then they also have to almost present the self-image of beliefs they cover and pretend the players feel as they do, which is definitely not the case."

Will Cain joined ESPN in 2015, just before Trump announced he was running for president, and left just as Trump was leaving the White House. He later joined Fox News, and has made no secret before, during, and after his time at ESPN that he was a conservative (although notably, not a Trump voter in 2016). And while Cain's radio show and First Take appearances largely left politics on the cutting room floor, it was still a unique spot, considering very few at the network were openly conservative during this time.

"At the same time that Donald Trump was driving every single news cycle within traditional media, Colin Kaepernick was taking a knee in sports media, and then Donald Trump commented on Colin Kaepernick taking a knee, and then all of a sudden, everything collided," Cain told me. "Everything became the same thing. Politics, culture, sports, it all seemed to become the same thing. For my own commentary, I tried to be very respectful, and I'm not patting myself on the back or trying to put myself in a holier-than-thou position, but maybe because I came from the world of news and politics before I went into sports, I didn't have an underlying itch to scratch. I wasn't dying to comment on politics, even if I had the experience and the qualifications to do so. And I do think there is a real desire within sports media, within the commentators within sports media, to be political commentators. I can't say why that is, but I think there definitely is a desire within sports media to be political media."

But as the sports media at ESPN shifted to the political media at ESPN, it only went one direction. "When I came into ESPN, there was an acknowledgment that they were already beginning to only voice opinions that reflected one segment of America. You know, John Skipper, who I respect and I like, was pretty open that the ideology of ESPN commentary was driven by progress and tolerance. And I think those two terms become Trojan horses or euphemisms for whatever is trending on the left in the moment. And if you are guided by what is trending on the left in the moment, in my estimation, you will ultimately end up regressive and intolerant," said Cain. "...I truly believe that John Skipper and many of those providing the editorial direction of ESPN were doing it from a place of authenticity, meaning they believed in these values. But they also understood that they were probably alienating a major segment or isolating or ignoring a major segment of their audience."

But there were so many forces at play, and despite still being the behemoth, ESPN was paying attention to smaller, less relevant platforms—and letting the whims of those platforms dictate the incentive structure defined by culture over finances. "The seeds of fear, I think, were planted in the years probably from 2010 to 2016," Cain told me, highlighting the "power at the time of Deadspin," a popular left-leaning sports blog. "Deadspin had a lot of ESPN executives running afraid of their criticism. And I feel like Deadspin was probably the seed or the precursor of the fear that eventually Twitter would inherit the mantle and take to an entirely new level."

The problem was once the executives allowed some conversation, it opened the door to much more. And the fear—internal and external—kept the conversation firmly in an isolated arena. "They did not want us to go quote unquote 'political.' They wanted it to be tied to sports. They wanted it to be connected to culture, and I respect them in seeing that line and understanding the audience. I don't think a lot of commentators had a success or desire to differentiate that line," said Cain. "So quickly what starts out as some cultural or sports conversation turns into whether or not Donald Trump specifically is a bad human being or a racist, or even further than that, anyone that supports Donald Trump is an ignorant human being or a racist... Towards the end of my tenure at ESPN, after George Floyd, which was a seminal moment in this country and in sports media, and I defended Drew Brees and I defended, very strongly, Drew Brees not being racist by the judgments of his actions in his life, the choices he's made, the money he's given, versus his opinion that you should stand for the national anthem. And I got a call. I got several calls. From inside of ESPN, from commentators. And I will say this—from outside of ESPN, from the most famous sports figures you can imagine, who said you are the only one who is saying this, and it is true."

A good example of the bizarre ways this new ESPN positioning manifested came in July 2021, just as the NBA Finals were about to kick off. The *New York Times*'s Kevin Draper published a gigantic piece about the internal fallout that was happening at the network for more than a year, and that "ESPN has been trying, and often failing, to deal with the scandal for months."[7]

The "scandal" boiled down to this: In July of 2020, Rachel Nichols, one of the star NBA hosts at the network, was unknowingly recorded in her hotel room having a private conversation with LeBron James's business advisor. In that conversation, which the *New York Times* published audio from, she expressed her disappointment that she was losing out on the NBA Finals hosting duties to Maria Taylor, another star NBA and NFL host at the network.

"I wish Maria Taylor all the success in the world," Nichols said in the tape. "If you need to give her more things to do because you are feeling pressure about your crappy longtime record on diversity—which, by the way, I know personally from the female side of it—like, go for it. Just find it somewhere else. You are not going to find it from me or taking my thing away."

Nichols's beef wasn't with Taylor—it was with ESPN, for pitting her against a fellow female host. But the underlying message in the confusing, poorly written *Times* story was that there was some sort of racial animosity in Nichols's comments about Taylor. (Nichols is white, and Taylor is Black.) The story didn't blatantly say it, but other head-lines did, like sports blog ClutchPoints, calling it a "racist rant."[8]

It's worth pausing for a minute to note that Nichols is not some conservative, like Cain. She's spoken out on George Floyd, and in support of Black Lives Matter. And what also was bypassed in the story was that Nichols herself was the victim—of this video recording of her from her hotel room without her knowledge or approval.

"I don't want my private conversations aired in pub-lic, but instead of making the obvious observation that she didn't say anything offensive, she didn't say anything bad, everybody had to react to the premise as though she did," Strauss told me. "Or at least not speak up in defense of her. And I know that a lot of conservatives probably cheered what happened to her because she was politically left in what she was saying. So there's a bit of hoisted on her own petard sentiment, but I just looked at it as illustrative of this current madness, where people often don't react with their honest take, but instead out of fear, just promote this idea that somebody did something bad, they did the bad thing, it's so bad. And the funny thing about it is that it was all inspired by an article in the New York Times on ESPN's lack of diversity, alleged. And the article itself had freaked out people in Bristol. They were in a tizzy over it, which caused them, I think, to try to shake up their demography. But if you look at the article, and you look at the New York Times comments section, which is a self-selected group of very lib-eral people, it was interesting because the top comments, the vast majority, it's a big yawn. It's a big 'I'm just tired of this.' They didn't find it compelling."

Still, it had a big impact—inside ESPN and outside of it. "Shoddy reporting by the *New York Times*, opinion-driven writing, poor editing by the *New York Times*," Bob Ley told me. "Nothing that Rachel said was wrong, that was a drive-by assassination of somebody. And one of the lesser moments I think in the chronology."

A "drive-by assassination"—and it was Nichols's career that was over at ESPN because of it. Shortly after the 2021 NBA season ended, Nichols was sidelined by the network, and sat out for the duration of her contract. Taylor didn't grab the slot she wanted over Nichols, though—she left ESPN almost immediately after the *New York Times* story was published for NBC, and was hosting the Olympics just weeks later. ESPN wasn't rewarded with goodwill. It was just a further mess. A mess exacerbated by the broken financial incentive structure that makes doing the right thing secondary to doing what keeps the base happy. Or in ESPN's case, a tiny vocal minority of the base—the loudest voices on Twitter.

CHAPTER 10

Newsroom Purges and Guilt Journalism

ON PAPER, THE HIRING OF Alexi McCammond by *Teen Vogue* to be its next editor-in-chief in March 2021 should have been greeted with cheers from the champions of diversity and equity. McCammond, a Black, female, accomplished journalist, was taking over the reins of the media brand at the age of just twenty-seven years old as it shifted focus from fashion to politics.

The celebration was short-lived. The Daily Beast reported the staff was in revolt over McCammond's "anti-Asian" tweets from when she was a teenager.[1] The staff of *Teen Vogue* banded together to tweet out a statement that called out their new boss's past "racist and homophobic" tweets, saying that "in a moment of historically high anti-Asian violence and amid the on-going struggles of the LGBTQ community, we as the staff of *Teen Vogue* fully reject those sentiments."[2]

What were the tweets in question? Back in 2011, when she was just seventeen or eighteen years old, McCammond tweeted things like "Now googling how to not wake up with swollen, asian eyes…" and "outdone by an Asian #whatsnew."

These aren't tweets to be proud of. But they were a decade earlier, and McCammond had already apologized for them two years prior to the *Teen Vogue* job.[3] Also, apparently these twenty *Teen Vogue* staffers outraged by decade-old tweets didn't have a problem with working for an organization that was running sponsored content for Saudi Arabia—not a noted bastion of openness on progressive issues—including one article headlined "Why Saudi Should Land on Every Culture Lover's Radar."[4]

McCammond apologized again. "You've seen some offensive, idiotic tweets from when I was a teenager that perpetuated harmful and racist stereotypes about Asian Americans. I apologized for them years ago, but I want to be clear today: I apologize deeply to all of you for the pain this has caused," she said, in part.

The organization that hired her, Condé Nast, initially stood by her. "Alexi McCammond was appointed editor-in-chief of *Teen Vogue* because of the values, inclusivity and depth she has displayed through her journalism," a statement said. "Throughout her career she has dedicated herself to being a champion for marginalized voices."

Days later came a joint statement by McCammond and the "*Teen Vogue* Staff," that said, "As a team, we've had frank, thoughtful, and real conversations over the last days about inclusivity and the way forward," and promised "those will only continue as we grow from here."

The reconciliation didn't last long. Within weeks, McCammond was out at *Teen Vogue*. It wasn't a decision spearheaded by her bosses or the executives who run *Teen Vogue*. It wasn't about the financial impact of her hiring (despite the fact that one major advertiser, Ulta Beauty, paused its ads with the publication during the controversy). It wasn't about her editorial performance. McCammond was gone because a small but vocal group of young staffers wanted her out.

The newsroom uprising won. And in a media world with a broken financial incentive structure, newsroom purges of those perceived to be insufficiently ideologically pure are a side effect. They happen in this particular moment in time in the media for one reason only—because they can. They are allowed to. The power dynamics of the newsroom, of media organizations, of the cultural conversation around the press—these all have softened the ground for these sorts of obscene cancelations.

The kids run the newsroom not because it makes sense by any real metric. It's because the overall business is weakened, the cultural penalties feel enormous, and the Acela Media is full of cowards who will stay silent so they can keep their cushy jobs. Until, of course, the newsroom purge comes for them next.

Perhaps the most valuable case study to examine happened the year before McCammond was unceremoniously cast out of the vaunted *Teen Vogue* ecosystem. And it happened at the (unsarcastic this time) vaunted *New York Times*.

Case Study: Tom Cotton Op-Ed

On May 25, 2020, George Floyd was killed while in police custody by Minneapolis police officer Derek Chauvin. Chauvin was later convicted of murder for his actions that day, which were seen in excruciating detail thanks to Darnella Frazier, who captured the entire incident in a video on her phone—video that showed the original police incident report was misleading. Chauvin kneeled on Floyd's neck for more than nine minutes, including several when it was clear Floyd was no longer resisting arrest, or even moving.

The shocking video of Floyd, who was Black, and Chauvin, who was white, came into the public consciousness as the COVID pandemic was heating up. Many people had barely left their house in two months. What came next was a wave of outrage and protest. Social justice marches were all over America, as were some instances of violence, looting, and arson. It was a particularly perilous time in the country—one that also happened to be a mere five months before a presidential election that could determine whether the country would have four more years of Donald Trump.

This context is important because context is always important—but also because on some level it helps explain the bizarre and extremely concerning actions that were to come, from a journalistic perspective.

Into this cultural firestorm came an opinion column in the *New York Times* by Senator Tom Cotton. Cotton was a young, first-term, conservative senator from Arkansas, who had previously served in the military and done tours in Afghanistan and Iraq. He's a graduate of Harvard, both undergrad and law school. And, notably, he was a frequent contributor to the *New York Times* opinion section. Earlier in 2020, he wrote a column headlined "The Case for Killing Qassim Suleimani," which came out shortly after Suleimani was killed.[5] The prior year he wrote "We Should Buy Greenland."[6]

The piece published nine days after George Floyd's death, at the height of the social justice movement, would prove to be far more controversial. Originally headlined "Send in the Troops," and shortly after publication changed to "Tom Cotton: Send in the Troops," Cotton's op-ed makes the case that the military should potentially get involved in stopping the violence that was erupting as an offshoot to the protests.[7]

Cotton's column is less incendiary than the headline—which he didn't write—might make it seem. He notes the "revolting moral equivalence of rioters and looters to peaceful, law-abiding protesters. A majority who seek to protest peacefully shouldn't be confused with bands of miscreants," while concluding, "One thing above all else will restore order to our streets: an overwhelming show of force to disperse, detain and ultimately deter lawbreakers. But local law enforcement in some cities desperately needs backup, while delusional politicians in other cities refuse to do what's necessary to uphold the rule of law."

I find the column to be mostly uncompelling, and fairly obvious—is it any surprise that Tom Cotton would write a column like this?

Many of the most vocal *New York Times* employees were outraged. And they shared their displeasure in a unique, coordinated way. Dozens of staffers, former staffers, and friends of the paper shared a screenshot of the headline, while tweeting "Running this puts Black *New York Times* staff in danger."

Express your disagreement with the column—even with the *New York Times* for running the column. But "danger"? And what was with the coordinated response? The next day *New York Times* opinion editor James Bennet responded on Twitter: "Times Opinion owes it to our readers to show them counter-arguments, particularly those made by people in a position to set policy. We understand that many readers find Senator Cotton's argument painful, even dangerous. We believe that is one reason it requires public scrutiny and debate."

This point is obviously true—and while I understand some may disagree with it, you'd like to think the people who would most agree with it would be journalists, and particularly journalists who occupy a spot at the most prestigious newspaper in the country, if not the world.

Instead, inside the *New York Times* it was even more chaotic and hysterical after the publication of the column than it appeared to those watching from the outside. Shawn McCreesh, now of *New York* magazine, was an opinion staffer at the *New York Times* at the time the Cotton op-ed ran. He shared that it was a day he will never forget. "I absolutely loved working at the *New York Times*. I was there for almost five years and I was always so proud to represent the paper, and it was just this really wonderful place," he told me. "But that was just the weirdest day in the almost five years I worked there."

He told me everything "snowballed really quickly," largely organized on Slack—the chat tool many in the media use to dish with colleagues while theoretically working. "There was like this giant communal Slack chat for the whole company that became sort of the digital gallows," he told me. "And all these angry backbiting staffers were gathering there and demanding that heads roll and the most bloodthirsty of the employees were these sort of weird tech and audio staffers and then a handful of people who wrote for like the Arts and Leisure section, and the Style section, and the magazine, which, in other words, you know, it was no one who was actually out covering any of the protests or the riots or the politics. It was just sort of like a bunch of Twitter-brained crazies kind of running wild on Slack. And the leadership was so horrified by what was happening. They just completely lost their nerve."

Picture a giant media organization—but everyone is at home, spending their time on Zoom and Twitter, afraid to go outside because of COVID, angry about the Floyd killing. And then—the Cotton op-ed drops a bomb into the virtual newsroom. "Before we knew it, we were in all these series of town hall meetings basically watching James Bennet defend himself before the Star Chamber, and it was awful," McCreesh said. "James is a really great guy. We all really respected him, and you can have arguments about the op-ed or whether it should have been run or the editing process. This was something else. It was like a Maoist struggle session. The town hall that was for just the opinion staff—there was one for the whole company, and then there was one for the opinion staff, which was about a hundred people—that was the one that got really weird. There was this white guy, Charlie Warzel, who wrote about tech and lived on a farm in the middle of nowhere. And he got on and he began crying and saying that none of his friends wanted to talk to him anymore because he worked for this horrible evil newspaper that would print this op-ed, and it was just so bizarre what was happening."

I asked James Bennet and Charlie Warzel for comment. Both declined to speak on the record.

"The worst part was that a lot of the people who were stabbing James in the front were the ones that he hired and brought to the newspaper," said McCreesh. "It was like Caesar on the floor of the Roman Senate or something. Just this sort of horrible moment, and I remember closing my laptop and pouring a huge glass of wine, even though it was at like noon. Because I was so fucking freaked out by what we had just witnessed. And most of the adults in the room figured that what we were witnessing would pass, and it was just sort of this weird moment where everybody kind of had to get all the shit out of their system and we'd move on. Very few people realized that what we were witnessing in real time was like a murder. And it was gross."

By the next day, the *Times* announced the op-ed "did not meet our standards" and, among other actions taken as a result, they would be "reducing the number of op-eds we publish." The day after that, a lengthy editor's note was added to the top of the column, which noted, in part, that "the tone of the essay in places is needlessly harsh and falls short of the thoughtful approach that advances useful debate."

Two days after that, the hammer—Bennet "resigned" as the editor of the opinion section. He apologized internally days earlier, but he "declined to comment" to his own paper as they wrote about his demise.[8]

McCreesh said the "murder" had a long-lasting effect, and that for a lot of people at the *Times*, "the morale never fully rebounded" after the Bennet incident. "I always thought that none of this would have ever happened if it weren't for the pandemic, because you have to remember most editorial types are sort of shy and awkward and a little weird, and I think it's really easy to be like a keyboard cowboy, but it's so much harder to fling mud at your colleagues when you have to look them in the face," he said.

But the big sticking point to me was the way the orchestrated campaign against Bennet went public—to describe it as a "danger." It amplified the severity by a significant margin, without a doubt. Did dozens of journalists really believe that? There's no doubt some did. Others likely felt a pressure to conform—to support their colleagues and be a proper ally.

"Was it really traumatic to read a newspaper op-ed?" asked McCreesh. "... I just think there's a real problem with the type of person who comes into journalism these days, which is somebody who does not ever want to be confronted with views they don't like, and is just really lacking a fundamental curiosity that's necessary to do this job well."

McCreesh recalled how it was an "insane time," but that the reaction in the Washington bureau (the site of a lot of the insanity) was quite different from the "culture warriors sitting back in the office on Eighth Avenue" in New York City:

> There was a very well-respected reporter there who said something very smart that I remembered, which is that as a news reporter, especially in DC, when you're trying to win the trust of Republicans and people who think that the *Times* isn't going to give them a fair shake, they see op-eds or really hard, tough columns and they say, 'Well, the paper's not going to treat me fairly.' And the news reporters would always say, 'That's the opinion side. I have nothing to do with that. That doesn't reflect on my coverage.' And this person said this was the first time that actually the news side reached into the opinion, and told them we don't like what you've written. It was this weird role reversal where it was the newsroom that got up in arms, and that really shredded a lot of credibility for reporters in Washington who then had to go try to say with a straight face to Republicans that we're going to treat you fairly, when the entire staff couldn't even handle an op-ed that was written by one of the party's leading senators.

Amy Chozick was a *New York Times* reporter for close to a decade who reported on Hillary Clinton and others on the campaign trail. She remains a "writer at large" for the outlet but was not involved in the 2020 Tom Cotton discussions personally. "What was interesting about that, and I think is legitimate, and super fucking interesting, as we contemplate a media future, is that there is a generation of young kids who believe that objectivity is akin to white supremacy," Chozick told me. "I'm not saying I disagree with them, or I agree with them. I'm saying there is a real debate here happening."

Chozick notes the Cotton op-ed story was an offshoot of this debate. "There is a school of thought that to be objective—if you have no skin in the game, you can be objective," she said. "And so I think that's great, it's incredible that different types of voices and different people with different life experiences are entering newsrooms, and I think they have like real questions about what objectivity is and I don't know the answer and I'm not saying they're wrong. I'm not saying the old school is wrong, I'm just saying to me that debate, that interaction, whatever happened in the *New York Times*, brought to life this simmering thing that you're hiring a new crop of young journalists who don't reflexively feel like journalism has to be, both sides, has to be objective... You put out that fire, whether it was James Bennet getting ousted or corrections or apologies or whatever town halls, like you put out that fire, but that's still brewing, and that's still a debate. But I don't know if anyone is ready to have it or knows how to settle it."

Ben Smith was the media columnist for the *New York Times* when the Cotton op-ed was published. He thinks the fallout was a symptom of the time, but had long-lasting ramifications. "A lot of companies and government entities were trying to figure out how to deal with their employees who were suddenly really animated about racial justice, and also was this incredibly strange time in the middle of a pandemic.

It's a little hard to separate from that moment in time. Which isn't to say it didn't have a really lasting impact on the brand, and how people saw the brand," he told me. "...I just think people, readers in particular, saw James Bennet's firing as like a symbolic act in a way that I don't think the *Times* ownership thought about it or intended it, but that doesn't really matter in terms of how it was perceived."

Olivia Nuzzi watched what happened from the outside, as a reporter for *New York* magazine. "There was a rather sudden moving of the goalposts that kept happening throughout that," she told me. "At first it was the op-ed itself that was the problem. And then suddenly the line became 'oh no, he fucked up all these other things, and anyone saying otherwise, they don't understand because they're not a part of this.' It felt like it often feels on the internet when it comes to fraught subject matter. Like it was kind of impossible to engage in earnest debate, and I think that's the death of an honest public intellectualism in a way. If you can't be certain that you're engaging with someone with whom you disagree, and I'm not saying this applies to any of the *New York Times* staffers who said they felt unsafe, I'm saying in general the way that story moved very quickly and took on a different shape in real time...On speech, it represented a really clear shift."

Jane Coaston wasn't at the *New York Times* at the time of the op-ed, although she's there now. "I think it said a lot about when people feel as if they are lacking in power they will go towards the place where they feel like they do have power," she told me. "...When people are attempting to foist their power off on someone else, where it's like 'The

New York Times staffers have all the power,' and then it's like, 'No, all the people in the Senate have all the power.' The Senate, I would argue, has more power than we do, but we both do. And so I think that was where these two forces came running headlong at each other, and it went poorly."

Joel Cheatwood had been in the media business for decades and was surprised by what he saw—the coordinated push by journalists to claim the publication of the op-ed was dangerous. "Jesus, I mean, come on. That's not how journalism is done. That's not what we do. We present stories, and if we need to present a counter we do, because that's what journalists do. We don't just say it doesn't meet our belief or standard, so we're not going to do it," he told me. "...I don't know what's in their mind and heart, but I can tell you that I think it's a very convenient reason and excuse. The reality is, there are stories told every day that put somebody's life in danger, potentially. You do the best you can. But that was a new one on me because I'd never really heard a media organization or a group of people within that organization say, 'Well, we can't do that story because I might get hurt.' That's just the opposite of really what being a journalist is all about."

Before he became a TV news star, Piers Morgan was a newspaper editor in England. He saw the fallout at the *Times* as a truly unique moment. "I've totally disagreed with what Senator Cotton wrote, but I thought what happened afterwards was completely outrageous. The guy's a serving US senator. He's entitled to his opinion. It was an honestly held opinion. And he was exploring one way of dealing with what was going on at the time, which some people agree with and some people didn't," he told me. "I thought in a democracy, that's what senators are supposed to do. And the idea that a serving senator is commissioned to write a piece with a provocative opinion, and starts a debate which is quite a useful, interesting debate about how you manage that kind of situation. And the fact that he is then hounded himself by having that view is fine, but the fact that senior *Times* executives lost their jobs for allowing him to argue that point in the *New York Times* was utterly breathtaking.

"We have the same problem with the BBC in the UK. They're very fine organizations. I watch the BBC a lot. I avidly read the *New York Times*, but when they behave like that, they do themselves a massive disservice. It looks like they're anti-conservative on principle, which is no place for the *New York Times* to be, in my opinion," said Morgan. "They should be a broad church for all views, but also the idea that senior talented executives lose their jobs for offering a platform to a senator to explore a debate is mind-boggling."

The promise by the *Times* to publish fewer op-eds came to an absurd conclusion the next year, in April 2021, with the announcement that there would be no more op-eds at all published by the media outlet. Instead, they would be renamed "guest essays"—a designation that would "appear prominently above the headline."[9]

It's hard not to see this action as a direct result of the Cotton fallout. It's not just that they'd be publishing fewer columns in general—and certainly fewer from anyone deemed to be a potential purveyor of "Unacceptable Thought" (like a Republican, perhaps). No, now they've found a term to put an even greater distance between the opinion and the paper. Look, this person is just a guest here. If you don't like what they say, please don't blame us!

It was the embarrassing degradation of a once great institution—that still does some great work too. But now everyone is on notice. You step outside the bounds of acceptability, you try to introduce some thought-provoking opinion into the intellectual ecosystem, you cross the kids in the newsroom? You might be next.

Concept: Guilt Journalism

This necessity for the leadership of news organizations today to bow to the whims of their junior staff is really a self-preservation instinct. The loudest voices on Twitter have the perceived power, and they can wield that power if their elder bosses get out of line. The bosses have less power because the business incentives no longer supersede the cultural incentives.

But what is the self-preservation, at its core? It's a version of what is commonly known as "cancel culture." The newsroom purges of those deemed unacceptable are removing the improperly "woke." And while cancel culture has become a sort of catch-all phrase, it's a very real factor in certain corporate media decision-making.

Which brings us to a new activity that can best be described as a precaution against cancel culture. It's a preemptive shield—or at least an attempt to prevent a possible cancel culture swipe of the sword, which could be lurking behind any corner. It's Guilt Journalism.

Guilt Journalism takes place when a media property knows it has committed some current cultural sin in its past, and is now trying to survive in this new environment by attempting to absolve its guilt in as performative a way possible so as not to be potentially canceled down the road. It's a survival mechanism for a corporate press that wants to show clear and obvious repentance.

Cosmopolitan magazine is best known as a publication offering tips on how to get flatter abs, or have better sex, or find the perfect lipstick. It would often feature an actress on the cover in a sexy pose.

But in January 2021, it went a different direction. Various overweight women graced the cover that month. The headline said simply "This Is Healthy!" with a sub-headline, "11 Women on Why Wellness Doesn't Have to be One-Size-Fits-All." Most of the cover models were non-white.[10]

In the accompanying article, there's very little on exactly why *Cosmo* has determined these women are "healthy"— at least not by any traditional definition of the word. No, instead it's about body positivity, body shaming, and a screed against "fatphobic" comments.

And look: I'm against body shaming. But "this is healthy"? And even if there suddenly was a body positivity beauty magazine on the market, that's one thing. But it's pretty rich coming from *Cosmo*, which was certainly one of the reasons there was "fatphobia" and body shaming in the first place. For years, *Cosmo* put a skinny, white model on its cover and offered tips on how to get skinnier. But this is of course no longer a culturally acceptable way of running a magazine.

There's no doubt *Cosmo* feels guilty about the body shaming they've done in the past and inflicted on their readers. So we get their guilt in the form of Guilt Journalism. No, they scream it on their cover. "This is healthy!" With an exclamation mark, as if they're trying to convince themselves as much as they are their readers. "Please forgive us!" they shout. "Don't cancel us over our past body shaming! We'll try to do better! See, this is healthy! We're sorry!"

Guilt Journalism shows up not only in what gets covered, and how, but also what doesn't. Shawn McCreesh now writes features for *New York* magazine. And the industry business of feature writing has changed, because of "sensitivity readers" who try to anticipate the type of content that might get a writer, or a publication, "canceled"—or at least draw the ire of Twitter for a few hours. "The big thing with this is you're no longer allowed to really write about what people look like anymore," McCreesh told me. "…If somebody is drop-dead gorgeous, I think that's a relevant detail that the reader needs to know. And this isn't about gender, I've described the outfit and the images of men and women alike, and I always do, or at least I would if I weren't always having to cut things out, because God forbid someone might get offended, but when you go back and you read all the great stuff from the old magazines, those writers can really paint a picture. You felt like you were there with those people. And they weren't being neutered this way. And guess what, the average reader who doesn't spend every waking second scrolling through rageaholic Twitter but still lives in the real world, and pays for the subscriptions to read all this crap, is the person that suffers."

If you're a publication with something that could get you deemed unacceptable that's in your past, get out in front of it by showing how sorry you are in the most performative way possible. Don't describe what a person looks like because you might offend someone. Until the incentive structure changes, Guilt Journalism will only grow and become more absurd.

———

The purges in the newsrooms, and the Guilt Journalism we see from publications and journalists, all stem, on some level, from fear and power. And this fear and power can manifest in interesting ways—and ways you may not expect.

Sharon Osbourne was a host of *The Talk*, who was essentially fired after an on-air spat with a couple other co-hosts. You could assume this particular incident is a variation of the "newsroom purge" trend we've seen in the media, but instead, it's actually more of the Guilt Journalism variety.

Piers Morgan made comments about Meghan Markle that some ungenerously deemed to be racial in nature. Sharon Osbourne then defended her friend Morgan on Twitter. The next day on *The Talk*, through two excruciating segments, Osbourne defended Morgan, and then herself, while two of her co-hosts, Sheryl Underwood and Elaine Welteroth, attacked her for coming to Morgan's defense. It was emotional and raw. And then, shortly after, Osbourne was gone from *The Talk* for good.

But what really happened was revealed later in a leaked audio recording from Osbourne's dressing room, which the *Daily Mail* published. It's uncomfortable—Osbourne is sobbing throughout much of it. But what transpired is fascinating and illuminating.[11]

Osbourne confronts Welteroth, whom she considered a friend (like Underwood), wondering why this would transpire on the air the way it did. "I'm just so sorry that went the way it went," Welteroth tells Osbourne. "It's so fucked up."

Welteroth then admits, "I didn't even read the tweets" that Osbourne put out, but explained she had to go after her co-host anyway. "Sheryl and I are held to a different standard by Black people and people of color out there, who expect us to say something about every racist anything," Welteroth told Osbourne. "And it puts us in such a fucked-up position. That even if we don't have information, if we don't even really care, if we don't really want to engage, it feels like a spotlight is on us."

Later, Welteroth said, "There's this pressure to demonstrate how to talk about this stuff. But we haven't ever been guided on how to fucking do this. I'm not a DEI expert. I don't know how to do that."

Welteroth didn't personally want to smear Osbourne with the insinuation that she too was a racist. She didn't want to go down that road at all. But she did so because of guilt and fear. She knew that going easy on Osbourne would ultimately backfire on her—and because of the warped and broken incentive structure in the media today, a bit of social media backlash would be too much to handle. Instead, she chose to go the Guilt Journalism route and throw Osbourne under the bus.

It's a sad reality of the current media ecosystem. And one that exists largely because of one insular platform—Twitter.

CHAPTER 11

"Influencers" and Anti-Speech Activism

Tucker Carlson has been the subject of boycotts for much of the time he's hosted a primetime show at Fox News. (I suppose if you want to go back even further, he was one of the subjects of a boycott of sorts by Jon Stewart during his *Crossfire* days on CNN.)

In 2018, Jack Shafer wrote a great column about the latest round of boycotts aimed at Carlson, urging people to boycott Carlson by not watching the show, rather than trying to shame advertisers into dropping their sponsorship of his program. Shafer described how "partisan watchdogs" like Media Matters and Sleeping Giants were "leading the charge," and had successfully persuaded various advertisers to drop the show. Shafer concluded: "If you hate Carlson's show, send letters of protest to Fox. Sign petitions protesting his show. Picket Fox headquarters. Cancel your cable

TV package...But please keep your hands off of Carlson's advertisers. In the long run, you'll be hurting only yourself."[1]

This was, essentially, a journalistic argument. We talk a lot about the First Amendment being "freedom of speech," but it's also "freedom of the press," and boycotting media you don't like is not a winning strategy. But what's interesting about that moment is Shafer was countering the "watchdogs" who were leading the charge—the political organizations. Fast-forward to January of 2021. Margaret Sullivan is a columnist for the *Washington Post*, having previously served as the ombudsman, the internal journalism ethics check, at the *New York Times*, and was an editor in Buffalo, New York. If anyone should theoretically understand freedom of the press, it should be Sullivan.

And yet here she was arguing that Fox News was "a hazard to our democracy," and, as such, should be destroyed: "Corporations that advertise on Fox News should walk away, and citizens who care about the truth should demand that they do so (in addition to trying to steer their friends and relatives away from the network)."[2]

When she tweeted the column, she attached a second link to the thread, to Media Matters—one of those "political watchdogs" that Shafer had called out a few years earlier. Sullivan was explicit, directing her followers to the Media Matters link of "a list of Fox's biggest advertisers."[3]

The message was clear—go get them! From a political operative, this point of view is expected. But from a journalist, or, I suppose, a former journalist, like Sullivan, what was this bizarre turn? I've described it as "anti-speech activism," and later this chapter I'll explore it in more depth.

But the other element to this story is how Sullivan could have become emboldened into this position—this extreme perspective that speech she doesn't like, and deems to be a "hazard," must be eliminated from the marketplace. Sullivan's story went viral on Twitter, with thousands of retweets and admiration from her more than 100,000 followers. But if Twitter didn't exist, would she have written the column? Would she have held that position at all? What role did that cesspool of narcissistic insular self-gratification have in crafting the current journalistic mindset?

It's of paramount importance to remember that Twitter is wholly unrepresentative of the country, because it is used by such a small minority of Americans. According to the Pew Research Center, just 23 percent of American adults use Twitter at all—far less than the 81 percent who use YouTube, 69 percent who use Facebook, 40 percent who use Instagram, or even 25 percent who use Snapchat. Unlike the user numbers of other social media platforms, that number has plateaued over the last few years, and has not been growing at all.[4]

But it's not just that few people actually use Twitter. What "Twitter" even is is unrepresentative of the 23 percent figure. The most active 10 percent of Americans on Twitter account for approximately 80 percent of all the tweets from Americans.[5] Or, put another way, the most active 25 percent account for 97 percent of the tweets.[6]

Therefore, less than 3 percent of all American adults are responsible for 80 percent of what Twitter "is." And less than 6 percent make up essentially all of Twitter. It is truly an echo chamber, and one in which we see a self-fulfilling prophecy about what actually matters, or what "Americans" actually think. It's a huge detriment to the way the media works. And it's the fifth and final problem with the modern media.

But before we dig into where we are now, let's look back at where this started.

Case Study: Rick Sanchez

Rick Sanchez joined CNN in 2006, the same year Twitter was founded. As Sanchez began hosting his own weekend show with the network within a couple years, he was unique in that he was one of the few Latino hosts on cable news. But he'd soon find another way to differentiate himself from the pack—he embraced social media, and specifically Twitter, as part of his broadcast.

This was in the very early days, when few actually were on Twitter. The vitriol and coordinated attacks that are what the platform would come to be known for were absent at that time. It was people having a conversation, virtually. And then, suddenly, it became incorporated into a TV show.

"Was it the *New York Times* or was it PBS that wrote, 'Rick Sanchez was tweeting before Twitter was cool'? And I guess I feel good about being considered by many a pioneer engaging in social media and in particular Twitter, and combining it with the thought process and the news process," Sanchez told me.

But Sanchez didn't come up with the idea himself. "We were sitting at the National Association of Hispanic Journalists conference, where I was going to be on a panel, and

Jon Klein, the president of CNN, asked me to have breakfast with him," said Sanchez. "And he said, 'Join me upstairs.' I sat down, and he says, 'Have you heard of this Twitter thing?' And I said, 'Why?' He goes, 'There's this thing called Twitter. And it's really cool. And I'm going to explain it to you.' So he kind of took me through it. And he says, 'It's a way of engaging virtually and in real time with people,' and I thought, 'So how does that involve what you and I do for a living, which is present the news on CNN?' And he said, 'I wouldn't even dare say this to anybody else there because I don't think anybody else would be able to manifest this. But knowing you, Rick, you seem to be the kind of person who would probably be willing to engage in conversations because it's part of your personality. And why don't we try, if there's some way you could figure out a way to do it, how to see if we can somehow involve Twitter in the news process.' "

Sanchez started using the instant conversation as part of his linear television broadcast shortly after that conversation with Klein. "I looked at the camera and I said, 'We're going to try something new here as we start this newscast. I have my laptop in front of me. And I'm going to go on something called Twitter. So it's www dot,' and I explained it to people," Sanchez told me. "I said go to this place and during the commercial breaks, which are going to be three minutes long, send me your thoughts on the stories I'm sharing with you. And if you have any information or something you think I should know about, send me that too.' Son of a bitch. This thing—within that show—I started seeing 'ding ding ding,' and I told my producer, Angie, I said, 'What the hell's going on?' She goes, 'I don't get it, but there's people who want to talk and there's people who are really interested in this.' So they just started dinging and dinging and dinging. And before you knew it, we had a couple hundred, and then a couple thousand, and then by the end of that weekend, I think we had close to 100,000 people who were contacting me and telling me I want to talk to you."

Sanchez said he was told that the demographics of his show were unique to CNN too—with more Latino, Black, and young viewers than other programs. He attributed that to the "Twitter engagement" he was bringing to the show.

While it was successful almost instantly, Sanchez said within a few months more executives got involved and changed the dynamic. "I think it lost its authenticity. I think, in the outset, when we first started doing it, I used it, I think this is the general approach that made the most sense, as a democratizing tool. For the first time, it was going to feel like we could literally connect to the viewer," Sanchez said. "...I started feeling resistance about six months to a year in, where it felt like people were looking at me like 'This guy's breaking the rules of the institution, this is not who we are...This is going to get us in trouble. This is gonna be a problem.' And then the first thing they did is they canceled the scroll, they said no more scroll. 'We don't like the scroll, because some stuff is going through there that people are reading and it could get us in trouble and the legal department worried. All right, we'll lose the scroll.' And then, 'Who's choosing the tweets?' We are, me and Angie and a couple guys on the team. 'We need to be involved in that now as well.' And after a while I saw it kind of losing its authenticity, its democratizing force."

Sanchez was out at CNN in 2010—a few months before I joined the network. I worked to incorporate Twitter into *Piers Morgan Tonight* as digital producer on the program—my first job at the channel. I later served as senior digital producer, overseeing the digital and social output of all the network's US television programs. In that role, I was in the production van during all 2012 debates, when we'd surface potential tweets to ask during the debate too. By 2013, as we put together tweets for a special after the killing of Trayvon Martin, I was already starting to see the drift on the platform. More people were on it, but it wasn't just the scale and scope—it was the tone.

More concerning than how the average user engaged on Twitter was how the media members used it. When Rick Sanchez was spearheading the movement, he was curious and respectful. The whole conceit was that he was one of the people—listening, responding, engaging in real time. He was taking in feedback introspectively, and not preening in egomaniacal glory. He wasn't chasing clout.

Maybe clout is what really changed. Or, rather, Klout. In the early 2010s, a new app called Klout hit the market, and everyone in the media was fascinated by it. Klout took your social media interactions, mainly on Twitter, and through their own proprietary algorithm, gave you a score for how "influential" you were—at least theoretically. I know Klout was popular among the insular media bubble because I was in the insular media bubble, and I talked about Klout with other media people in the bubble incessantly. I'd wonder why my Klout score went down a point, or how my Klout score might be affected thanks to a retweet from a big account. In retrospect, it was all very gross.

Klout eventually shut down, but in many ways it solidified the way Twitter would be used by the media for years to come—and altered the media landscape forever. Gone were the days of Rick Sanchez quaintly reading tweets from viewers live on the air, or responding for hours to people who asked legitimate, good-faith questions with legitimate, good-faith answers. No, the game had been officially changed.

In the current media environment, a journalist can now become an "influencer." They have "followers"—tens of thousands, hundreds of thousands, even millions. They put something out and get instant feedback, often from their adoring "fans." Conversely, the more popular, famous, and influential they are, the more likely they have a small but vocal percentage of detractors. These "haters" bring them the inverse sort of feedback—they see these nameless, faceless digital foes as their enemy.

And all of this, ultimately, has nothing to do with the actual work.

"Are people more informed than they were? Are the media holding the powerful to greater account than they were? Is the country calmer? Is the democracy more functional? Are we more united than we were? No, no, no, no, no. Twitter's not the only cause of this. But clearly the way that we communicate, which is to say electronically over the internet, via social media or any other means, has divided us into warring camps," Tucker Carlson told me.

"It's like a million fish darting this way, darting that way, and coming at you all at once and the effect is overwhelming. It's exhausting. And one of the things that you see mainstream news organizations deal with, with some of their more talented and prominent people, is that those individuals, however talented they are and however, in some ways, effective they are, still get affected by Twitter, and still get just the emotional ramifications of Twitter, and you see it, the combativeness," NPR's David Folkenflik said. "...There's a younger generation that is closer in tune with their belief systems and their passions and bring that to their journalism, and that sometimes fuels some terrific journalism, but it's often of a different nature, and big news organizations that are kind of legacy outfits are often trying to figure out ways to channel that without harming the integrity of both the substance and the perception of what they provide the public. Twitter can be punishing. Twitter can be cruel. Twitter can be unbelievably distorted, both of the facts and of a sense of balance or what people actually think about something. Journalists often say to each other Twitter isn't real life, and then they get obsessed by what's said on Twitter anyway."

The *New York Times*'s Katie Rosman explained how Twitter has become both essential and inessential for a modern journalist. "I had a really prominent journalist reach out to me recently, who I had known from the *Wall Street Journal*. He was a really big deal at the *Wall Street Journal* when I was not, and I don't say that to diminish myself or be self-deprecating. There was a difference in our stature. And he has written a book that is authoritative and deeply reported and years in the making. And I think it was very well reviewed," she told me. "...He wants more press for the book. He feels like it's not on the radar. And he said, 'I've never been on social media. I don't feel comfortable with the self-promotion. It's never been my way.'...It revealed to me a profound lack of understanding of what social media stands for—far more than me posting pictures of my kids, which I'm absolutely guilty of on Instagram. But I see Twitter and Instagram in a different way. [Twitter] is where ideas are shared, are made, take on importance, take on controversy. Yes, take on division. And a lot of negative attributes too, but it is the marketplace of ideas and to disconnect from that, in a pearl-clutching sort of way, is to say I'm going to opt out of the conversation, listening to the conversation, adding to the conversation, observing the conversation."

So Twitter is where a conversation is—at least a conversation by journalists and for journalists—but what does it actually add up to? "What do the follower counts mean? What do they convert into in the long term? And maybe it's fame and wealth and being somebody whose ideas get listened to broadly in the marketplace. Maybe it delivers the dream, but I just think we don't know," she told me. "We are in this two-second news cycle. As soon as we read it, it's over and we're on to the next thing. And I don't have a broad perspective on what this all means in terms of our individual legacy as purveyors of information and ideas. We just can't know. It's too young and we're too distracted."

Ben Smith sees the pros and cons to it as well. "It's essentially the beating heart of news. It's where news breaks, it's where news gets processed, and sort of, I think, elite opinion gets formed," he told me. "And it's much more small-d democratic than the previous spaces where that happened, which was backrooms, in newsrooms, followed by blogs, and now it's just sort of wide open social media space. And it is also open to manipulation, campaigns of manipulation, and to me increasingly, I felt like there was this golden era on Twitter where people were talking to each other and changing their minds. And now, increasingly, people form their opinions in DM groups or in Slack or in text groups or in other forums, and then come to Twitter to kind of brigade and fight with people and attack their enemies."

Smith ran a newsroom at BuzzFeed, and now will again at a new start-up, Semafor. He said he wants his journalists on Twitter, but he wants them to do it in a smart way. "I certainly want my reporters to be tweeting, but I don't want them to be tweeting like idiots," he said. "But I don't want them to give speeches and sound like idiots or write things and sound like idiots and, in fact, I would prefer they not be idiots. So I will try not to hire idiots. Sometimes when a journalist, including me, tweets something that's really stupid and wrong, it's because they really have something wrong. Like they're confused about reality in some way that people are yelling at them, but Twitter is helpful because Twitter is sort of revealing something about the way they misperceive the world. It's not really a social media problem. It's like a problem revealed by social media."

Sharon Waxman, founder of TheWrap, shares the

position on the dichotomy of Twitter—and sees the chilling effect it can have on a newsroom. "I think we've all seen Twitter at its best. And we've seen Twitter at its worst. I think I have seen my own reporters back off of aggressive stories or aggressive reporting out of fear of being attacked on Twitter, which I think is extremely regrettable," Waxman told me. "And I have been attacked many times on Twitter by people who don't know me, just jump on a bandwagon. I see it all the time, don't bother reading the article. Don't bother looking past, if someone says, 'Oh that person's a racist.' And off they go to the races. It's really painful, and it's most painful for me when I see it happening to one of my reporters, but I also see the impact of it, which is they don't want to put themselves out there, and I can hardly blame them."

"I want it to exist and I want it to survive for a lot of basic reasons, including the preservation of democracy," MSNBC's Ali Velshi told me. "I do want the idea you do have access and you do have a megaphone for your ideas, despite who you are. The fact is, just staying with Twitter for a moment, that's not really true...There's a lot of blue checkmarks on Twitter, but we tweet for each other, I think, sometimes. I say this a bit sarcastically because I don't tweet for 'each other,' I tweet for my viewers. But the reactions that matter—Twitter has a way to just check for what verified people have to say."

Amy Chozick, *New York Times* editor-at-large and now a television producer, has seen how Twitter has affected the way the Acela Media functions. "I think it's very dangerous when we start letting Twitter be our coverage assignment, or to use Twitter as a gauge of how people feel about an article," she told me. "It's a very specific vocal subset, and it's not to say it's not important, but I think you have to look at it as one small segment of the population... You want to share your stories, want to like chat about media and politics, cool, I get some news, I have some fun. I enjoy reading Twitter often. I just think it's really important for reporters to get out in the country and realize just how small [Twitter] is. And I keep seeing people posting like 'I'm doing a story on X, if this fits you, DM me' and I'm like no, you're reaching such a small subset of self-selecting people. Maybe I'm just too old school but I think it's a dangerous thing when you start to think it's reflective of the country."

Chozick says there's something very modern in how Twitter and social media exacerbate the divides in the media, and the goals of journalists:

> On one hand, divide of journalists being a brand or like toiling anonymously in a newsroom in pursuit of the truth. I think it's often covered generationally. And of course, younger people are more adept at social media, but I also think it's leaving out the economics, which is you used to be able to work in a regional newspaper and raise a family and send your kids to good public schools and send your kids to college, and I think the idea of raising a family in New York on a *New York Times* salary is a very difficult prospect for a lot of people. And I think it's like an imperative that you find other income streams, so often that is your personal brand, whether that's a CNN contract, a talking head on CNN, you're an

Instagram influencer, a book deal, and I say this as someone who wrote a book. So I'm not criticizing at all, I'm just saying, I think it's often too simple to say it's the Gen Z versus the old crusty Gen Xers. I think it's too simple. I think there's been a lot of economic turmoil in this industry. And you used to be able to support a family just covering city hall for a newspaper, and you can't do that now. So I think that puts pressure on every journalist.

The *New York Times*'s Jane Coaston agrees, and sees the focus on "brand" and social media as a survival mechanism for journalists in a broken industry. "The reason why people need to build brands as journalists is because you have to assume that at some point where you work could explode," she said. "And you have to exist in a world in which people will follow your work around even if you are no longer with X outlet...I've written at a bunch of different places, but that happened because I got laid off from MTV and I was like, 'Well, we have to pay rent.' So I will now write and do all of this work, that's what I did. So I think that it comes out of this terrible necessity. And I'm not going to wax rhapsodic about a time where you can work for your local newspaper for sixty years, until you keeled over. But I do think that the emergence of journalism as a brand and the need for journalists to brand themselves is not because we are all incredibly self-involved. It's because we all recognize that at any time someone invests in the wrong thing, or somebody pivots to something else, and you're just like, well, I have to go find something else to do."

But Chozick also described the very specific way Twitter became a companion to the Trump Era of the media. "The showboating in the White House press room is a good example—are you pressing the president to benefit the American people, or are you trying to get a moment that goes viral to help your own career? And I think news consumers are smart and can sense that," she said. "It turns you off if it looks like someone's just in pursuit of their own career, so I think it's mixed up with the economics, but I also think it has something to do with contributing to the distrust."

Fox News's John Roberts saw the way Twitter intersected with the Trump White House firsthand—and the way Trump himself embraced it. "Twitter was the driving force behind coverage of the Trump administration," he told me. "Both from his perspective, and from the news media's perspective. Trump would go over the heads of the news media by going to his followers directly on Twitter, and then the news media would engage him right back on their Twitter. And it wasn't exactly Trump responding to the tweets, because he didn't follow that many people. And so I don't think he saw most of what was out there. But if he saw something, if he read it in the newspaper or he saw it on TV or whatever, he would react to it. So it did become this kind of sub-level of communication. You had the communication at the network level. And then you had this sub-level of communication that was going on with Twitter, but it was huge."

On the other end of the podium from Roberts was Kayleigh McEnany, when she was the White House press secretary in 2020. "The briefings have been televised for a while, so I would say the biggest change is the social media aspect to it," she told me.

McEnany recalled an example from her time at the White House when Jim Acosta "asked a question about school re-openings and I said something to the effect of 'the science should not stand in the way on this.' " McEnany referenced the "American Academy of Pediatrics" and other "data points that undergirded the idea that science was on the side of schools reopening." But Acosta took "the science should not stand in the way on this" and ran with it. "It became a viral tweet. I remember walking back to my office, every chyron on MSNBC, 'the science should not stand in the way,' all based on this tweet from Jim Acosta, causing even his colleague Jake Tapper to rebuke him and saying, that's not what she said," McEnany said. "And then Jim Acosta puts the full quote out there, but as you know, the cleanup doesn't get the attention of the initial tweet. So I think that's a brief example of how Twitter is used and weaponized by leftists in the briefing room like Jim Acosta, to further a brand, to go viral, to cause headlines."

Ethan Strauss sees the way Twitter can be used as a tool—despite its small audience. "There's this sense of 'everybody is very animated over this, and you better not disagree or you will be ostracized and cast out of this community.' And that is quite powerful in getting people to conform and coercing them into having to mirror whatever they're seeing," he told me. "So I think it's huge at these corporations and it's especially big in media, and it's borne itself out. And I think it's unfortunate because anything that results in a lot of people falsifying their preferences and lying can't be good overall."

Meanwhile, social media has changed television—and not in a good way. "TV forever was sit back, shut up, we'll tell you what's important, that's your only job here, just be quiet and listen," Joel Cheatwood told me. "Facebook turned that into 'I don't have to do that anymore. I can not only consume the content, I can interact with the content. And I can talk to the person that's providing the content, and I can share the content, which means that it helps define my personality to friends and family. And I can almost be a co-owner in this.' And I think that was absolutely devastating to television."

Rich McHugh sees the way Twitter has truly affected coverage. "There's such vitriol, and it's just armchair vitriol directed at people, journalists. It's a platform that gives people a big voice and big opportunity to be heard, but we've reduced the conversations to these 140-character or whatever-it-is-now sound bites, and people spend more time crafting, like, the right bomb to drop on Twitter instead of worrying about the journalism or how it's reported," he said. "And so I think part of that bleeds over into the coverage itself, and you see some of the talking points on Twitter on TV, and you see some of the talking points trotted out by both sides, GOP or the Democrats, and it's kind of gross. [But] it's a necessary tool right now."

With the instant and public feedback, McHugh worries about how some journalists alter their work based on Twitter. "I think people in news organizations kind of wait to read the room a little bit. See who responds and how it gets handled, and unfortunately, when you work in these big news organizations, maybe I'm gonna get attacked for saying this, but there's groupthink. Everybody kind of falls in line," he said. "...There's certain voices that kind of set the news agenda. We used to say the *New York Times* set the news agenda of the morning, and now it's on Twitter, and whoever you follow, it's kind of like this echo chamber, but here are the ten voices I follow, who I agree with them, like if they're going to go hard on immigration, or they're going to go hard against transgender swimming. People like go all in on that. So it's a little bit like the cable news landscape where it's like an echo chamber of just reinforcement of what you believe and what you want to hear, unfortunately."

It's that fear in the newsroom that Erik Wemple of the *Washington Post* honed in on when I asked him about Twitter. He relayed a specific story about a Bloomberg Law reporter who reported something inaccurately about a figure in the Trump administration. The story had to be retracted, but what stood out to Wemple was the way Bloomberg dealt with the fallout—they asked their reporters not to tweet about it. "There you have what I view as a real-life concession or admission by editors that they are scared shitless of Twitter. They're scared shitless of backlash on Twitter," Wemple told me. "They're scared to look at the screen when things go bad."

Concept: Anti-Speech Activism

What is the true effect of Twitter on the media—what reverberations does this echo chamber have on the direction of the press?

First, let's acknowledge that it's a very real phenomenon

that public figures in the media get attacked on the platform—particularly women. "I've certainly been threatened before, like physically, for things I didn't even write, just for being me," Tara Palmeri of Puck news told me. "I've seen my Wikipedia page be updated multiple times to say that I'm a conservative writer when I'm not. I'm not a liberal writer either. I'm just a journalist. And it sort of just comes with the business. It can be really hard on women. I've heard people of color say it's really hard on them. And I've seen it, and I just think it's difficult. I think it's really difficult to get that kind of feedback. We're in a really tense, political environment right now stoked by our political leaders, and in some ways, maybe stoked by the polarization of the media. But people feel like everyone is their enemy, and the messenger is an easy person to shoot, right?"

So it is in this cesspool that journalists are spending a lot of time. Too much time. Everything feels far more important than it actually is. Everything is heightened. A couple hundred retweets can feel thrilling. A couple dozen negative replies can feel horrific. There's a psychological effect of this interaction, over and over, day after day.

"I think Twitter has incredibly unearned, [undue] influence on the American media," Will Cain told me. He cited how unrepresentative Twitter is on the political spectrum ("D +43" according to Cain), that while independent voices have flourished thanks to the freedom of social media, the overall effect is disastrous. "You could make the argument that Twitter is destroying the American media. It has compelled media executives to put people on television they believe are insightful or interesting to the American public and they have failed one after another. So it has destroyed talent cultivation and talent development. In the age of information we have coalesced into acceptable groupthink, so it has destroyed the potential for independent thought," he said. "...People have traded independent thought. They have traded insight, for essentially virtual coins. Likes. Little hearts on Twitter. What is that worth? I guess you could argue it's worth ultimately a sham of a media job that you will fail at. You'll get a few contracts out of it, maybe one, maybe two contracts out of it, but it's pretty cheap currency. It's pretty fraudulent currency."

This currency does have value, and it has empowered some in the Acela Media to gain a level of status, both real and perceived. But it's bigger than the media. Social media in general has burrowed into, and subsequently broken, our brains. Twitter and Instagram and other platforms allow us to carefully curate our feeds. We see only what we want, and nothing else. The platforms then amplify everything—they amplify outrage, and they amplify positivity and negativity. And Twitter in particular is public in a way where everything plays out in the open, adding to the performative nature of simply existing.

Now combine these factors, and see the toxic sewage the press is swimming in. Positive feedback on Twitter makes them feel artificially powerful. Negative feedback on Twitter makes them feel artificially targeted.

And bring in the tools at their disposal on Twitter. There are avenues to silence. There's a mute button, where you can stop hearing from those you wish to avoid, without them knowing it. There's the "block," where those people can no longer see what you're saying. In fact, there are tools you can download to preemptively block large swaths of the population already deemed "unacceptable," so you never have to encounter them, and they can stay, digitally, far away from you. If a particular user gets even more out of hand, you can implore the social media companies to suspend or ban that person.

Suddenly it's not just personal, but a mission—"Why should anyone have to hear from those who are putting out 'unacceptable' thoughts?" The allure of silencing metastasizes into an entire "block" culture. And then this mission of silence moves beyond just Twitter, and becomes an IRL (in real life) instinct too.

This is how we get an occupation that previously cared deeply about the First Amendment and free speech to shift gears and instead become "anti-speech activists." Journalists like Margaret Sullivan of the *Washington Post* are suddenly writing columns advocating for boycotts of cable news outlets, and tweeting advocacy links to spur her audience into action. CNN reporters are tacitly pressuring cable providers to drop channels like OAN and Newsmax after the 2020 election and the January 6 riot.[7]

This anti-speech activism began during the Trump Era, and was contained to politics. It was disappointing to see the shift in the media, and telling, but it got even more concerning during COVID. Suddenly "misinformation" became the enemy, and one item after another became the target of the anti-speech activists. First it was the lab leak theory, then it was masks, then it was vaccines.

During one segment on CNN in July 2021, Dana Bash

asked Surgeon General Vivek Murthy about the role of social media and the conservative press in spreading "misinformation." Murthy said the tech companies weren't doing enough, and that "health misinformation harms people's health. It costs them their lives."[8]

"Do you think conservative media, like Fox News, are doing the same?" Bash pressed, while Murthy avoided directly answering. He was the guest—but the anti-speech activist was the host on the other side of the table.[9]

This interview came as the White House laid out the "disinformation dozen" (disinformation being an even more dire and awful version of misinformation) and told reporters that Facebook was literally "killing people."[10] President Biden wasn't called out by the press—they reported on the "dozen" completely uncritically. They were part of the exercise. The goal was to shame the social media outlets into taking more severe action to curb speech, and the anti-speech activists were more than happy to push this point of view.

As was the case with the Hunter Biden laptop story in October 2020, the anti-speech activists in the press are a key cog in the elite censorship collusion racket. There are the government, the tech companies, and the media—and a media that cared about speech as paramount would ruin the whole equation. Instead, the Acela Media's instinct to give outsized weight to Twitter is what ultimately brings them to a position of anti-speech activism. And it allows the racket to continue.

"If you believe in free speech, then you believe in protecting offensive speech, the right for people to speak offensively, but not their right to not suffer consequences for that," Josh

Rogin, a notably non-anti-speech activist in the media today, told me. "...I think people should have the right to say offensive things and then other people should have the right to not like that in the sense of not supporting that person. But giving that power over to Twitter mobs just seems insane to me, because it doesn't result in the kind of nuance that we need to apply to this difficult societal issue. And it's because it's just a bunch of animals throwing feces at each other."

It is. But one that has so much clout to offer. Bask in the spotlight, while silencing those who have unacceptable positions. It's a combination that leads to massive distrust from an American public that neither cares very much about what happens on the platform, nor believes as strongly that opposing viewpoints should be shut down.

CHAPTER 12

The Transparency Paradox

As Kayleigh McEnany began her job as Trump White House press secretary in April 2020, she was profiled in the *New York Times*. It was a fascinating look at the thirty-two-year-old rising star in the GOP, a Harvard graduate. It was hardly fawning—it referenced "racist" tweets she put out eight years earlier—but it included interesting details, like her friendships at her old job as a CNN contributor with Democratic contributors Donna Brazile and Van Jones.[1]

Soledad O'Brien, the former CNN host, hated it. She described in a series of tweets the "biggest failure" of the *New York Times* as "the many ways it normalizes the abnormal." She said the piece "on a press secretary who has no core beliefs, who lies easily and chronically and who's a racist is bad."[2]

O'Brien thought she knew the reason for the profile—access journalism. "In an administration full of losers and a revolving door, you need a good source to feed you info. One way to do it is the positive profile. This is a good example," she tweeted. "Anyway I won't link to it because it's a waste of your time to read it."

Never mind that this completely misrepresents the piece, makes zero logical sense, and teaches the future journalists of America all the wrong lessons. This was O'Brien's MO. A couple days earlier she responded to a journalist by simply tweeting, "Aww, babe. You are an idiot."

O'Brien is a talented journalist, but she is smug and self-aggrandizing. I was at CNN the same time O'Brien was, for several years, and for a few months had a desk right outside her office. I watched as her own staff would be forced to wait outside her office door, calling her name gently until she allowed them to enter and address her directly.

No one would get to see this off-air side of O'Brien—were it not for Twitter. O'Brien is a prolific tweeter. She has 1.3 million followers, and somehow follows 431,000 people (I'm convinced this is some strategy she employs with an intern or social team, because it's absolutely psychotic to follow that many people). She has tweeted more than 116,000 times.

Twitter provides us a window into the real Soledad O'Brien. And O'Brien has certainly amassed a large following by being her true self on the platform. But what does the average American consumer of O'Brien's journalism think if they see her on Twitter first? They certainly won't be expecting anything approaching objectivity.

Transparency in journalism can be a positive thing. You want to show the audience how a news story came together, or the reality of an interview. Or transparency can be when a news organization makes a mistake—being honest with the consumer about what went wrong, and owning up to the errors. Twitter, theoretically, can be a transparency window for the press, allowing others to see the process. But that's the transparency paradox—because what if, when we get that peek behind the curtain, the audience doesn't like what it sees? What if the transparency undermines the work, rather than bolstering it? What if the audience becomes more alienated, instead of more trusting, after the veil gets dropped?

We'll get to specific examples. But there's another form of transparency that was popularized during the Trump Era, which also dovetails with the anti-speech activism of the press.

Concept: Fact-Checking Fetish

This new era of "transparency"—at least, a form of transparency—brought other areas in which journalists finally got a chance to embrace their true selves. For years prior to the election of Donald Trump they were forced into a façade of objectivity. Now they could finally let their opinion fly.

Acela Media reporters began spilling their unvarnished thoughts on Twitter. CNN started writing snarky, opinionated lower-third chyrons. Objectivity began to be seen as a negative, derisively referred to as "both-sidesism" that wasn't honest with readers and viewers.

The NBC Nightly News anchor Lester Holt, who has a stellar reputation and actually was at one time a registered Republican, declared in a speech that "fairness is overrated," and that "the idea that we should always give two sides equal weight and merit does not reflect the world we find ourselves in."[3]

There was a push to call statements from Trump and others in the GOP "lies"—rather than couch them as "untrue" or "incorrect." The unwritten rules of journalism that existed for so long were no longer applicable. This was a special moment, which called for special rules, at least according to the elites in NYC and DC newsrooms.

And this new instinct to call balls and strikes led to a focus on, and eventual love affair with, "facts." In this structure, the "fact checkers" received pop star status. The left and the media groupies swooned over the fact checks of Trump and others on the right. We saw the birth of the "fact-checking fetish."

During the Trump presidency, the *Washington Post* began a massive project to "fact-check" every false statement Donald Trump made. By the time his presidency was over, the *Washington Post* found he had made "more than 20,000 false or misleading claims."[4]

Don't bother asking, by the way, how many false claims Joe Biden has made during his presidency. The *Washington Post* shut down the fact-checking project shortly after Biden took office.

The *Post* got plaudits from the Twitter crowd, but no one turned the Acela Media and its #Resistance fans on quite like Daniel Dale, the bespectacled Canadian transplant who joined CNN from the *Toronto Star* in June 2019.

Dale has a cult following on Twitter, where he's amassed more than a million adoring fans. And I should say—Dale is talented. But the response he gets is what makes the exercise so bizarre. One particular moment stood out as a crowning achievement of Dale's. In August 2020, a three-minute on-air fact check of President Trump's convention acceptance speech got the fact-check fetish crowd drooling.

"This president is a serial liar, and he serially lied tonight," he began. Strong start!

He then listed a dozen or so "lies" told by Trump, which included Trump's statement that "I have done more for the African American community than any president since Abraham Lincoln," which seems more like an un-fact-checkable boast rather than a lie or misleading statement.[5]

Twitter was totally turned on. "He is a machine gun of truth," tweeted one colleague.[6] One MSNBC host equated Dale to Nas, and Trump to Jay-Z, and compared it to the infamous diss track "Ether."[7] *The Atlantic*'s Derek Thompson described it as "one of the most impressive things I've ever seen on live TV."[8] Ever!

But perhaps no one's response was more orgasmic than Jay Rosen's, a frequent press critic who has barely been an actual journalist and yet teaches journalism at New York University. "He lets the terms that best describe this propaganda method—flood the zone with sh*t, the firehose of falsehood—inspire his own performance," he tweeted. "His is a flood of evidence for their lying, a firehose of refutation."[9]

Dale and others who are tasked with the "fact-checking" were scratching an itch for their audience. It wasn't so much a fetish about "facts," but one where a version of the truth could be a hammer to pound away at a political foe. The faux transparency gives another paradoxical window into the journalistic process—one that feeds a certain subset of the "extremely online" population of America exactly what it wants, hitting a sort of truth erogenous zone, but ultimately turning off a much larger subset of the public that sees through it.

Dale is still at CNN, and his Twitter profile says his job is "fact-checking the president and others." But in the Biden Era, "others" is much more his focus, as he sometimes goes months between fact checks of the current commander-in-chief, instead focusing on lesser-known GOP congresspeople and internet memes.

The fact-check fetish has subsided, now that the focus shifted.

Case Study: Taylor Lorenz

For modern media members, there's the work, and then there's the extracurricular activities surrounding the work. It may seem like Twitter is part of a journalist's job, and in some ways it is—for many in the press, listening on Twitter, observing the cultural conversation on the platform, is necessary for reporting in the current era. But participating in the discourse is not work. It's extracurricular.

And as the transparency paradox exposes, sometimes great work can be overshadowed by extracurricular social activities. And even more perniciously, great work can be undermined by what the "transparency" on Twitter and elsewhere reveal.

Taylor Lorenz is a prominent journalist with a very modern media beat—loosely responsible for covering "influencers" as part of her jobs at various publications, from Business Insider to the Daily Beast to the *New York Times* to the *Washington Post*. She has developed a large following, with more than 300,000 followers on Twitter and an even bigger presence on the more Gen-Z-focused social platform, TikTok, where she has more than 500,000 followers and more than 8 million likes. TikTok has a special relationship in the Lorenz oeuvre. It's where she cultivates her sources, as she writes about the insular world of teen culture. It's also a platform she often writes about positively, in contrast to her coverage of other platforms like Instagram or Facebook. This, despite the fact that TikTok is quite literally owned by the Chinese government, which purchased a stake in TikTok's parent company, ByteDance.

Lorenz has done some excellent reporting—she is well sourced in the world she covers, and in the broader tech space. But she often gets herself into trouble for the extra-curricular side of the equation. In late 2020 she took a great interest in the start-up app called Clubhouse, which was growing in popularity among the tech and media crowd. The app essentially allowed users to create live podcasts, where virtual audience members could call in as guests. At launch, you needed a special invite to be on the app, so it felt a bit like a roped-off "clubhouse."

Lorenz began tracking what she described as "harassment, abuse, misinformation, and other Clubhouse moderation issues," mostly by tweeting out what she heard. She was essentially serving as a de facto hall monitor or tattletale. What were these "issues," according to Lorenz? Things like a white speaker saying, "I just think racism is so overblown," or a room that was called "sex work is unacceptable." These are simply beyond the pale for this anti-speech activist.[10]

But then Lorenz went from broadcasting her non-journalistic opinions to getting something entirely, factually, wrong. She tweeted that during one Clubhouse conversation the venture capitalist Marc Andreessen used a "slur"—"retard." The reference was a description of what users of a Reddit forum affectionately called themselves, but the bigger issue was that Andreessen was not the person who said it. Lorenz eventually back-pedaled and said she simply heard a male voice make the remark. It turns out it actually was entrepreneur Felicia Horowitz, who happens to be a Black woman.[11]

This error was bad for Lorenz's journalistic credibility, and yet it happened outside of her "work" environment. It's like when Lorenz found George and Kellyanne Conway's fifteen-year-old daughter, Claudia, on TikTok, and began amplifying the comments of the teenager about her parents to Lorenz's hundreds of thousands of followers. This undermines her work, but it's not even her "work."[12]

But Lorenz can't stay away from Twitter and other social outlets. In March 2021, she tweeted, "It's not an exaggeration to say that the harassment and smear campaign I've had to endure over the past year has destroyed my life. No one should have to go through this... The scope of attacks has been unimaginable. There's no escape. It has taken everything from me."[13]

And yet, there was an escape. She could stop using social media so much. And this "harassment" she endured did not in fact take everything from her. She was a highly successful journalist at the most prestigious journalistic institutions in America. Yet, in time, this sloppiness that happened extra-curricularly would seep into her work too. In a June 2022 story about "creators" and the Johnny Depp–Amber Heard trial, a lengthy, two-paragraph editor's note had to be added to Lorenz's report, correcting multiple errors. Lorenz blamed her editor for the mistake and tweeted incessantly about the "bad faith" campaign being waged against her.[14]

Getting off social media wasn't an option. That "transparency" would continue—because Lorenz and other journalists in her mold can't let the work speak for itself. The work is only a part of the whole. There's a "brand" to be mindful of too. Lorenz covers influencers. But she has positioned herself as one as well—intentionally or not.

Lorenz's one-time colleague at the *New York Times* Astead Herndon is a political reporter, who now hosts a political podcast at the news outlet. Like Lorenz, he does some excellent reporting. The "work" can be solid. But then comes Twitter—the non-work. And Herndon provides the sort of transparency that can be illuminating for all the wrong reasons.

Like Lorenz, Herndon talks openly about his "brand" as well. "I encourage young black ppl in media to protect their byline/image/brand in a way that even goes past their well-connected, institutionally rooted, and usually white contemporaries," he tweeted in 2020. "When the time comes, those structures will insulate them from blowback in a way unavailable to u."[15]

So okay—Herndon tweets about his brand and other meta journalistic analyses for all to see. But fast-forward to November 2, 2021: election day in America. In this off-year election, the biggest race being watched was the Virginia governor contest between Terry McAuliffe and Glenn Youngkin, a race that Youngkin went on to win. As results were coming in, showing what looked to be a Youngkin victory, Herndon took to Twitter. "Bc race as discussed in political media rarely includes whiteness, stories abt dem erosion in white, rural areas come from one direction," he wrote. " 'why Ds lost these voters by going too far' and not how this version of Rs, thru an open embrace of grievance politics, are winning them anew."[16]

Suddenly, Herndon's non-work was intersecting with his actual work. A few days later, he published a story headlined "Democrats Thought They Bottomed Out in Rural, White America. It Wasn't the Bottom."[17]

With a dateline of "Hot Springs, Virginia," Herndon and a co-author reported on the Virginia race "from a town of 500 on the VA/WV border," according to his tweet of the article. You'll never guess what happened next. Of course he reported out his instant analysis on Twitter from election night, and found some racist white people to prove his thesis. Herndon's analysis—which is a kind way of saying his "opinion"—on Twitter was then laundered as "truth" and "news" and "objectivity" by the *New York Times.*

Of course, the actual truth was that more than 1.6 million people voted for Glenn Youngkin, for all sorts of reasons (economy and education—and specifically COVID-caused school closures—were two big ones, based on exit polls).[18]

But that wasn't what Herndon was going for. Instead, he talked to "a dozen white, rural voters," and for them, according to his news article, "policy was less important than grievance and their own identity politics. And the voters, fueled by a conservative media bubble that speaks in apocalyptic terms, were convinced that America had been brought to the brink by a litany of social movements that had gone too far."

This is not to say that these twelve individuals didn't actually convey this sentiment. But thanks to Herndon's initial tweet, we see the sausage-making process, and the transparency ultimately undermines the validity of the reporting. From the piece, a photo caption read, "John Wright said he had become so frustrated with the mainstream media that he consumes only pro-Trump programming." The construction of the piece only justifies Wright's frustration—set up from before he was even identified to fit a narrative that was crafted live on Twitter days earlier.

Some who engage in this undermining radical transparency on social media remain protected, because the standards are different depending on the individual. A key example of this is what happened with Joy Reid of MSNBC.

In July of 2020, Joy Reid was promoted to the 7 p.m. hosting slot at MSNBC, nearly to the coveted primetime. She had hosted shows on the weekend, and earlier in the day, for years. Now she was getting a big promotion. She talked to the *New York Times* ahead of the show's launch, and was asked about a controversy from several years earlier. "It's two years ago, so I don't spend a whole lot of time thinking about that old blog," said Reid. "What I genuinely believe is that I truly care about the LGBT people in my own life. I care about being a good ally, a good person, and making sure that my voice is authentic, that I can make a difference."[19]

What were the circumstances of "that old blog"? In 2018, blog posts at a now deleted blog of Joy Reid's from 2006 were unearthed, and they included some blatantly homophobic writing, among other offensive commentary. In one, she wrote that "most straight people cringe at the sight of two men kissing," and acknowledged, "Does that make me homophobic? Probably." In another, she wrote that "adult gay men tend to be attracted to very young, post-pubescent types." Other posts appeared to be Islamophobic. While she issued a version of an apology at the time, she also claimed a peculiar explanation—she was hacked. "I learned that an unknown, external party accessed and manipulated material from my now-defunct blog, The Reid Report, to include offensive and hateful references that are fabricated and run counter to my personal beliefs and ideology," she said in a statement to Mediaite at the time. "We notified federal law enforcement officials of the breach. The manipulated material seems to be part of an effort to taint my character with false information."[20]

Shortly after, Reid's lawyer announced the FBI had opened an investigation. And then—there was no resolution. In 2020, I asked Reid, MSNBC, and the lawyer what the resolution of the FBI investigation was, and whether Reid still believed her blog was hacked. I got no explanation.

"I can't prove that Joy Reid is lying about the FBI hack. But she, as far as I know, has shown no evidence for her claim that she was hacked," the *Washington Post*'s Erik

Wemple told me. "And if I were MSNBC, I would want to see that evidence. I don't have any evidence that they looked for that...This idea of distancing yourself from authorship, when all these technological sleuths say that there's no evidence of hacking, and you sort of clam up when pushed on, where's this investigation? That's a real problem. It's a really big problem. And as far as I'm concerned, this case is not closed. And any additional scrutiny she gets, she has invited. And it makes it harder for me to trust her judgment."

Wemple was one of the few media reporters who dared to cover the story when it happened—and stayed on it beyond the first day. Another was David Folkenflik of NPR.

"It's hard to look at that and not conclude that NBC and MSNBC just decided to ride it out. That she had a strong base, she was a good performer for them, smart lady, audience connects—ride this thing out," Folkenflik told me. "That's not a journalistic value. That's not a transparency value on a human level...I think it's really unfortunate. I think news organizations in a corporate life need to try as best they can to live up to their journalistic ideals that supposedly are the point of their operation. And there are times where certain kinds of personnel confidentiality are legit concerns and they're competing imperatives here. But I think you live your values in a time of crisis as best you can. One thing I'll say about NPR, for all of our flaws, I think there's an effort most of the time, and I can say this as the guy who often covers these things, is that NPR lives our values. And the way that I know it does is that I have great liberty with my editors to cover the things, however unflattering they are to NPR, if necessary. And we don't do terrible things all the time, but when I think it's newsworthy, and we make a mistake, or there's controversy, we cover it, and MSNBC needed to do that for itself."

No, MSNBC just wanted it to go away. And it did. Reid wasn't cast out. Instead, she continued to be promoted, gaining more status and fame. And I want to be clear—I don't think Joy Reid should be "canceled" for what was on her blog more than fifteen years ago. I'm against it for everyone, including those who want to use those same tools to cancel others. But it's just important to acknowledge the obvious double standard.

Meanwhile, Reid continued causing controversy, accused of Islamophobia again, this time in 2020, when she said that "in the Muslim world" there was "a lot of violent talk and encourage their supporters to be willing to commit violence, including on their own bodies in order to win against whoever they decide is the enemy" (seeming to conflate all Muslims with Islamic terrorists).[21]

After multiple calls to apologize, she went on to focus on the topic in a later segment, and acknowledged her framing "obviously did not work." But no apology. Why should she? In this new world of transparency, some who provide the peek behind the curtain remain protected from repercussions in the traditional sense. She wasn't the target of anti-speech activists—instead, she was part of their team. She was cozy with the right powerful people. Her thoughts, mostly, were seen as "acceptable." She said the right things, and retained her powerful position—introspection-free, in her geographically isolated Acela Media bubble.

CHAPTER 13

On the Other Hand

MOST OF THE POTENTIAL SOURCES I wanted to interview for this book who ultimately said no did so for one of.
two reasons—they weren't allowed to because of their current occupation, or they felt some level of fear in speaking
openly and honestly with me about the industry they were
in or around. I don't fault them, necessarily, and certainly
if I filled this book up with on-background and anonymous
quotes, many more people would have talked and given a lot
of juicy stories. But it worked out. I'm very grateful to the
more than two dozen individuals who agreed to go on the
record to give their perspective.

There was one person who ultimately said no to an interview whose reason stood out, though. A media executive I
greatly respect declined because he believed the focus of the
book was completely misplaced and misguided. According
to this executive, the big story of the media's decline was one
outlet and one outlet only—Fox News.

According to him, Fox News represented a unique threat

because it spun dangerous misinformation to its audience, while remaining far closer to the GOP and Trump than other media outlets were to the Democrats.

So let's play this perspective out for a minute. The January 6 committee revealed a window into the coziness between host Sean Hannity and the Trump White House, showing text messages between Election Day and Biden's inauguration between the two sides, talking everything from strategy to personal friendship.[1] We also know that Roger Ailes, who ran Fox News, advised Trump before his debates after Ailes was ousted from the network during the general election.[2]

Of course, it's worth noting that Hannity is an opinion host. He spoke at Trump rallies before too, but is his coziness with the GOP surprising to anyone—his fans or his foes? Hannity, it seemed, was mostly the same on air as he was off it.

And it's also true that it's not particularly surprising that Ailes was advising Trump, but more importantly, he wasn't the only network head to be doing so. We found out later through tapes released by Tucker Carlson that CNN's Jeff Zucker was giving Trump's lawyer Michael Cohen advice to pass to the candidate during the primary election (and also discussing the possibility of a weekly show on CNN if and when Trump lost the general election).[3]

Fox News is without a doubt the most watched cable news network, and depending on your metrics, competes with the broadcast outlets too. It has an enormous presence on social media and a strong digital outlet. But Fox News also doesn't have the cachet that others like the *New*

York Times and CNN have. And that can be a positive and negative—it operates largely autonomously from the larger media apparatus. There are the obsessed watchers like Media Matters or certain media reporters. But as a whole, Fox News simply doesn't have the prestige of other lesser-consumed media properties.

But the other big factor is that Fox News is far more honest about what it is. Fox has news properties, like Bret Baier's *Special Report*. It has reporters like John Roberts that do great, objective journalism. But Fox News caters to a right-leaning audience as a counterbalance to the rest of the media industry. Fox News's mirror on the left would be MSNBC, although that network has far fewer viewers. Still, MSNBC has news, and it has opinion. It is also, like Fox, mostly opinion. But it is honest about what it is.

Compare that to outlets like CNN, or the *New York Times*, or the *Washington Post*. These journalistic entities have sold their audience a promise of objectivity, while often ignoring that charge. Don Lemon on CNN is considered the host of a "news" hour of programming. It's illogical, it's unnecessary, and ultimately it's far more harmful to the audience than Fox News's non-news hours, which make no pretensions about what they are.

So I disagree with this person, but ultimately, I appreciate the thought exercise. Throughout the process of writing this book I have often thought, "What if I'm wrong?" I don't have any apprehension about interrogating my beliefs and conclusions, in this or anything. I hope you do that with me.

Take "geographic bias," which I argue is more pernicious than a political bias. Some, who perhaps hold the opposite political views of the guy above who wasn't happy this entire book wasn't about Fox, might say that geographic bias is all well and good, but the liberal bias in the media is a far greater problem. That ideology pervades every element of the press, and it makes fixing the media impossible unless that ideological shift, or balance, occurs.

I don't agree. You could make the argument the corporate media has always leaned left—at least it has for decades. And yet something tangible has shifted, broadly speaking, in the last decade, or even in the last seven years. In that way, I believe a corporate press that remains just as liberal as it is now can still serve the public in a fair and responsible way. Other changes would have to occur, but ideology alone will not fix the problem, nor is it the root cause.

I think too about the concept of "coziness with power." Others I've spoken to about this book point to the need to not paint with a broad brush when it comes to this as an underlying issue. Just because members of the press interact casually with those in power—in government, in entertainment, in tech, in corporate America—it doesn't necessarily invalidate their work. It perhaps complicates it, but there's a way to do the job while still maintaining personal friendships.

And in some ways I suppose it is inevitable, when the Acela Media power centers are in NYC and DC. But I hope I'm not leaving you with the impression that everyone who makes up the Acela Media is corrupted by their coziness with power. Surely there are excellent journalists who also have powerful friends and are able to separate their personal and professional lives in impressive ways. This is the same for all the problems I raise in the book. There are journalists who can use Twitter regularly, give viewers a look behind the curtain and bring a level of transparency, without undermining their actual work. They can use Twitter and not become self-obsessed narcissists. (I'd like their advice on how to do it.)

But that doesn't make the critiques less valid either. A corporate media that's cozy with power will ultimately drift toward a level of corruption that is inevitable. And a more defined distance from power—a true Fourth Estate that's closer to the people than to the powerful—will inevitably improve the media output.

At least, that's my take. And perhaps I'm wrong. I'm open to that possibility. But I don't believe whether I've correctly diagnosed the problem is ultimately what matters most. I think the key is how we fix the industry. I don't want to burn it all down. I love the media. I want to help make it better.

CHAPTER 14

Defibrillation

THE AMERICAN MEDIA IS SICK, but it is not dead. Let's bring it back to life—better than it was before.

The first issue I discussed was the geographic bias of the media, and I do believe that's perhaps the easiest to fix—at least in theory. The *New York Times* has journalists that live throughout the country. CNN has small "bureaus" in cities like Dallas and Chicago. But there is never any confusion about where the staff that matters are located. The media that matters in this current era are based in New York City and Washington, DC—and that's a problem.

"Go to Iowa and have a town hall," said Kaleigh Mc-Enany. "I'm not talking about a town hall where you invite Joe Biden, you preselect the voters. You don't even go shake their hand or talk to them, but you have them stand up and ask the question as you're the almighty moderator talking to Joe Biden. That's not what I'm talking about. But have a town hall. Do what Salena Zito did. She wanted to understand a phenomenon that was happening across the country,

one that, on separate poles, Van Jones and Kayleigh Mc-
Enany seemed to grasp, because we're both people who
don't just sit in echo chambers, but be like Salena Zito, take
your car. She doesn't take air travel. She drives, she wants
to see the signs in people's yards, the bumper stickers, the
landscape. Have a town hall, go to these places, do listening sessions, because CNN, in particular, and MSNBC have
gone very far askew from where the American people stand.
Go out and listen to them. Go out and talk to them. CNN's
got a new president? Go out and listen to the American people, see what you're doing wrong. I get an earful about what
they're doing wrong. So I'm sure you will too."

But I'd go one step further. All these outlets would be
well served to not just helicopter into Iowa or another flyover state, but to embed reporters in these communities—
for good. Decentralize your media hubs. It's fine to keep a
presence in places like NYC and DC, but start hiring reporters in—or moving reporters to—towns outside the typical
locations.

Find places that are big and small, red and blue (and even
better—purple), thriving and struggling. But more important than the location is the longevity. Salena Zito spent her
life with these people, which is why she was able to drive to
a town and start reporting right away. It doesn't have to be
the middle of nowhere either. Stay in New York, but base the
reporter in Buffalo.

And then go bigger—build a real presence, filled with top
talent and executives, outside of the east coast Acela Media
hubs. Dallas is nice.

On the issue of a lack of introspection, so much can be

solved by what gets incentivized. As of this moment, news outlets are almost disincentivized from drawing attention to their mistakes—or correcting faulty reporting with newer, better information. There's a cottage industry on pointing and laughing at editor's notes, or corrections—and that comes from the right as well as the left. We need to embrace media outlets that get introspective and transparent. Humility should be welcomed, and if they feel the incentives shift to an environment in which updates are viewed as a positive—a hypocritical corrective that focuses more on the correction and less on the hypocrisy—more outlets will follow suit.

To that point, "ombudsmen" or those like it should become a greater part of the press. These staffers are tasked with reporting on the internal activities of the media outlet. They, perhaps more than anyone in the newsroom, are quite literally serving the public—another term for an ombudsman is a "public editor." Media outlets are inevitably leery of giving these individuals power to call out the outlet on a regular basis, but that autonomy will ultimately help consumers trust the outlet even more. Some outlets are going the opposite direction—the *New York Times* eliminated its "public editor" position in May 2017.[1]

It doesn't have to be a formal position either—I'm thankful to have two of the media reporters who serve ombudsman-like roles at their outlets quoted throughout this book (David Folkenflik at NPR and Erik Wemple at the *Washington Post*). But this single hire could go a long way toward re-establishing trust with the public.

As Rich McHugh sees it, opinion is the key roadblock.

"If CNN really is trying to go back to its roots, I think that's an awesome thing. I would love to see that for all networks," he told me. "I think just having networks on the right and on the left does no good for anybody except the people who want to sit at home at 8 p.m. and drink a scotch and be reinforced about what they believe. I think more independent journalism being lifted up that is unafraid to call it out on both sides, platforms like that being funded, being elevated. My hope is that in a few years, we won't just be in the same spot where it's so politically divided."

Coziness with power is perhaps the greatest challenge to overcome because it's so closely tied into the other issues with the press. Solve the geographic bias problem, and coziness with power will inevitably subside. Gain a level of introspection, and the powerful suddenly seem less alluring. But there are other ways to go about correcting this. Whether based in the Acela corridor or somewhere else in the country, news outlets should recruit new journalistic talent that, frankly, DGAF (don't give a . . . you get it). These people exist, but perhaps they are not the kinds of individuals graduating from the top journalism schools in America. Great reporters don't need a degree in journalism. They don't need a degree, period. It's a mentality. You need a brain, a spine—and a relentless curiosity. Find better people who don't care about how many Twitter followers they have or whether their report might piss someone off.

This dovetails with the next category of challenge, which is the broken financial incentive structure. But one area to make the media less cozy with power is to embrace and lift up the independent journalists. The Glenn Greenwalds and

Matt Taibbis of the world—and the countless others far less prominent—are building themselves a platform outside the mainstream. These individuals gain the ability to fully go after power, without the interconnected mess that corporate structures bring. But they don't have the backing needed in some instances for bigger, bolder reporting. They don't have the legal departments to fight a frivolous lawsuit, for example. The corporate press can help get less cozy with power by unofficially, and officially, partnering with and propping up these independents. Make them "microbrands" disassociated with the mothership. Find a financial arrangement that works for all parties. Corporate media would be smart to help build brands that can connect with audiences disenchanted with corporate media—that aren't afraid to ruffle feathers.

Because the solution to all of this is not a fully independent press—a giant disassociation away from all legacy media. I believe in institutionalism too. There can be real value in it. "We need the *New York Times* in our society," Shawn McCreesh told me. "You want to open that paper on Sunday and have some great, crazy six-byline investigation into some shit. And just nobody can do it at the level that they do it, and so yeah, people like Rogan are entertaining or whatever and they're filling a gap and a need. Maybe this sounds like hubris, but I just don't see how anything could even come close to replacing that core function of what that newspaper does. That 'A' section is so important and still so good."

We need to strengthen the media institutions into outlets that deserve the trust of the public. If we do that, they'll receive the trust they crave. But we need to find a balance too. The broken financial incentive structure that exists means we have outlets that are less interested in casting a wide net when it comes to audience. The *New York Times*, or ESPN, or CNN, may not feel like they need to earn the trust of all Americans to be financially viable anymore. They are not wrong to feel the erosion of the audience happening beneath their feet, and grasp onto the lowest hanging fruit to survive. But if they can embrace an intellectual diversity in the way they've embraced diversity through DEI initiatives, they'll find there's a path to have it both ways.

Disassociated brands under a wider umbrella can alleviate the cultural punishment while reaping the financial reward. The independent press shouldn't run and hide from the corporate behemoths that want to find ways of partnering up. It can be mutually beneficial. And in this way you can improve the perception of the larger media entity not through direct change to the product but through association.

When it comes to the rise of the media "influencer," we have to acknowledge that social media, and Twitter in particular, is not going away. Platforms may ebb and flow, but our current oversharing environment is a long way from seeing the pendulum swing in the other direction.

"The word I use when I speak with young students, especially early years in college, is a voice. You need to distinguish yourself in the marketplace, or in a workplace, whether you're going to work in a large newsroom or whether you're going to be part of the gig economy," Bob Ley said. "But when I make the point about developing your own voice to be distinctive, I try to make the point it's based on, how many people know how to write well? Even people who are working. Express yourself cogently and well, and be fair and be accurate, so you have a platform of credibility upon which you can offer that voice. But so many people—it's addictive."

The entrepreneur Jarrod Dicker wrote a great piece in 2020 equating media outlets to record labels—showing how the "talent" at your media company may be associated with your outlet, or "label" for a time, but that the relationship is fleeting, and the institutional heft that once existed has evaporated.[2]

The truth is that people in the media need to stop sharing every thought they have on a public platform like Twitter if they want to improve the reputational standing of the media as a whole. There's no way around it. But as Dicker makes clear, this is not going to be accomplished through edicts from *Washington Post* or CNN management. In fact, those could actually have the adverse effect—driving the most online talent away from the institution, toward the independent route, and then ultimately putting us in the same precarious position.

But I have a different solution: unions. Now I have mixed feelings about unions—and you may feel strongly about them one way or the other. But unions have been on the rise in the corporate press. While management can't impress to the workers of these media institutions that social media activity could be embarrassing and deleterious to the outlet, unions can make the point to their members about it. Tweets that expose the staff to backlash, tweets that undermine reporting of other members, tweets that hurt the institution of journalism—these are areas the unions should compel their members to avoid. And if the brand-building outbursts are de-emphasized, the anti-speech activism in the press will subside as well as a result of the quieter landscape overall.

If the Acela Media adopts all these ideas, we surely haven't fixed the problem of the press. But I believe it's a start. I've talked a lot in this book about incentives—incentives that lead to coverage, incentives that lean away from coverage, incentives that lead to business decisions that hurt the editorial product. And incentives that lead to complacency and inaction.

"Everyone's walking on eggshells," Shawn McCreesh told me. "There are a lot of obviously great changes happening, and progress is hard, but I think that there are certain young people who began working in newsrooms or places in liberal America in the last couple years—a bad example or precedent has been set, because I think they see that smearing your way to the top is a viable career path. And if you can get worked up enough, you might get a promotion. And I think that's driving a lot of this."

This is an incentive that will keep the media's growth at a standstill. If there's one change that needs to happen, we need to recalibrate around reality.

BONUS CONVERSATIONS

I HAD SO MANY GREAT CONVERSATIONS with the media players in this book that didn't fit into the overall structure, so I wanted to highlight a few extra here.

Ben Smith on the symbolism of WikiLeaks and the Steele Dossier:

"There's a way in which a document's symbolism can mean more than its substance in a way I'm still sort of trying to figure out. I remember being at an event once in Jersey just before the '16 election, it was a Trump event. There's a guy out front with a sign that said WikiLeaks, and he was chanting 'WikiLeaks, WikiLeaks.' And I happened to have spent the morning reading through WikiLeaks emails, which were mostly pretty banal. And I was like, 'Which WikiLeaks? Like what do you think? Is there something specific in there you're upset about?' And he's like, 'No, they just all show how corrupt she is.' But like which ones, and in what way? It was like the fact of WikiLeaks, the notion of this secret bad information was more important than any specific thing in a way that I still sort of find a little disorienting and scary...It became a totem for people."

Josh Rogin on his specialty, China, and the American media:

"There's no US media literacy on China. And by that I mean China is such an important country, such a big country, such a powerful country, with such a massive, massive worldwide propaganda and influence operations infrastructure. That is unlike anything, makes the Russian interference machine look like child's play. You thought like Facebook groups and stealing John Podesta's emails was bad. Wait 'til you hear about this, folks. Tens of billions of dollars pumped into our institutions, through proxies, and corporations, and Americans, and corruptions, and Wall Street, and academia. And grassroots astroturf community organizations, and English language media, and Chinese language media, and research grants and fellowships and think tank programs, and tech partnerships, and VC investment schemes, and IPOs, and all of them and that's a thousand times more dangerous than Russian Facebook groups and hacking John Podesta's emails. We don't cover that.

Too complicated. And then when they come after our media, which they do in a number of ways, by buying into it when they can, making corrupt partnerships with American media organizations when they can, by infusing their propaganda into our media through these partnerships when they can, by taking American journalists on corrupt junkets to China, paid for by cutouts and proxies and other crooks, and by convincing the US media at its very base level that their propaganda is actually their policy. And we see this right now with the war in Ukraine, because their propaganda is that China believes in sovereignty and non-interference and they're very conflicted about the war in Ukraine. And maybe they could help solve the thing and they could mediate it and they love the Ukrainians, and it's really unfortunate what's happening. That's the lot. That's the propaganda. And the truth is that the Chinese Communist Party under Xi Jinping is a co-conspirator in Putin's war, and underwriting it in a number of ways, which you can read all about in my columns, and the US media has fallen for the propaganda mostly with a couple of exceptions, myself included. So we don't have a media literacy in dealing with China. We don't understand that the Chinese Communist Party is attacking our media environment in much more strategic ways than the Russians ever dreamed of. By forming relationships and by corrupting our institutions from the inside to disable the antibodies of a healthy democracy. And that includes in the Fourth Estate."

Tucker Carlson on Bernie Sanders and Donald Trump selling out their voters:

"It turns out Sanders is a total fraud and a weakling and sold out his own voters and he's like a contemptible figure, but it's not about him. It's about the fact that all the energy in the Democratic primary was behind Bernie Sanders for one reason—because he was talking about economics. Everyone else was talking about trans and you know illegal aliens are better, and all this stuff. Okay, fine. You know, I have strong views on those things too. But ultimately, the business of government is the business of allocating money and where does it go, and why all of a sudden is J. P. Morgan richer than ever? They're doing a better job with banking? What is this? No, they're getting money from the Fed, and it's making a small number of people very, very rich. And it's destroying the middle class and like, that's true, and nobody was talking about it on either side except Bernie Sanders and to some extent Trump, who also sold out his voters completely the second he got there, Steve Mnuchin in Treasury, it's like, this is like *Animal Farm*. But anyway, I'm watching Sanders and I'm like, I hate the lifestyle liberalism stuff because it's just too stupid, and anti-family, but the economic stuff was like—he's onto something."

Jane Coaston on the nuance of coastal versus flyover cities and states:

"I talk a lot about the problem of the nationalization of politics, especially because you see that if you don't live in these places, New York, Washington, Los Angeles, any number of these places become ideas, and not real places. I was talking earlier about how much I hate the 'this town' narrative because it talks about people who live in Washington, DC, as this very small cabal of people, and I've never met any of those people. I don't hang out with those people...People talk about New York where it's either that you're the wealthiest scion, the wealthiest person, or you're homeless. There's no in between, which is not true. And I think that it means that people have a warped view of these coastal cities, and the people who look on the places that aren't on the coasts have a warped view of them, and it becomes both derogatory in terms of thinking about flyover country, or it becomes this idea that these places are more real than DC."

Sharon Waxman on how tech companies have destroyed new media upstarts:

"Google and Facebook ate their business model. Very simply, Google ate their business model. Facebook ate their business model. Anybody who had a business model that was in any way tied to Facebook, royally fucked over, you can use the f-word, because that's how strongly I feel about how Facebook betrayed people they promised partnership to. Bullshit. Luckily, I won't say including us because we never sought that out, but we're in a much more privileged position than the Vices of the world and also any of those other companies…A digital media company that was attempting to achieve scale and was attempting to survive by advertising and offering advertisers scale compared to say an *LA Times*, which only offers you say 40 million eyeballs a month in the LA region, which has a lot of value too. But they're fine to say, you know, we can hit whatever it would be, 100 million people, and they just were completely out-competed by Facebook, which in every case is going to give an advertiser more scale, more data, more ability to target a particular advertising goal."

Olivia Nuzzi on introspection in the Trump years:

"There was this sort of ugly impulse that I recognized in myself and I found myself disgusted by, to kind of throw reporting chum at the Resistance. And that's not to say I was manufacturing anything, exaggerating anything, but the same way I would with any other newsworthy detail with anyone I'm writing about, but you think, 'Someone's gonna react this way to this or someone's gonna react this way to that.'

I hated knowing that I was about to report something or say something that was going to give me short-term satisfaction, because people were praising me for it. It's just true that there's no constituency for critical or even just even-handed, nuanced, not complimentary reporting on Joe Biden, and you're not going to be 'Yas Queened' to death if you report something unflattering about him. And that was absolutely the case with Donald Trump."

Ali Velshi on the state of the media:

"This would be a much easier question twenty years from now. When we look back and say, 'Remember that really interesting time where content distributors and content creators were merging in a way that would have given a whole lot of antitrust people a lot of agita many years ago.' We don't seem to worry about this as much anymore, now that the creators and the distributors are the same people. So I think we're looking at a sort of a battle. Is there content supremacy, or do you need really good content and really good distribution?...I don't know where we are right now. I'd like to think that good creators of content, whether it's news or entertainment, win, but it does seem that it's harder to win if you don't have a distribution mechanism behind you. Then a counterpoint to that is CNN+. They've got the distribution. It's impossible to believe that anyone looked at three weeks of results and said, this isn't gonna work. I think it's a directional shift. So I think we're all sort of planting our flags, but it might take a while before anything happens with those flags. And it might be years. It might be you gotta establish what that product you're creating is going to look like, but something's going to happen in a world where people stop subscribing to cable and start subscribing to things on a bespoke basis. And I think we're literally right in the middle of it right now."

ACKNOWLEDGMENTS

I've done a lot of writing in my life, but I've never undertaken a project quite like this. It's an exercise that gets you thinking about the totality of your career. And in that spirit, I want to start by thanking all the bosses and mentors who have had a huge impact on my life and work: Horace Corbin, my first boss, at the *Westfield Leader*, Chris Ariens and Laurel Touby at TVNewser, Colby Hall and Dan Abrams at Mediaite, Piers Morgan, Jonathan Wald, Bart Feder, and Christa Robinson at CNN, Chris Balfe and Joel Cheatwood at The-Blaze, and Mark Denesuk at Commerce House.

Now I'm thankful to work with Chris Balfe again, and also am honored to work every day with the incomparable Megyn Kelly, as the executive producer of *The Megyn Kelly Show*. A special thank-you to Megyn, and everyone on the whole fantastic team we've built at the show.

Most importantly, I want to thank my wife, Meghan, and my kids, Jack and Mia, for providing the important life perspective that's necessary—what really does matter.

Thanks to my research assistants and copy editors who worked for free—my parents. To my sister, Alison. And a special note to my grandparents—my grandma in Florida, now ninety-five and going strong, and my grandma and grandpa from New Jersey, who passed away in 2016—all of whom were so supportive of my career.

Thank you to my agents, Keith Urbahn and Dylan Colligan, for helping put the proposal together. And a big thanks to Alex Pappas, my editor, who actually came up with the idea for this in the first place and saw it through every step of the way.

Alex was one of the readers of my Fourth Watch newsletter, which launched in December 2019. You never know who might be reading—but I'm so glad to have the tens of thousands of subscribers who have been game to think about the media differently.

This book would not have been possible without the candid and insightful conversations with those in and around the industry, all who displayed a bit of bravery to agree to go on the record. Thank you to: Maria Bartiromo, Jay Bhattacharya, Will Cain, Tucker Carlson, Joel Cheatwood, Amy Chozick, Jane Coaston, David Folkenflik, Bob Ley, Marty Makary, Shawn McCreesh, Kayleigh McEnany, Rich McHugh, Piers Morgan, Olivia Nuzzi, Tara Palmeri, John Roberts, Josh Rogin, Katie Rosman, Rick Sanchez, Ben Smith, Ethan Strauss, Ali Velshi, Sharon Waxman, Eric Wemple, and Salena Zito.

And thanks to all of you for reading this book. In the spirit of transparency and introspection, I'd love to hear what you think—email me at UncoveredSK@gmail.com. Let me know what you loved or, more importantly, what you didn't.

NOTES

Prologue: The Laptop

1. Emma-Jo Morris and Gabrielle Fonrouge, "Smoking-Gun Email Reveals How Hunter Biden Introduced Ukrainian Businessman to VP Dad," *New York Post*, October 14, 2021, https://nypost.com/2020/10/14 /email-reveals-how-hunter-biden-introduced-ukrainian-biz-man-to-dad/.
2. Jake Sherman, Twitter post, October 15, 2020, 11:42 a.m., https:// twitter.com/JakeSherman/status/1316781581785337857.
3. Andy Stone, Twitter post, October 14, 2020, 10:10 a.m., https://twitter .com/andymstone/status/1316395902479872000.
4. Kyle Griffin, Twitter post, October 14, 2020, 8:50 a.m., https://twitter .com/kylegriffin1/status/1316375735179780096.
5. Marshall Cohen, Zachary Cohen, Michael Warren, Evan Perez, Alex Marquardt, and Mark Morales, "US Authorities Investigating if Recently Published Emails Are Tied to Russian Disinformation Effort Targeting Biden," CNN, October 16, 2021, https://www.cnn.com/2020/10/16 /politics/russian-disinformation-investigation/index.html.

Introduction

1. Megan Brenan, "Americans' Trust in Media Dips to Second Lowest on Record," Gallup, October 7, 2021, https://news.gallup.com/poll/355526 /americans-trust-media-dips-second-lowest-record.aspx.
2. Felix Salmon, "Media Trust Hits New Low," Axios, January 21, 2021, https://www.axios.com/2021/01/21/media-trust-crisis?s=04&fb clid=IwAR0EMuwk7_b1XxHZozx59LktSK9bK-sv66CHwrgr6S0S -0UNR_9R6N7wTjE.
3. Tom Bevan, Twitter post, January 4, 2022, 9:29 a.m., https://twitter .com/tombevanrcp/status/1478388129144918016?s=11.

4. Last Call with Carson Daly, Twitter post, February 16, 2017, 5:35 p.m., https://twitter.com/lastcalllcd/status/832372841542610944.

Chapter 1: The Way It Was, and How It Got Weird

1. "CNN Hosts Display Own Controversial 'Hands Up,' " YouTube video, December 14, 2014, https://www.youtube.com/watch?v=ha1ljAbOPnY.

2. Emanuella Grinberg, "Why 'Hands Up, Don't Shoot' Resonates Regardless of Evidence," CNN, January 11, 2015, https://www.cnn.com/2015/01/10/us/ferguson-evidence-hands-up/index.html.

3. Erik Eckholm and Matt Apuzzo, "Darren Wilson Is Cleared of Rights Violations in Ferguson Shooting," *New York Times*, March 5, 2015, https://www.nytimes.com/2015/03/05/us/darren-wilson-is-cleared-of-rights-violations-in-ferguson-shooting.html.

4. Glenn Kessler, "The Biggest Pinocchios of 2015," *Washington Post*, December 14, 2015, https://www.washingtonpost.com/news/fact-checker/wp/2015/12/14/the-biggest-pinocchios-of-2015/.

5. Jonathan Capehart, " 'Hands Up, Don't Shoot' Was Built on a Lie," *Washington Post*, March 16, 2015, https://www.washingtonpost.com/blogs/post-partisan/wp/2015/03/16/lesson-learned-from-the-shooting-of-michael-brown/.

6. Department of Justice, "Ferguson Police Department Report," March 4, 2015, https://www.justice.gov/sites/default/files/opa/press-releases/attachments/2015/03/04/ferguson_police_department_report.pdf.

7. Mark Berman and Wesley Lowery, "The 12 Key Highlights from the DOJ's Scathing Ferguson Report," *Washington Post*, March 4, 2015, https://www.washingtonpost.com/news/post-nation/wp/2015/03/04/the-12-key-highlights-from-the-dojs-scathing-ferguson-report/.

8. Wesley Lowery, "In Ferguson, *Washington Post* Reporter Wesley Lowery Gives Account of His Arrest," *Washington Post*, August 14, 2014, https://www.washingtonpost.com/politics/in-ferguson-washington-post-reporter-wesley-lowery-gives-account-of-his-arrest/2014/08/13/0fe25c0e-2359-11e4-86ca-6f03cbd15c1a_story.html.

9. Michael Calderone, "Trey Yingst, Journalist Arrested in Ferguson, Wins Settlement from St. Louis County," HuffPost, August 3, 2015, https://www.huffpost.com/entry/trey-yingst-journalist-arrested-in-ferguson-wins-settlement-from-st-louis-county_n_55b7f4bfe4b0224d88345c7d.

10. Brian Stelter, "6 More Journalists Arrested in Ferguson Protests," CNN, August 19, 2014, https://www.cnn.com/2014/08/19/us/ferguson-journalists-arrested/index.html.

11. Niraj Chokshi, "Ferguson-Related Charges Dropped against *Washington Post* and Huffington Post Reporters," *Washington Post*, May 16, 2016,

https://www.washingtonpost.com/news/post-nation/wp/2016/05/19
/ferguson-related-charges-dropped-against-washington-post-and
-huffington-post-reporters/.

12. Steve Krakauer, "Intellectual Discomfort Will Heal America," Fourth
Watch, June 2, 2020, https://mailchi.mp/thefirsttv/fourth-watch-jun-2.

13. Major Garrett, "The Pen, Phone and Stray Voltage," CBS News, April 16,
2014, https://www.cbsnews.com/news/the-pen-phone-and-stray-voltage/.

14. Jon Greenberg, "CNN's Tapper: Obama Has Used Espionage Act More
than All Previous Administrations," Politifact.com, January 10, 2014,
https://www.politifact.com/factchecks/2014/jan/10/jake-tapper/cnns
-tapper-obama-has-used-espionage-act-more-all-/.

15. Kim Zetter, "Obama Administration Secretly Obtains Phone Records
of AP Journalists," Wired, May 13, 2013, https://www.wired.com/2013
/05/doj-got-reporter-phone-records/.

16. "Obama Administration Spied on Fox News Reporter James Rosen,"
Yahoo News, May 20, 2013, https://www.yahoo.com/news/blogs/ticket
/obama-admin-spied-fox-news-reporter-james-rosen-134204299.html.

17. Hadas Gold, "Risen: Obama Administration Is Greatest Enemy of Press
Freedom," Politico, February 17, 2015, https://www.politico.com/blogs
/media/2015/02/risen-obama-administration-is-greatest-enemy-of-press
-freedom-202707.

18. James Risen, "If Donald Trump Targets Journalists, Thank Obama," New
York Times, December 30, 2016, https://www.nytimes.com/2016/12/30
/opinion/sunday/if-donald-trump-targets-journalists-thank
-obama.html.

19. David Samuels, "The Aspiring Novelist Who Became Obama's Foreign-
Policy Guru," New York Times, May 5, 2016, https://www.nytimes
.com/2016/05/08/magazine/the-aspiring-novelist-who-became-obamas
-foreign-policy-guru.html.

Chapter 2: Geographic Bias

1. Tristan Justice, "Exclusive: Investigation Reveals White House Press
Corps is 12 to 1 Democrat," The Federalist, July 6, 2022, https://
thefederalist.com/2022/07/06/exclusive-investigation-reveals-white
-house-press-corps-12-to-1-democrat/.

2. CNN, Twitter post, February 28, 2020, 9:00 a.m., https://twitter.com
/cnn/status/1233406525491814400?s=11.

3. Brad Toelle, Twitter post, February 28, 2020, 9:01 a.m., https://twitter
.com/elleot1/status/1233406837166399489.

4. Wine Industry Network, "5WPR Survey Reveals 38 percent of Beer-
Drinking Americans Wouldn't Buy Corona Now," February 27, 2020,

https://wineindustryadvisor.com/2020/02/27/5wpr-survey-38-beer
-drinking-americans-wouldnt-buy-corona-now.

5. Amanda Mull, "Georgia's Experiment in Human Sacrifice," *The Atlantic*, April 29, 2020, https://www.theatlantic.com/health/archive/2020/04/why-georgia-reopening-coronavirus-pandemic/610882/.

6. Scott Morefield, "'No Major Spike in Cases': NBC Nightly News Airs Segment On Georgia Reopening," Daily Caller, May 25, 2020, https://dailycaller.com/2020/05/25/nbc-nightly-news-georgia-brian-kemp-coronavirus-reopening/.

7. Mike Moffitt, "China Study Suggests Outdoor Transmission of COVID-19 May Be Rare," SF Gate, April 28, 2020, https://www.sfgate.com/science/article/China-study-suggests-outdoor-transmission-of-15229649.php.

8. Christina Maxouris, "As Death Toll Nears 100,000, Some Americans Break from Social Distancing during Holiday Weekend," CNN, May 25, 2020, https://www.cnn.com/2020/05/25/health/us-coronavirus-memorial-day/index.html.

9. Anderson Cooper 360, Twitter post, May 25, 2020, 7:46 p.m., https://twitter.com/AC360/status/1265081740890116103.

10. "Large Gatherings Seen Across US as Battle against COVID-19 Continues," *TODAY*, March 8, 2021, https://www.youtube.com/watch?v=ZpQZDbp59OQ.

11. Townhall.com, Twitter post, December 21, 2021, 8:53 p.m., https://twitter.com/townhallcom/status/1473305692714983439?s=11.

12. Amir Vera and Ed Lavandera, "It's Been 2 Weeks Since Texas Lifted Its Mask Mandate. Here's How Business Owners Are Handling It," CNN, March 22, 2021, https://www.cnn.com/2021/03/22/us/texas-mask-mandate-business-owners/index.html.

13. Andy Lancaster, Twitter post, August 18, 2021, 9:21 p.m., https://twitter.com/andylancaster/status/1428180302845861895.

Chapter 3: Laziness and Incompetence vs. Conspiracy

1. Vinay Prasad, "At a Time when the U.S. Needed Covid-19 Dialogue between Scientists, Francis Collins Moved to Shut It Down," Stat News, December 23, 2021, https://www.statnews.com/2021/12/23/at-a-time-when-the-u-s-needed-covid-19-dialogue-between-scientists-francis-collins-moved-to-shut-it-down/.

2. Joseph R. Wulfsohn, "CNN Blasted for Now Declaring 'Wuhan Virus' as 'Racist' after Weeks of Network's 'China's Coronavirus' Coverage," Fox News, March 12, 2020, https://www.foxnews.com/media/cnn-china-wuhan-coronavirus.

3. UnfilteredSE, Twitter post, January 19, 2019, 6:57 p.m., https://twitter.com/unfilteredse/status/1086789656207810561?lang=en.

4. SE Cupp, Twitter post, January 21, 2019, 9:26 a.m., https://twitter.com/secupp/status/1087370828499558401?lang=en.

5. "Jussie Smollett Tells Cops Attacker Shouted 'MAGA Country'…'Empire' Calls in Armed Security," TMZ, January 29, 2019, https://www.tmz.com/2019/01/29/empire-star-jussie-smollett-attacked-hospitalized-homophobic-hate-crime/.

6. Steve Krakauer, Twitter post, February 18, 2019, 2:25 p.m., https://twitter.com/SteveKrak/status/1097593081761796099.

7. BuzzFeed, Twitter post, January 29, 2019, 4:15 p.m., https://twitter.com/BuzzFeed/status/1090372767013310465.

8. CNN Newsroom, Twitter post, January 29, 2019, 3:40 p.m., https://twitter.com/CNNnewsroom/status/1090364116181622785.

9. Yamiche Alcindor, Twitter post, January 29, 2019, 10:41 a.m., https://twitter.com/Yamiche/status/1090288879482085377.

10. "Jussie Smollett FULL Interview on Alleged Attack," YouTube video, ABC News, February 15, 2019, https://www.youtube.com/watch?v=pXLx5OY21Bk&t=427s.

11. Steve Krakauer, Twitter post, February 21, 2019, 2:06 p.m., https://twitter.com/SteveKrak/status/1098675339310579715.

12. Philip Rucker, Robert Costa, and Josh Dawsey, "Trump Seeks to Bend the Executive Branch as Part of Impeachment Vendetta," *Washington Post*, February 12, 2020, https://www.washingtonpost.com/politics/trump-seeks-to-bend-the-executive-branch-as-part-of-impeachment-vendetta/2020/02/12/8b712e18-4dc9-11ea-9b5c-eac5b16dafaa_story.html.

13. Ken Meyer, "Sen. Tim Kaine Rips Trump's Influence over AG Barr, Believes 'This Is How Democracies Die,'" Mediaite, February 13, 2020, https://www.mediaite.com/tv/sen-tim-kaine-rips-trumps-influence-over-ag-barr-believes-this-is-how-democracies-die/.

14. Max Boot, "This Is How Democracy Dies—in Full View of a Public that Couldn't Care Less," *Washington Post*, February 15, 2020, https://www.washingtonpost.com/opinions/2020/02/15/this-is-how-democracy-dies-full-view-public-that-couldnt-care-less/.

Chapter 4: Lack of Introspection

1. Sara Fischer, "The Media's Epic Fail," Axios, November 14, 2021, https://www.axios.com/2021/11/14/steele-dossier-discredited-media-corrections-buzzfeed-washington-post.

2. Evan Perez, Jim Sciutto, Jake Tapper, and Carl Bernstein, "Intel Chiefs Presented Trump with Claims of Russian Efforts to Compromise Him," CNN, January 12, 2017, https://www.cnn.com/2017/01/10/politics/donald -trump-intelligence-report-russia/index.html.

3. Ken Bensinger, Miriam Elder, and Mark Schoofs, "These Reports Allege Trump Has Deep Ties to Russia," BuzzFeed, January 10, 2017, https://www.buzzfeednews.com/article/kenbensinger/these-reports -allege-trump-has-deep-ties-to-russia.

4. David Frum, "It Wasn't a Hoax," *The Atlantic*, November 25, 2021, https://www.theatlantic.com/ideas/archive/2021/11/trump-russia -senate-intelligence-report/620815/.

5. Anne Applebaum, Twitter post, November 17, 2021, 6:40 a.m., https:// twitter.com/anneapplebaum/status/1460950967936069636?s=11.

6. #1718—Sanjay Gupta, Joe Rogan Experience podcast, October 2021, https://open.spotify.com/episode/6rAgS1KiUvLRNP4HfUePpA?si =mGuW2Sw_RkiQ1eUoX9baXg&dl_branch=1&nd=1.

7. Vanessa Romo, "Joe Rogan Says He Has COVID-19 and Has Taken the Drug Ivermectin," NPR, September 1, 2021, https://www.npr .org/2021/09/01/1033485152/joe-rogan-covid-ivermectin?utm_term =nprnews&utm_medium=social&utm_campaign=npr&utm _source=twitter.com.

8. Steve Krakauer, Twitter post, September 1, 2021, 9:19 p.m., https://twitter .com/SteveKrak/status/1433253115734671361.

9. Nobel Prize, press release, October 5, 2015, https://www.nobelprize.org /prizes/medicine/2015/press-release/.

10. CDC, Oversees Refugee Health Guidance, https://www.cdc.gov/immi grantrefugeehealth/guidelines/overseas-guidelines.html.

11. Steve Krakauer, Twitter post, October 14, 2021, 1:50 p.m., https:// twitter.com/SteveKrak/status/1448722909925498881.

12. Ian Sample, "Boys More at Risk from Pfizer Jab Side-Effect than COVID, Study Suggests," *Guardian*, September 10, 2021, https:// www.theguardian.com/world/2021/sep/10/boys-more-at-risk -from-pfizer-jab-side-effect-than-covid-suggests-study.

13. Emily Anthes and Noah Weiland, "Heart Problems More Common After COVID-19 Than After Vaccination, Study Finds," *New York Times*, August 25, 2021, https://www.nytimes.com/2021/08/25/health/covid -myocarditis-vaccine.html.

14. Brian Stelter, Twitter post, May 23, 2020, 9:33 p.m., https://twitter.com /brianstelter/status/1264383878803927041?s=11.

15. "The Coronavirus Death Toll," The New York Times Store, May 2020, https://store.nytimes.com/products/an-incalculable-loss-newspaper ?variant=31754326671430.

16. GMA, Twitter post, April 5, 2021, 6:06 a.m., https://twitter.com/gma /status/1379027701470748676?s=11.

17. Steve Krakauer, Twitter post, July 7, 2020, 8:56 p.m., https://twitter .com/SteveKrak/status/1280682014128115713.

18. Jim Salter and Leah Willingham, "Teacher Deaths Raise Alarms as New School Year Begins," Associated Press, September 9, 2020, https:// j7dfh9pbumnyhazfmcsfgm9m.apnews.com/article/mississippi-education -michael-brown-randi-weingarten-virus-outbreak-3e97872bf3c d8697064014efcf2ec622.

Chapter 5: The Trump Addiction

1. MSNBC, "Exclusive Donald Trump Interview: 'I Love China,' " YouTube video, June 18, 2015, https://www.youtube.com/watch?v=Tsh _V3U7EfU&t=51s.

2. CNN, "Donald Trump: 'I'm the Least Racist Person,' " YouTube video, December 9, 2015, https://www.youtube.com/watch?v=XRDmWPAtHiA.

3. Steve Krakauer, Twitter post, February 14, 2020, 9:42 a.m., https:// twitter.com/SteveKrak/status/1228343772053987328.

4. Matt Lewis, "Dems Say Sexist Attacks Are Wrong. Someone Tell Sarah Palin!" The Daily Beast, August 11, 2020, https://www.thedailybeast .com/dems-say-sexist-attacks-are-wrong-someone-tell-sarah-palin.

5. Sharri Markson, Twitter post, June 1, 2021, 10:41 p.m., https://twitter .com/SharriMarkson/status/1399934149666934784.

6. Jason Leopold, Twitter post, June 1, 2021, 4:19 p.m., https://twitter .com/JasonLeopold/status/1399838023412420614.

7. John Haltiwanger, "Dr. Fauci Throws Cold Water on Conspiracy Theory that Coronavirus Was Created in a Chinese Lab," Business Insider, August 18, 2020, https://www.businessinsider.com/fauci-throws-cold -water-conspiracy-theory-coronavirus-escaped-chinese-lab-2020-4.

8. Paulina Firozi, "Tom Cotton Keeps Repeating a Coronavirus Fringe Theory that Scientists Have Disputed," Washington Post, February 17, 2020, https://www.washingtonpost.com/politics/2020/02/16/tom-cotton -coronavirus-conspiracy/.

9. Eliza Barclay, "The Conspiracy Theories about the Origins of the Coronavirus, Debunked," Vox, March 12, 2020, https://www.vox.com/2020 /3/4/21156607/how-did-the-coronavirus-get-started-china-wuhan-lab.

10. Chris Cillizza, "Tom Cotton Is Playing a Dangerous Game with His Coronavirus Speculation," CNN, February 18, 2020, https://www.cnn.com/2020/02/18/politics/tom-cotton-coronavirus/index.html.

11. Lindsey Ellefson, "NY Times COVID Reporter Deletes Tweet Claiming 'Racist Roots' of 'Lab Leak Theory' After Backlash," TheWrap, May 27, 2021, https://www.thewrap.com/new-york-times-covid-lab-leak-apoorva-mandavilli/.

12. Josh Rogin, "State Department cables warned of safety issues at Wuhan lab studying bat coronaviruses," Washington Post, April 14, 2020, https://www.washingtonpost.com/opinions/2020/04/14/state-department-cables-warned-safety-issues-wuhan-lab-studying-bat-coronaviruses/.

13. Nate Silver, Twitter post, May 27, 2021, 6:26 a.m., https://twitter.com/NateSilver538/status/1397876974434066432.

14. Tim Teeman, "Omar Mateen Committed LGBT Mass Murder. We Must Confront That," The Daily Beast, June 12, 2016, https://www.thedailybeast.com/omar-mateen-committed-lgbt-mass-murder-we-must-confront-that.

15. Melissa Jeltsen, "Everyone Got the Pulse Massacre Story Completely Wrong," HuffPost, April 4, 2018, https://www.huffpost.com/entry/noor-salman-pulse-massacre-wrong_n_5ac29ebae4b04646b6454dc2.

16. Jeremy Herb, Phil Mattingly, Lauren Fox, and Manu Raju, "How a Swift Impeachment Was Born under Siege," CNN, January 14, 2021, https://www.cnn.com/2021/01/13/politics/democrat-impeachment-plans-behind-the-scenes/index.html.

Chapter 6: This Was CNN

1. "Exclusive: Dozens of CIA Operatives on the Ground during Benghazi Attack," CNN, August 1, 2013, https://security.blogs.cnn.com/2013/08/01/exclusive-dozens-of-cia-operatives-on-the-ground-during-benghazi-attack/.

2. Joe Hagan, "The Apprentice's Sorcerer," New York Observer, February 12, 2007, https://observer.com/2007/02/ithe-apprenticeis-sorcerer/?__s=xxxxxxx.

3. Fox News, "New Audio: CNN Chief Jeff Zucker Cozies up to Michael Cohen," YouTube video, September 8, 2020, https://www.youtube.com/watch?v=7cdNZCI1nXM.

4. William Langewiesche, "What Really Happened to Malaysia's Missing Airplane," The Atlantic, June 17, 2019, https://www.theatlantic.com/magazine/archive/2019/07/mh370-malaysia-airlines/590653/.

5. Reliable Sources, Twitter post, December 27, 2020, 12:51 p.m., https://twitter.com/ReliableSources/status/1343268288424501249.

6. Brian Flood, "CNN's Jake Tapper Urged Republican Sean Parnell Not to Run against Democrat Rep. Conor Lamb," Fox News, September 10, 2020, https://www.foxnews.com/media/cnn-jake-tapper-republican-sean-parnell-democrat-conor-lamb?__s=xxxxxxx.
7. Tom Elliott, Twitter post, July 3, 2020, 3:24 p.m., https://twitter.com/tomselliott/status/1279148978576261120.

Chapter 7: Coziness with Power

1. Karen S. Schneider, "A Magical Merger," *People*, February 7, 2005, https://people.com/archive/a-magical-merger-vol-63-no-5/.
2. Steve Krakauer, "Trump's Wedding to Melania Was 15 Years Ago. It Explains So Much about Our Cultural Moment," NBC News, January 22, 2020, https://www.nbcnews.com/think/opinion/trump-s-wedding-melania-was-15-years-ago-it-explains-ncna1120236.
3. Laura Bradley, "Ronan Farrow Alleges That Harvey Weinstein Used Matt Lauer Blackmail to Pressure NBC," *Vanity Fair*, October 9, 2019, https://www.vanityfair.com/hollywood/2019/10/harvey-weinstein-matt-lauer-ronan-farrow.
4. Sharon Waxman, " 'Harvey Weinstein's Media Enablers?' The New York Times is One of Them," TheWrap, October 8, 2017, https://www.thewrap.com/media-enablers-harvey-weinstein-new-york-times/.
5. Landon Thomas, Jr., "Financier Starts Sentence in Prostitution Case," *New York Times*, July 1, 2008, https://www.nytimes.com/2008/07/01/business/01epstein.html.
6. David Folkenflik, "A Dead Cat, A Lawyer's Call, and a 5-Figure Donation: How Media Fell Short on Epstein," NPR, August 22, 2019, https://www.npr.org/2019/08/22/753390385/a-dead-cat-a-lawyers-call-and-a-5-figure-donation-how-media-fell-short-on-epstei.
7. Alexandra Wolfe, "Katie Couric, Woody Allen: Jeffrey Epstein's Society Friends Close Ranks," The Daily Beast, April 1, 2011, https://www.thedailybeast.com/katie-couric-woody-allen-jeffrey-epsteins-society-friends-close-ranks.
8. David Folkenflik, "ABC News Defends Its Epstein Coverage after Leaked Video of Anchor," NPR, November 5, 2019, https://www.npr.org/2019/11/05/776482189/abc-news-defends-its-epstein-coverage-after-leaked-video-of-anchor.
9. Lachlan Cartwright and Kate Briquelet, "Jeffrey Epstein Gave Bill Gates Advice on How to End 'Toxic' Marriage, Sources Say," The Daily Beast, May 16, 2021, https://www.thedailybeast.com/jeffrey-epstein-gave-bill-gates-advice-on-how-to-end-toxic-marriage-sources-say.

10. Kenzie Bryant, "The Bill Clinton Portrait Is Not Even the Most Sinister Décor Found in Jeffrey Epstein's Mansion," *Vanity Fair*, August 15, 2019, https://www.vanityfair.com/style/2019/08/jeffrey-epstein-mansion -bill-clinton-painting.

11. Charlie Savage, Eric Schmitt, and Michael Schwirtz, "Russia Secretly Offered Afghan Militants Bounties to Kill U.S. Troops, Intelligence Says," *New York Times*, June 26, 2020, https://www.nytimes.com/2020 /06/26/us/politics/russia-afghanistan-bounties.html.

12. *AM Joy*, "NYT Reporter Covering Russia's Bounty on US Troops Gives Analysis," MSNBC, June 27, 2020, https://www.msnbc.com/am-joy /watch/trump-knew-of-russian-bounty-on-troops-before-late-march -report-86147653508.

13. Charlie Savage, Michael Crowley, and Eric Schmitt, "Trump Says He Did Not Ask Putin about Suspected Bounties to Kill U.S. Troops," *New York Times*, July 29, 2020, https://www.nytimes.com/2020/07/29/us /politics/trump-putin-bounties.html.

14. Adam Rawnsley, Spencer Ackerman, and Asawin Suebsaeng, "U.S. Intel Walks Back Claims Russians Put Bounties on American Troops," *The Daily Beast*, April 15, 2021, https://www.thedailybeast.com/us -intel-walks-back-claim-russians-put-bounties-on-american-troops? source=politics&via=rss.

15. "White House: Intel on Russian Bounties on US Troops Ahaky," Associated Press, April 15, 2021, https://apnews.com/article/joe-biden-donald -trump-afghanistan-russia-vladimir-putin-928ebdf775268b10e121d 3160af2da42.

Chapter 8: The Interconnected Mess

1. Paul Farhi, "Media, administration deal with conflicts," *Washington Post*, June 12, 2013, https://www.washingtonpost.com/lifestyle /style/media-administration-deal-with-conflicts/2013/06/12/e6f98314 -ca2e-11e2-8da7-d274bc611a47_story.html.

2. Michael Grynbaum and Sydney Ember, "CNN Corrects a Trump Story, Fueling Claims of 'Fake News,'" *New York Times*, December 8, 2017, https://www.nytimes.com/2017/12/08/business/media/cnn-correction -donald-trump-jr.html.

3. Manu Raju and Jeremy Herb, "Email Pointed Trump Campaign to WikiLeaks Documents," CNN, December 8, 2017, https://www.cnn .com/2017/12/08/politics/email-effort-give-trump-campaign-wikileaks -documents/index.html.

4. Donna Brazile, "Inside Hillary Clinton's Secret Takeover of the DNC," Politico, November 2, 2017, https://www.politico.com/magazine/story/2017/11/02/clinton-brazile-hacks-2016-215774/.

5. Alexander Burns, Jonathan Martin, and Nick Corasaniti, "Buttigieg and Klobuchar Endorse Biden, Aiming to Slow Sanders," *New York Times*, March 2, 2020, https://www.nytimes.com/2020/03/02/us/politics/pete-buttigieg-joe-biden-endorsement.html.

6. Reed Richardson, "Chris Matthews Freaks Out about Socialism, Says He Might've Been Executed in Central Park if 'Castro and the Reds' Had Won Cold War," Mediaite, February 8, 2020, https://www.mediaite.com/election-2020/chris-matthews-freaks-out-about-socialism-says-he-mightve-been-executed-in-central-park-if-castro-and-the-reds-had-won-cold-war/.

7. Steve Krakauer, Twitter post, February 9, 2020, 1:15 p.m., https://twitter.com/SteveKrak/status/1226585333866934278.

8. BernForBernie20, Twitter post, February 22, 2020, 4:47 p.m., https://twitter.com/bernforbernie20/status/1231349788769124353?s=11.

9. Justin Baragona and Maxwell Tani, "MSNBC Benches Contributor Who Smeared Bernie Sanders Staffers," The Daily Beast, February 26, 2020, https://www.thedailybeast.com/msnbc-benches-contributor-jason-johnson-who-said-bernie-sanders-staffers-are-island-of-misfit-black-girls.

10. Tom Kludt, "Fox Has Been 'More Fair': Why Bernie's Team Has Had It With MSNBC," *Vanity Fair*, February 18, 2020, https://www.vanityfair.com/news/2020/02/fox-has-been-more-fair-why-bernies-team-has-had-it-with-msnbc.

11. Caleb Howe, "Bernie Supporters Drag CNN For 'No Clear Leader' Headline on Poll with Sanders Clearly in Lead," Mediaite, January 11, 2020, https://www.mediaite.com/politics/bernie-supporters-drag-cnn-for-no-clear-leader-headline-on-poll-with-sanders-clearly-in-lead/.

12. MJ Lee, "Bernie Sanders Told Elizabeth Warren in Private 2018 Meeting that a Woman Can't Win, Sources Say," CNN, January 13, 2020, https://www.cnn.com/2020/01/13/politics/bernie-sanders-elizabeth-warren-meeting/index.html.

13. Chris Cuomo, Twitter post, May 20, 2020, 8:21 p.m., https://twitter.com/ChrisCuomo/status/1263278630408531974.

14. Cristina Cuomo, "Cristina Cuomo Corona Protocol, Week 3," The Purist Online, April 2020, https://thepuristonline.com/2020/04/cristina-cuomo-corona-protocol-week-3/.

15. National Library of Medicine, "Hydroxychloroquine: From Malaria to Autoimmunity," April 2012, https://pubmed.ncbi.nlm.nih.gov/21221847/.

16. Yaron Steinbuch, "Chris Cuomo Makes 'Official Re-entry' from Basement after Coronavirus Quarantine," Page Six, April 21, 2020, https://pagesix.com/2020/04/21/chris-cuomo-re-emerges-from-basement-after-coronavirus-quarantine/.

17. Peter Hasson, "Chris Cuomo Has Yet to Ask Andrew Cuomo about New York Nursing Home Deaths. Here Are 9 Questions He Asked Instead," Daily Caller, May 19, 2020, https://amp.dailycaller.com/2020/05/19/chris-andrew-cuomo-new-york-nursing-home-deaths.

18. Jesse McKinley and Luis Ferre-Sadurni, "Ex-Aide Details Sexual Harassment Claims against Gov. Cuomo," New York Times, February 24, 2021, https://www.nytimes.com/2021/02/24/nyregion/cuomo-lindsey-boylan-harassment.html.

19. Brynn Gingras and Elizabeth Hartfield, "Cuomo Denies Former Aide's Sexual Harassment Allegations," CNN, February 25, 2021, https://www.cnn.com/2021/02/25/politics/andrew-cuomo-lindsey-boylan-allegation/index.html.

20. Luis Ferre-Sadurni and Jesse McKinley, "Aide Says Cuomo Groped Her, as New Details of Account Emerge," New York Times, March 10, 2021, https://www.nytimes.com/2021/03/10/nyregion/andrew-cuomo-sexual-harassment.html.

21. Amy Brittain, Josh Dawsey, Hannah Knowles, and Tracy Jan, "Cuomo's Behavior Created 'Hostile, Toxic' Workplace Culture for Decades, Former Aides Say," Washington Post, March 6, 2021, https://www.washingtonpost.com/politics/cuomo-toxic-workplace/2021/03/06/7f7c5b9c-7dd3-11eb-b3d1-9e5aa3d5220c_story.html.

22. Eric Lach, "Who Ordered a Smear Campaign Against Andrew Cuomo's First Accuser?" New Yorker, March 9, 2021, https://www.newyorker.com/news/our-local-correspondents/who-ordered-a-smear-campaign-against-andrew-cuomos-first-accuser.

23. Bernadette Hogan and Lee Brown, "Former Aide Lindsey Boylan Alleges Cuomo 'Sexually Harassed' Her about Looks," New York Post, December 13, 2020, https://nypost.com/2020/12/13/lindsey-boylan-alleges-cuomo-sexually-harassed-her-about-looks/.

24. Nicholas Fandos, Michael Gold, Grace Ashford, and Dana Rubenstein, "Chris Cuomo Played Outsized Role in Ex-Gov. Cuomo's Defense," New York Times, November 29, 2021, https://www.nytimes.com/2021/11/29/nyregion/chris-cuomo-andrew-cuomo-sexual-harassment.html.

25. Luis Ferre-Sadurni and Michael Gold, "How the Fallout from Andrew Cuomo's Resignation Spread to Jeff Zucker," *New York Times*, February 3, 2022, https://www.nytimes.com/2022/02/03/nyregion/andrew-chris -cuomo-jeff-zucker.html.

Chapter 9: Broken Financial Incentive Structure

1. Steve Krakauer, "Jimmy Fallon and *Late Night*: The Future of Broadcast TV," Mediaite, December 14, 2009, https://www.mediaite.com/tv /jimmy-fallon-and-late-night-the-future-of-broadcast-tv/.

2. Richard Deitsch, "ESPN Suspends Bill Simmons for Criticism of Roger Goodell," *Sports Illustrated*, September 24, 2014, https://www.si.com /nfl/2014/09/25/espn-bill-simmons-roger-goodell-suspension.

3. Richard Sandomir, "ESPN Suspends Keith Olbermann for Remarks on Penn State," *New York Times*, February 24, 2015, https://www.nytimes .com/2015/02/25/sports/keith-olbermann-suspended-by-espn-for -remarks-about-penn-state.html.

4. Ryan Parker, "ESPN Suspends Jemele Hill over Social Media Use," *Hollywood Reporter*, October 9, 2017, https://www.hollywoodreporter.com /news/general-news/espn-suspends-jemele-hill-social-media-use-1047149/.

5. Paul Kasabian, "Report: Adrian Wojnarowski Suspended Without Pay by ESPN after Email to Senator," Bleacher Report, July 11, 2020, https:// bleacherreport.com/articles/2899824-report-adrian-wojnarowski -suspended-without-pay-by-espn-after-email-to-senator.

6. "Bob Ley Retires after 40 Years as ESPN Anchor," ESPN, June 26, 2019, https://www.espn.com/espn/story/_/id/27058914/bob-ley-retires-40 -years-espn-anchor.

7. Kevin Draper, "A Disparaging Video Prompts Explosive Fallout Within ESPN," *New York Times*, July 4, 2021, https://www.nytimes.com/2021 /07/04/sports/basketball/espn-rachel-nichols-maria-taylor.html.

8. R. P. Salao, "Rachel Nichols Bombshell Racist Rant against Maria Taylor from 2020 Caught on Hot Mic," ClutchPoints, July 4, 2021, https:// clutchpoints.com/rachel-nichols-bombshell-racist-rant-against-maria -taylor-caught-on-hot-mic/.

Chapter 10: Newsroom Purges and Guilt Journalism

1. Maxwell Tani, "*Teen Vogue* Staff Rails Against New Editor-in-Chief's Past Tweets Mocking Asians," The Daily Beast, March 8, 2021, https://www.thedailybeast.com/teen-vogue-staff-rail-against-new -editor-in-chiefs-past-tweets-mocking-asians.

2. Allegra Kirkland, Twitter post, March 8, 2021, 5:43 p.m., https://twitter .com/allegrakirkland/status/1369071340544753665.

3. Alexi McCammond, Twitter post, November 20, 2019, 5:08 p.m., https://twitter.com/alexi/status/1197290613701513217.

4. Josh Barro, Twitter post, March 8, 2021, 11:40 p.m., https://twitter.com /jbarro/status/1369161256217817089?s=11.

5. Tom Cotton, "The Case for Killing Qassim Suleimani," *New York Times*, January 10, 2020, https://www.nytimes.com/2020/01/10/opinion /soleimani-iran-tom-cotton.html?searchResultPosition=22.

6. Tom Cotton, "Tom Cotton: We Should Buy Greenland," *New York Times*, August 26, 2019, https://www.nytimes.com/2019/08/26/opinion /politics/greenland-trump.html?searchResultPosition=8.

7. Tom Cotton, "Tom Cotton: Send in the Troops," *New York Times*, June 3, 2020, https://www.nytimes.com/2020/06/03/opinion/tom-cotton -protests-military.html.

8. Marc Tracy, "James Bennet Resigns as *New York Times* Opinion Editor," *New York Times*, June 7, 2020, https://www.nytimes.com/2020/06/07 /business/media/james-bennet-resigns-nytimes-op-ed.html.

9. Kathleen Kingsbury, "Why the *New York Times* Is Retiring the Term 'Op-Ed,'" *New York Times*, April 26, 2021, https://www.nytimes .com/2021/04/26/opinion/nyt-opinion-oped-redesign.html.

10. Lottie Lumsden and Annabelle Lee, "11 Women Who Prove Wellness Isn't 'One Size Fits All,'" *Cosmopolitan*, January 1, 2021, https://www.cosmopolitan.com/uk/body/a34915032/women-bodies -wellness-healthy-different-shape-size/.

11. Karen Ruiz, "EXCLUSIVE: 'I Know You're Not Racist!' The Talk's Elaine Welteroth consoled sobbing Sharon Osbourne and admitted she was 'set up' in explosive AUDIO clip after on-air blow-up with Sheryl Underwood— before stabbing star in the back to CBS," *Daily Mail*, July 14, 2021, https:// www.dailymail.co.uk/news/article-9784399/Elaine-Welteroth-heard -comforting-Sharon-Osbourne-air-spat-Sheryl-Underwood.html.

Chapter 11: Media "Influencers" and Anti-Speech Activism

1. Jack Shafer, "Stop the Stupid Tucker Carlson Boycott," Politico, December 19, 2018, https://www.politico.com/magazine/story/2018/12/19 /stop-the-stupid-tucker-carlson-boycott-223387/.

2. Margaret Sullivan, "Fox News Is a Hazard to Our Democracy. It's Time to Take the Fight to the Murdochs. Here's How," *Washington Post*, January 24, 2021, https://www.washingtonpost.com/lifestyle/media/fox-news -is-a-hazard-to-our-democracy-its-time-to-take-the-fight-to-the-murdochs

-heres-how/2021/01/22/1821f186-5cbe-11eb-b8bd-ee36b1cd18bf_story
.html.

3. Margaret Sullivan, Twitter post, January 24, 2021, 7:27 a.m., https://
twitter.com/Sulliview/status/1353333489777696769.

4. Brooke Auxier and Monica Anderson, "Social Media Use in 2021,"
Pew Research Center, April 7, 2021, https://www.pewresearch.org
/internet/2021/04/07/social-media-use-in-2021/.

5. Stefan Wojcik and Adam Hughes, "Sizing Up Twitter Users," Pew
Research Center, April 24, 2019, https://www.pewresearch.org/internet/
2019/04/24/sizing-up-twitter-users/.

6. Colleen McClain, Regina Widjaya, Gonzalo Rivero, and Aaron Smith,
"Comparing Highly Active and Less Active Tweeters," Pew Research
Center, November 15, 2021, https://www.pewresearch.org/internet/2021
/11/15/2-comparing-highly-active-and-less-active-tweeters/.

7. Oliver Darcy, Twitter post, January 17, 2021, 10:35 a.m., https://twitter
.com/oliverdarcy/status/1350844159956017152.

8. Chandelis Duster, "US Surgeon General on Tech Companies' Fight to
Stop COVID Misinformation: 'It's Not Enough,'" CNN, July 18, 2021,
https://www.cnn.com/2021/07/18/politics/vivek-murthy-surgeon-general
-social-media-misinformation-cnntv/index.html.

9. State of the Union, Twitter post, July 18, 2021, 8:51 a.m., https://twitter
.com/cnnsotu/status/1416757640529600518?s=11.

10. TheHill, Twitter post, July 16, 2021, 2:03 p.m., https://twitter.com
/thehill/status/1416111364419035141.

Chapter 12: The Transparency Paradox

1. Elizabeth Williamson, "In Kayleigh McEnany, Trump Taps a Press
Fighter for the Coronavirus Era," New York Times, April 27, 2020,
https://www.nytimes.com/2020/04/27/us/politics/kayleigh-mcenany
-trump-coronavirus.html.

2. Soledad O'Brien, Twitter post, April 28, 2020, 7:19 a.m., https://twitter
.com/soledadobrien/status/1255109468888629250.

3. Dominick Mastrangelo, "NBC's Lester Holt Warns Media against Giving 'Platform for Misinformation,'" TheHill, March 31, 2021, https://
thehill.com/homenews/media/545803-lester-holt-warns-media-against
-giving-a-platform-for-misinformation/.

4. Glenn Kessler, Salvador Rizzo, and Meg Kelly, "President Trump Has Made
More Than 20,000 False or Misleading Claims," Washington Post, July 13,
2020, https://www.washingtonpost.com/politics/2020/07/13/president
-trump-has-made-more-than-20000-false-or-misleading-claims/.

5. Oliver Darcy, Twitter post, August 27, 2020, 11:10 p.m., https://twitter .com/oliverdarcy/status/1299197751373303809.

6. Bill Weir, Twitter post, August 28, 2020, 11:26 a.m., https://twitter.com /BillWeirCNN/status/1299382807001661440.

7. Tiffany Cross, Twitter post, August 28, 2020, 6:05 a.m., https://twitter .com/TiffanyDCross/status/1299301962777874432.

8. Derek Thompson, Twitter post, https://twitter.com/DKThomp/status /1299328508376875010.

9. Jay Rosen, Twitter post, August 27, 2020, 11:44 p.m., https://twitter .com/jayrosen_nyu/status/1299206271606960128.

10. Taylor Lorenz, "Clubhouse Moderation Issues and Incidents," Taylor Lorenz, Medium, January 26, 2021, https://taylorlorenz.medium.com /clubhouse-moderation-issues-and-incidents-726a88a1b4bd.

11. Rudy Takala, "NY Times Reporter Locks Twitter Account after Falsely Accusing Tech Entrepreneur of Using a Slur," Mediaite, February 8, 2021, https://www.mediaite.com/news/ny-times-reporter-locks-twitter -account-after-falsely-accusing-tech-entrepreneur-of-using-a-slur/.

12. Greg Evans, "George & Kellyanne Conway Tell Journalist to Stay Away from Daughter Claudia; She Doesn't Take It Well," Deadline, July 3, 2020, https://deadline.com/2020/07/claudia-conway-george-kellyanne -twitter-sorry-marriage-failed-1202977251/.

13. Steve Krakauer, "Protect the Family," Fourth Watch, March 11, 2021, https://mailchi.mp/thefirsttv/fourth-watch-mar-11-21?e=5674ff1082.

14. Erik Wemple, "Taylor Lorenz Said an Editor Was to Blame. Is That Okay?" Washington Post, June 10, 2022, https://www.washingtonpost .com/opinions/2022/06/10/washington-post-taylor-lorenz-correction -editor-mistake/.

15. Astead Herndon, Twitter post, July 2, 2020, 9:35 a.m., https://twitter .com/AsteadWesley/status/1278698781802979328.

16. Astead Herndon, Twitter post, November 2, 2021, 7:47 p.m., https:// twitter.com/asteadwesley/status/1455698122101960711?s=11.

17. Astead Herndon and Shane Goldmacher, "Democrats Thought They Bottomed Out in Rural, White America. It Wasn't the Bottom," New York Times, November 8, 2021, https://www.nytimes.com/2021/11/06 /us/rural-vote-democrats-virginia.html.

18. "Exit Poll Results: Virginia Voters Explain Which Issues Mattered Most to Them," Associated Press, November 2, 2021, https://wset.com/news/local /exit-poll-results-virginia-voters-explain-what-mattered-most-to-them.

19. Steve Krakauer, "That Old Blog," Fourth Watch, July 19, 2020, https:// mailchi.mp/thefirsttv/fourth-watch-jul-19?e=5674ff1082.

20. Caleb Ecarma, "Exclusive: Joy Reid Claims Newly Discovered Homophobic Posts from Her Blog Were 'Fabricated,'" Mediaite, April 23, 2018, https://www.mediaite.com/online/exclusive-joy-reid-claims-newly-discovered-homophobic-posts-from-her-blog-were-fabricated/.

21. Hayley Miller, "Muslim Groups Call on MSNBC's Joy Reid to Apologize for 'Islamophobic' Comments," HuffPost, September 2, 2020, https://www.huffpost.com/entry/msnbc-joy-reid-islamophobic-comments_n_5f4fa79bc5b6fea874634fc3.

Chapter 13: On the Other Hand

1. "Read: 82 Texts between Sean Hannity and Mark Meadows," CNN, April 29, 2022, https://www.cnn.com/2022/04/29/politics/mm-sh-texts/index.html.

2. Maggie Haberman and Ashley Parker, "Roger Ailes Is Advising Donald Trump Ahead of Presidential Debates," *New York Times*, August 16, 2016, https://www.nytimes.com/2016/08/17/us/politics/donald-trump-roger-ailes.html.

3. Joe Concha, "CNN's Zucker Discussed Weekly Trump Show, Offered Debate Advice in 2016 Call: Audio," TheHill, September 9, 2020, https://thehill.com/homenews/media/515633-cnns-zucker-discussed-weekly-trump-show-offered-debate-advice-in-2016-call/.

Chapter 14: Defibrillation

1. Dara Lind, "The New York Times is getting rid of its public editor for exactly the wrong reasons," Vox, May 31, 2017, https://www.vox.com/2017/5/31/15719278/public-editor-liz-spayd-new-york-times.

2. Jarrod Dicker, "The Next Media Opportunity: Talent, Reputation, and Lessons from Record Labels," Jarrod Dicker, Medium, May 28, 2020, https://jarroddicker.medium.com/the-next-media-business-talent-reputation-and-lessons-from-record-labels-e14b695c43b.

INDEX

ABOUT THE AUTHOR

Steve Krakauer is a journalist and media critic who has worked at CNN, Fox News, NBC, and TheBlaze. He authors the Fourth Watch media newsletter, hosts the Fourth Watch Podcast, and is the executive producer of *The Megyn Kelly Show*. He first covered the media as a TV writer and editor at TVNewser, and Mediaite, where he was a founding editor. He is a graduate of Syracuse University's Newhouse School. He lives in Dallas, with his wife and two kids.